Contents

D1086419

Overview Map

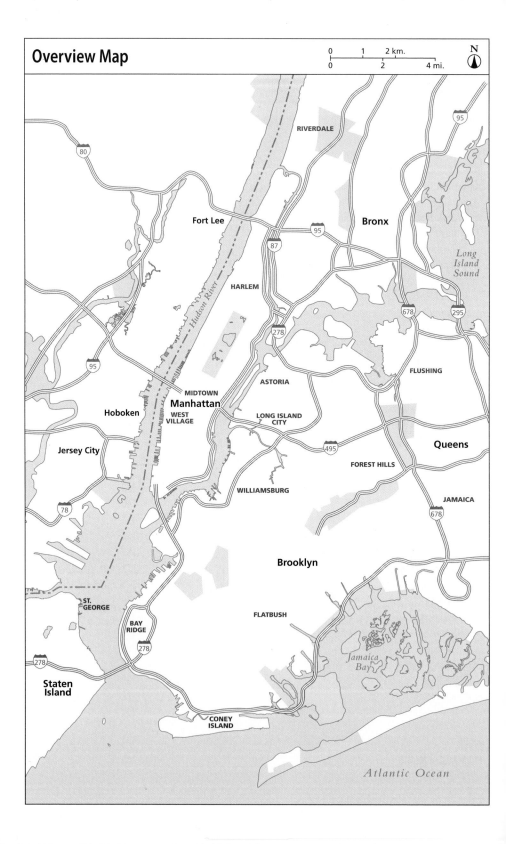

Introduction

R ock & roll may not have been born in New York, but this is one of the places it grew up and blew up and presented itself to the world. From the churches and street corners of Harlem and the Bronx to the underground clubs of the East Village, New York City has been a musical Mecca for generations, and *The Rock & Roll Explorer Guide to New York City* is a historical journey through its development across all five boroughs.

The Rock & Roll Explorer Guide to New York City restores a sense of time and place to music history by identifying and documenting critical points of interest spanning genres and eras and delineating the places in New York City critical to its musical development and ultimate triumphs and tragedies. Through this lens, we can see and understand how bands came together, scenes developed, and classic songs were written. In some cases, the buildings are still there, in others only the address remains, but you still get a sense of the history that happened there.

🚫 Look for the no-access symbol to indicate buildings that have been demolished. The structures are no longer there, but the stories remain.

Among the many locations in this book are addresses musicians and other key rock & roll figures once called home. In a very few instances we've included current addresses, but only when the location is historically significant and widely known; otherwise, we consciously left current residences out. *The Rock & Roll Explorer Guide to New York City* is intended as a fun travel guide through music history rather than a means of locating famous musicians. Most New Yorkers understand that everyone has a right to privacy. That's one of the reasons many of these artists live here.

Because of the city's rich history, this book cannot be a comprehensive encyclopedia of music, rock venues, or the music industry; nor do we present the definitive biographies of the musicians included. The artists and locations chosen represent a sometimes broad look at the history of rock & roll in the city, with an eye on those who either grew up or spent their formative years here. But there's so much more we couldn't include, and we hope readers will be inspired to go even further, whether they're hitting the streets themselves or experiencing the city vicariously from afar. Artists come and go, neighborhoods change, venues open and close, but the music lives on.

ROCK AND ROLL EXPLORER GUIDE TO NEW YORK CITY

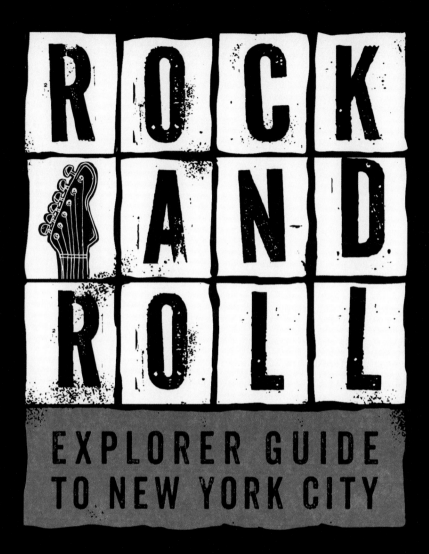

ROCK AND ROLL

EXPLORER GUIDE TO NEW YORK CITY

MIKE KATZ AND CRISPIN KOTT

FOREWORD BY LEGS MCNEIL

Globe
Pequot

Guilford, Connecticut

Globe
Pequot

An imprint of The Rowman & Littlefield Publishing Group, Inc.
4501 Forbes Blvd., Ste. 200
Lanham, MD 20706
www.rowman.com

Distributed by NATIONAL BOOK NETWORK

British Library Cataloguing in Publication Information available

Library of Congress Cataloging-in-Publication Data available

ISBN 978-1-63076-316-9 (paperback)
ISBN 978-1-4930-3704-9 (e-book)

∞™ The paper used in this publication meets the minimum requirements of American National Standard for Information Sciences—Permanence of Paper for Printed Library Materials, ANSI/NISO Z39.48-1992

Printed in the United States of America

Foreword

When I was a kid the world moved at such an excruciatingly slow pace that I thought the planet would never change. The hands on the clock seemed to be revolving backwards, and the only way to judge time moving forward was when a new copy of *Mad* magazine hit the magazine rack at Morton's Pharmacy. I'd sit at the soda-fountain counter with my Vanilla Coke and Ring Dings, with my thumbs in my ears, trying to absorb the entire issue in one sitting since I couldn't afford to buy it.

Other than a new issue of *Mad*, nothing much happened.

But somewhere along the way the world moved into hyper drive, I don't know exactly when that was, maybe it was at the end of the '70s when everyone started doing cocaine in an attempt to crash into next week? Or maybe it was in the '80s when MTV made it seem like more was happening than it was? Or maybe the '90s when the internet suddenly made the world very small? Or the 2000s when all the rules changed?

Yeah, somewhere along the line, technology launched us into the future, and before anyone had time to catch their breath, we became nostalgic for yesterday. Yeah, the more we fear the future, the more we recycle the past, which is probably why you're holding this book in your hand.

Yeah, I know, you were born too late. I know you'd like to go back to your favorite time in rock & roll history, and maybe, just maybe, imagine yourself being there when the Beatles stepped off the plane at JFK Airport? Or hanging out at the Apollo Theater with Little Richard and Buddy Holly tearing up the place? Or puking backstage at Max's Kansas City with Johnny Thunders and Sid Vicious?

Yes, the possibilities are endless!

And, thanks to this book and a bit of imagination, you can go anywhere and be anyone you want, because this isn't really a book! I'll let you in on a little secret, what you're holding in your hand is actually a rock & roll time machine! *That's right, a time machine!*

If you operate this book correctly, it will transport you back to those wondrous days of yesteryear when rock & roll was the only language spoken here, and the only thing that mattered was whether you had tickets to see the Stones at Madison Square Garden tonight!

Or Patti Smith performing at the St. Mark's Poetry Project with Lenny Kaye!

Or Danny Fields introducing Iggy Pop to David Bowie at Max's!

Geez, I'm getting pretty nostalgic myself right now, making me think, "Which part of the past would I like to revisit?"

Hmmm, I'd like to go back to my first threesome at the Punk Dump at 365 10th Ave., the *Punk Magazine* offices that also doubled as our apartment. That's when I thought I wasn't being kinky enough, so I dumped maple syrup over the two girls during the sex and ended up glued to the sheets in the morning after my companions left.

That's when I learned that food and sex don't mix.

Or maybe I'd head over to Nancy Spungen's apartment a few blocks away on West 23rd Street to take a shower and watch Nancy practice her new striptease routine over a plate of scrambled eggs she cooked for me. (Nancy was a lot nicer than you've been lead to believe.)

Or maybe I'd go over to Anya Phillips' apartment on St. Marks Place between 1st Ave. and Avenue A (which later became Café Mogodor) to take a bath? Did I mention we did not have a shower at the Punk Dump? I was so dumb that when Anya suggested she tie me to the bed and watch her masturbate, I answered, "Why the fuck would I wanna do that?"

I was not well-versed in the art of S&M culture.

Instead, I had her make me a peanut butter and jelly sandwich, which I ate in the tub while Anya played the new Talking Heads record. Hey, I was hungry, okay?

But most of all I'd like to go back to Arturo Vega's loft at 6 E. 2nd St., right around the corner from CBGB's, and hang with Joey Ramone, Robin Rothman, and Tammy Scott, the little redhead that was always dressed in a cute little Girl Scout uniform at CB's.

Or maybe it was a Brownie uniform?

Robin Rothman would always be giving me shit for me suggesting the Ramones do a benefit concert to provide bulletproof vests for NYC policemen, since they had to buy them with their own money. Yeah, NYC was really that broke back then.

Robin was a real hippie and didn't appreciate the irony of a bunch of Bowery losers like ourselves providing lifesaving equipment for the cops, and we'd spend the morning arguing until I eventually talked her into lending me a buck fifty to buy a quart of beer and a pack of Marlboros. Yeah, things really were that cheap.

Joey would just stand there, twirling his hair, with that sly smile of his, as Robin and I quarreled, waiting for it to be night again.

Or maybe I'd like to take the subway up to 34th Street, to Madison Square Garden, the closest subway stop to the Punk Dump, and stare at the *Hustler* magazine ads that read "Think Pink," and appreciate how truly pornographic New York City was. And I'd think how lucky I was to live in a city that had a half dozen "Happy Ending" massage parlors on every midtown street corner! Yeah, NYC really was that filthy, in dirt and in mind!

So take this book, read it, and then go explore all the dreams, desires, and fantasies of the past, and know that you're not alone. Then put this book away, and go start living them.

The future belongs to you!

—Legs McNeil

Rock & roll journalist, co-author of *Please Kill Me: An Uncensored Oral History of Punk*

TOM'S RESTAURANT
2880 Broadway

Suzanne Vega was a student at nearby Barnard College and working as a receptionist when she became a regular patron here, writing the tune "Tom's Diner" in 1982. The a cappella recording, first appearing in *Fast Folk Musical Magazine* in 1984, recounted her observations as she sipped coffee in the morning before catching the subway. The song later turned up on Vega's 1987 album *Solitude Standing*. In 1990 the British duo DNA dubbed her original vocal to a bouncy electronic backing track and released it as a bootleg entitled Oh Suzanne! Vega's label bought the recording, and it sold an astounding three million copies. Tom's is immediately recognizable as the diner from *Seinfeld*.

COLUMBIA UNIVERSITY
116th St. and Broadway

Columbia has been one of the nation's preeminent universities since its inception in the 18th century and has contributed mightily to America's cultural landscape. In the 1940s Columbia was the crucible of the nascent Beat movement with Jack Kerouac, Allen Ginsberg, Lawrence Ferlinghetti, William Burroughs, and others setting the stage for the coming countercultural revolution in the ensuing decades. They had a particular influence on the music of the '60s and '70s via Bob Dylan, Patti Smith, Lou Reed, and others.

Columbia grads Vampire Weekend (Chris Baio, Rostam Batmanglij, Ezra Koenig, and Christopher Tomson) formed on campus in 2006 and played their first gig at the Lerner Party Space. The cover for their first album was photographed at an early gig in **St. Anthony Hall (434 Riverside Dr.)**.

Many significant musicians of the rock era have attended Columbia, including Art Garfunkel, Lauryn Hill, Vanessa Carlton, Alicia Keys, Suzanne Vega, Jim Carroll, and the retro vocal group Sha Na Na.

THE MCMILLIN THEATRE
2960 Broadway

The McMillin famously hosted an evening on February 5, 1959, with Allen Ginsberg, Gregory Corso, and Peter Orlovsky that horrified many in the Columbia faculty, yet delighted the students in attendance. The McMillin later hosted a variety of recording artists in the rock era,

The McMillin/Miller Theatre

including Simon & Garfunkel, Frank Zappa, and Lou Reed. Today it's known as the Miller Theatre.

THE COLUMBIA/PRINCETON ELECTRONIC MUSIC CENTER
632 W. 125th St.
The Columbia/Princeton Electronic Music Center was established in 1959 and was an important pioneer in many aspects of electronic music, including the development of the synthesizer. Robert Moog did early work on his products here. Today it's known as the Computer Music Center.

CARL SCHURZ MEMORIAL
116th St. and Morningside Drive

One of the most iconic photographs of the Who was taken by Art Kane in 1968 when he shot the group feigning sleep while huddled beneath the Union Jack. The photo, used for the cover of *The Kids Are Alright* soundtrack in 1979, was taken

Carl Schurz Memorial

at the Carl Schurz Memorial with the group leaning against the wall just to the left of the steps that lead up to the statue.

MANHATTANVILLE JUNIOR HIGH SCHOOL, JHS 43
509 W. 129th St.

It was here in 1953 at the annual talent show that the Carnations, an energetic teenage vocal harmony group led by Earl Carroll, was spotted by Lover Patterson. Patterson was a songwriter, talent scout, and eventual manager of the Five Crowns (a.k.a., the second Drifters), another Harlem group. He brought the Carnations down to the **Shaw Artists Corporation (565 5th Ave.)**, a talent agency that handled the careers for many R&B acts of the time. Here they met Esther Navarro, who renamed them the Cadillacs. They went on to become known for their frenetic choreography, and had several successful singles, including "Gloria," "I Wonder Why," and their signature tune, "Speedoo," inspired by Carroll's nickname. Earl left the group in 1959 and sang for many

years with the Coasters before coming back to New York and working as a janitor at **PS 87 (160 W. 78th St.)**. In 1979, Carroll reformed the Cadillacs for a Subaru commercial and performed with them on weekends. He eventually retired from the school in 2005 but continued with the Cadillacs for several years longer. Carroll passed away in 2012.

MARCATA RECORDING
3280 Broadway, Suite 319

Originally opened as a studio and rehearsal space by three members of indie outfit the Walkmen after the dissolution of their former group, Jonathan Fire*Eater, Marcata Recording was located in a building that was supposedly used in the early 1950s to build Nash Ramblers. In addition to the Walkmen, groups like the Kills and the French Kicks recorded here. Marcata's house engineer, Kevin McMahon, has since relocated the studio to Gardiner, a small town outside of New Paltz in upstate New York.

HIGH SCHOOL OF MUSIC AND ART
443-465 W. 135th St.

Established in 1936 as one of New York City's specialty public schools, Music and Art, known as "the Castle on the Hill," educated many creative and influential people who made an impact on contemporary music. In 1984 it was absorbed into LaGuardia High School of Music

The former Manhattanville High School is today the Urban Assembly School for the Performing Arts.

The school is known today as the A. Philip Randolph Campus High School.

and Art and Performing Arts near Lincoln Center. Graduates include Peter Yarrow, Laura Nyro, Paul Stanley, Janis Ian, Slick Rick, Billy Cobham, and Bela Fleck. Kurtis Blow was also a student here, but he was reportedly expelled for selling marijuana.

WADLEIGH JUNIOR HIGH SCHOOL
214 W. 114th St.

Known today as the Wadleigh Secondary School for the Performing Visual Arts

One of the greatest and most beloved of New York's vocal harmony groups, the Harptones, had their beginnings in the schoolyard at Wadleigh in 1951. The pre-Harptones group, the Skylarks, originally consisted of William Dempsey James, Curtis Cherebin, and Freddy Taylor. They practiced at Wadleigh and later participated in an Apollo amateur contest, where they were soundly booed from the stage. The group was eventually joined with another from the Lower East Side by songwriter and arranger Raoul J. Cita and became known as the Harps. This new group consisted of Willie Winfield, his brother Clyde, William "Dicey" Galloway, Cherebin, James, and Cita, who served primarily as pianist and musical director. They won first prize at another Apollo amateur night in November 1953 performing Louis Prima's "A Sunday Kind of Love."

They were invited to audition at **MGM Records (1650 Broadway)** but were kept waiting in the hallway, so they rehearsed. They were overheard by the owners of the fledgling Bruce label, who promptly signed them. The group, which by now consisted of Winfield, James, Galloway, Cita, Billy Brown, and Nicky Clark, were brought to the studio to record "A Sunday Kind of Love." Before its release, however, a name change was necessitated due to a gospel group also named the Harps. Thus, the Harptones.

They went through many personnel changes and a few labels, but the Harptones never hit the national charts despite being hugely respected and immensely popular in New York. Their small regional labels simply didn't have the marketing and distribution clout of the larger record companies. They appeared at Alan Freed's first Rock & Roll Jubilee Ball in 1955 at the **St. Nicholas Arena (69 W. 66th St.)** and later at another Freed show at the **Brooklyn Paramount (1 University Plaza)**. They even appeared in the film *Rockin' the Blues* in 1956.

HARLEM'S VOCAL HARMONY GROUP GEOGRAPHY

The phenomenon of teenage vocal harmony (doo-wop) groups in Harlem in the 1940s and '50s was inspired primarily by gospel music, as well as the commercial hits of recording artists like the Mills Brothers, Ink Spots, Charioteers, Three Chocolateers, Redcaps, and Delta Rhythm Boys. Groups typically came together in schools or neighborhoods, and usually sang together on street corners, often in friendly competition with one another.

Some of the best-known groups were formed and sang on these streets:

115TH STREET
(BETWEEN 5TH AND 8TH AVENUES)

- The Harptones
- The Willows
- The Wanderers
- The Five Crowns (who became the second edition of the Drifters)

119TH STREET
(AT PARK AVENUE, UNDER THE RAILROAD TRACKS)

- The Schoolboys
- The Jesters
- The Desires

131ST STREET, ST. NICHOLAS HOUSES

- The Dovers
- The Cadillacs

142ND STREET

- The Crows
- The Vocaleers (between Lenox and 7th Avenue)
- The Crystals (between Amsterdam & St. Nicholas)

When Billy Brown died unexpectedly in 1956, several hundred fans attended the funeral procession along 118th Street.

The Harptones continued, in various forms, until well into the 21st century.

THE HARLEM WORLD CLUB

129 Lenox Ave. (a.k.a. Malcolm X Blvd.)

An early hip-hop dance club, Harlem World featured performances by Grandmaster Flash, the Cold Crush Brothers, T-Ski Valley, Doug E Fresh, Kool Moe Dee, and the Treacherous 3. Although Harlem World was open only from 1979 to 1985, a zoning law required the space to be officially known as The Harlem World Cultural and Entertainment Complex.

MT. MORRIS (MARCUS GARVEY) PARK

Madison Avenue and 120th through124th Streets

Despite the fact that it featured top-flight performers and was professionally filmed for posterity, the Harlem Cultural Festival, sometimes referred to as Black Woodstock, has not entered the American consciousness the way other music festivals of the period have, though it was a historic confluence of great music, politics, and cultural pride. Over the course of seven Sundays between June 29 and August 24, 1969, luminaries such as Stevie Wonder, Nina Simone, the Fifth Dimension, Abbey Lincoln, Max Roach, Mahalia Jackson, Sly & the Family Stone, B.B. King, the Staple Singers, Gladys Knight &

the Pips, Hugh Masekela, and others performed for free at the park, accompanied by speakers such as the Reverend Jesse Jackson. Coming a little more than a year after the assassination of the Reverend Martin Luther King, Jr., the event had a distinct Black Power–inflected tone, and some of the artists included extended, sermon-like performances, such as the Staple Singers, and most prominently, Nina Simone. Security was provided by the Black Panthers despite the fact that the city had underwritten the event. Highlights were broadcast late at night on local station WNEW. Producer Hal Tochin filmed the event for eventual theatrical release but never found a distributor. Aside from the blistering Nina Simone set, the remainder of the event remains commercially unreleased to this day.

LENOX LOUNGE ⊘

288 Lenox Ave.

First opened in 1942, the Lenox Lounge was immediately unmistakable with its red art-deco exterior and large windows, enabling Harlemites to see who was at the bar that night. Live jazz could be enjoyed in the Zebra Room, a luxuriously decorated inner chamber that hosted legends such as Billie Holiday, Miles Davis, and John Coltrane. James Baldwin, Langston Hughes, and Malcolm X were regulars as well. Madonna filmed her video for "Secret" here in 1994. The Lenox underwent an extensive restoration from 1990 through 2000, and it would be featured in the 2000 remake of *Shaft*.

Sadly, a dramatic rent increase forced its closure in 2012. There were plans to reopen a few blocks north, but that never materialized, and what remained of the Lenox Lounge was finally demolished in 2017.

HOTEL THERESA
2070 7th Ave. (a.k.a. Adam Clayton Powell Blvd.)
In an era when many New York hotels were still segregated, the Theresa opened its doors to African Americans in 1940, and it immediately became a magnet for many of the top black musicians and celebrities and remained so for the next two decades. Many important entertainers stayed or spent time here, including Dinah Washington, Louis Armstrong, Ray Charles, Cab Calloway, Duke Ellington, Nat King Cole, Ella Fitzgerald, Lena Horne, Count Basie, Billy Eckstine, Ruth Brown, and Little Richard. In the '50s WLIB, then the preeminent black radio station in New York, established its broadcast center in the hotel, where Phil "Dr. Jive" Gordon was a prominent R&B disc jockey.

By the early '60s, the Theresa was clearly in decline but still an important symbol of Harlem. In 1960 Fidel Castro checked in when he came to speak before the United Nations and met with Nehru, Khruschev, and Malcolm X while a guest. In 1963 a young Jimi Hendrix became a resident at the Theresa and ingratiated himself into Harlem's musical community at the nearby **Palm Cafe (209 W. 125th St.), Small's Paradise, Club Baby Grand,** and the **Apollo**, where he won $25 at a Wednesday night amateur contest. The

The former Hotel Theresa

Theresa closed in 1966 and was converted into an office block known as the Theresa Towers.

GOLD LOUNGE
2074 7th Ave.

In his autobiography, *Le Freak*, Chic founder and renowned record producer Nile Rodgers claimed that in the early '70s, his rock trio New World Rising first played the Gold Lounge on the same day as a multiple homicide.

CLUB BABY GRAND
319 W. 125th St.

This longtime lounge and after-hours hangout attracted top talent from its opening in 1953 until the 1970s. Former bandleader Willie Bryant (a.k.a. The Mayor of Harlem) was one of the first great disc jockeys of the rock & roll era and broadcast live with Ray Carroll on WHOM from the front window here when he wasn't emceeing at the Apollo down the street. In its heyday, Club Baby Grand featured comedian Nipsey Russell as its Master of Ceremonies. In the early '60s, Lou Reed and John Cale occasionally busked here in their pre–Velvet Underground days.

BOBBY'S HAPPY HOUSE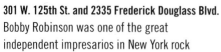
301 W. 125th St. and 2335 Frederick Douglass Blvd.

Bobby Robinson was one of the great independent impresarios in New York rock & roll history. He began by opening his own record store in 1946, one of the first black entrepreneurs to do so. By the early '50s, he began discovering and recruiting talent to record on the multitude of labels he'd created, including Fury, Fire, Enjoy, Red Robin, and Whirlin' Disc.

Among the artists he recorded were Wilbert Harrison, whose hit "Kansas City" sold more than one million copies, as well as the Shirelles, Champion Jack Dupree, Elmore James, Lee Dorsey, King Curtis, and Gladys Knight & the Pips. In the early hip-hop era, Robinson helped launch the careers of Grandmaster Flash, Doug E Fresh, and his own nephew, Spoonie Gee. Robinson operated the record shop continuously for six decades, eventually moving around the corner in the '90s. He was forced to close up shop permanently in 2008 due to increased development in the area. Bobby Robinson passed away in 2011 at the age of 93.

THE BRADDOCK HOTEL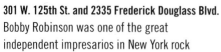
272 W. 126th St.

In an era when black performers were typically denied admittance to hotels south of 110th Street, The Braddock catered to many itinerant musicians beginning in the jazz era. Dizzy

Gillespie, Ella Fitzgerald, Billie Holiday, and many others frequented here and often played in the hotel lounge.

The hotel was also a regular hangout of young Malcolm Little, later known as Malcolm X. In 1938 two hugely influential pioneers of the electric guitar, Charlie Christian and Aaron Thibeaux "T-Bone" Walker shared a room here while playing with Benny Goodman and Les Hite, respectively. In 1943 The Braddock made headlines when an incident involving a black female guest and a white police officer sparked two days of rioting that resulted in 6 deaths and 600 arrests. In 1952 Ray Charles lived here when he began his relationship with Atlantic Records.

APOLLO THEATER
253 W. 125th St.
The theater that has become synonymous with great African-American entertainment was initially a whites-only venue known as **Hurtig and Seamon's New Burlesque Theater** when it first opened in 1914. It was not until 1934, when it was bought by Sidney Cohen and

refurbished as the Apollo, that it was open to both black patrons and entertainers. The Apollo changed hands again the following year when it was taken over by Frank Schiffman and Leo Brecher, whose families owned the theater for the next five decades. Very rapidly the Apollo established itself as the premier venue for jazz, comedy, and dance with appearances in those early years by Benny Carter, Bessie Smith, Billie Holiday, Bill "Bojangles" Robinson, Lena Horne, and Count Basie. In ensuing years Louis Jordan, Sarah Vaughan, Dinah Washington, Miles Davis, and Thelonious Monk graced the Apollo stage. It's no exaggeration to suggest that virtually every great black American musical artist played the Apollo at one time or another. It was easily the most prestigious theater of its kind in New York, and probably the country. Ella Fitzgerald, Pearl Bailey, Gladys Knight, King Curtis, Clyde McPhatter, and Jimi Hendrix were all winners at the highly competitive amateur night contests.

Beginning in 1955, DJ Tommy "Dr. Jive" Smalls helped introduce the Rhythm and Blues Revue, a hugely important showcase for emerging rock & roll acts. The same year marked the debut of the taped television program *Showtime at the Apollo* with host Willie Bryant and guests Sarah Vaughan, Big Joe Turner, Count Basie, and Nipsey Russell. Guests on later episodes included Nat King Cole, the Larks, Faye Adams, Ruth Brown, the Clovers, Amos Milburn, and Duke Ellington.

By the mid-'50s, rock & roll legends Chuck Berry, Bo Diddley, Fats Domino, and Little Richard had all played successful stands at the Apollo, even as they were also playing similar gigs at Brooklyn's Paramount for the white kids. In August 1957, in the first instance of reverse-crossover, Buddy Holly & the Crickets were booked for a week of gigs at the Apollo. At first, the black audience wasn't sure what to make of the hiccuping Texas rocker, but by the end of the stand he'd won them over.

On October 24, 1962, James Brown recorded his now classic album *Live at the Apollo*, which became a huge crossover hit, peaking at number two and spending 66 weeks on the pop charts. The Godfather of Soul recorded at the Apollo three more times in his career. When Brown died suddenly in 2006, his body was displayed on the Apollo stage in an open coffin so fans could pay their respects.

In the years to come, the Apollo provided a stage for all the great acts of the '60s and '70s, including Stevie Wonder, Otis Redding, Marvin Gaye, the Supremes, Jackson 5, B.B. King, Aretha Franklin, Sam & Dave, Bobby "Blue" Bland, and countless others.

On December 17, 1971, John Lennon and Yoko Ono appeared at a benefit for Attica prison-uprising families that also featured Aretha Franklin. It was only Lennon's second post-Beatles live appearance in the US.

By 1976 the Apollo was booked for only about half the year and the Schiffman family decided to close the theater. It opened for part of 1978 but closed again until 1981. Shortly after it was renovated, and the *Showtime at the Apollo* TV series was revived. In 1992 ownership was transferred to the state of New York, which leases it to the Apollo Theater Foundation, a not-for-profit organization that now operates the theater. The Apollo remains an important destination for a wide variety of performers to this day, and an historic anchor for a rapidly developing 125th Street.

ALHAMBRA THEATER
2116 Adam Clayton Powell Blvd.

Originally opened in 1905 as a vaudeville, concert, and dance hall, Alhambra Theater eventually became a movie theater with an upstairs ballroom that hosted Jelly Roll Morton, Billie Holiday, and Bessie Smith. It was here in 1927 that John Hammond, then a teenage prep school student, reportedly first heard Bessie Smith and developed a deep appreciation for African-American music. He eventually devoted his professional life to recording jazz and blues and played a pivotal role in the development of many important musical figures, including Holiday, Smith, Count Basie, and Aretha

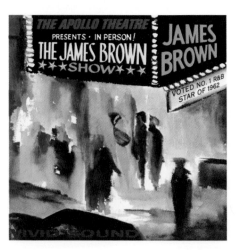

Facade detail of the Alhambra

Franklin. The Alhambra still stands as the Alhambra Ballroom.

SISTER ROSETTA THARPE'S HOME
55 W. 129th St.
Sister Rosetta Tharpe was the first gospel artist to cross over to the secular world of popular entertainment. Her brand of religious music was fiery and flashy, embracing both black and white audiences in nightclubs and theaters, much to the consternation of the religious community. She made her way to New York in 1938, where she recorded for Decca and performed at **Carnegie Hall (881 7th Ave.)** in one of John

Hammond's From Spirituals to Swing concerts. Later that year she played the **Paramount Theater (1501 Broadway)** with Count Basie. She became a popular attraction at the **Savoy Ballroom (596 Lenox Ave.)** and the **Cotton Club (200 W. 48th St.)**, where she appeared on a bill with Cab Calloway and the Nicholas Brothers. Other New York venues she performed in include the **Apollo (253 W. 125th St.)**, the **Town Hall (123 W. 43rd St.)**, and **Cafe Society (1 Sheridan Sq.)**. Tharpe had major crossover hits that included "Rock Me" (1938) and "Strange Things Happening Every Day" (1944), both of which are routinely pointed to as proto–rock & roll records. Beginning in the '40s, she began brandishing an electric guitar. She was certainly well known to blues musicians in the south and Chicago, and was a major influence on such figures as Willie Dixon, Little Richard, and Aretha Franklin.

55 W. 129th St.

She left this New York address in 1948 for Richmond, Virginia, but continued to tour regularly around the country. In the late '50s and early '60s she played successful tours in Great Britain, influencing a generation of artists there as well. Her last important gig in New York took place July 26, 1972, at Lincoln Center's **Alice Tully Hall (1941 Broadway)** as part of the Soul at the Center festival. She died the following year.

ELK'S RENDEZVOUS ⊘
464 Lenox Ave.
Louis Jordan was one of the foremost practitioners of jump blues, a vital link between the big bands of the '30s and the rhythm & blues of the '50s. He and his band, the Tympany Five, were particularly successful crossing over to the white audience and enjoyed a string of hits into the early '50s. His 1949 single "Saturday Night Fish Fry" is frequently cited as one of the very first rock & roll records. Jordan's frenetic and often comical approach to vocals was an enormous influence on Chuck Berry, Bill Haley, and Elvis Presley. He and his band played in many venues in Harlem but are famous for their several residences at this location.

MAMIE SMITH'S HOME ⊘
40 W. 135th St.
A native of Cincinnati, Mamie Smith was 37 when she recorded her breakout hit "Crazy Blues" in 1920 for Okeh Records. A veteran of cabaret and vaudeville, Smith had been cast in songwriter Perry Bradford's musical *Maid of Harlem*, where she performed her big number "Harlem Blues." Bradford, a staunch believer in the commercial viability of music recorded by black performers, shopped Smith around to various recording companies in New York without success. The conventional wisdom at the time (1917 to 1920 or so) was (incredibly) that African Americans simply would not buy records. Even within the black community, blues was looked down upon by those outside the South, and it was not typically performed

CRAZY BLUES
By PERRY BRADFORD

Get this number for your phonograph on Okeh Record No. 4169

unless dressed up and placed within the context of musical theater. Success for Smith came at Okeh, but not immediately. She initially recorded pop tunes "That Thing Called Love" and "You Can't Keep a Good Man Down" with white musicians. She imbued them with a bluesy vocal style, and they were modest hits by the standard of the day, thanks to support from the black press. Her stage hit "Harlem Blues" was retitled "Crazy Blues," but Okeh nearly gave the song to Sophie Tucker. Wiser heads prevailed, however, and on August 10, 1920, Smith, this time with her own band, the Jazz Hounds, made the recording that changed the American musical landscape forever. She had several other hits with Okeh, and other singers such as Alberta Hunter and Ethel Waters followed along the trail she blazed. Smith's recording career lasted into the early '30s. She made a comeback, but on the big screen this time, in the 1939 film *Paradise in Harlem*, singing her signature tune. She made a few other films, but evidently died destitute in 1946 and was placed in an unmarked grave. In 1964 fans from West Germany raised the funds to have her re-interred with respect and a proper headstone in Frederick Douglass Memorial Park (3201 Amboy Rd., Staten Island).

BLACK SWAN RECORDS

2289 7th Ave. (a.k.a., Adam Clayton Powell Jr. Blvd.) and 257 W. 138th St.
Black Swan Records holds the distinction of being the first black-owned record label to be commercially distributed in the US. Founded in 1921 by Harry Pace, the label was named for the opera singer Elizabeth Taylor Greenfield, known as the Black Swan.

257 W. 138th St.

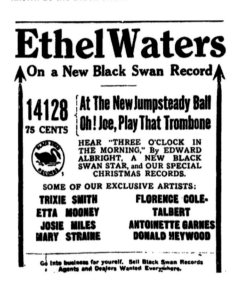

In its brief but historic life, Black Swan Records boasted some important names as part of its organization, including musical director Fletcher Henderson; W. E. B. DuBois was on the board of directors. The label featured primarily blues and jazz artists but also supported black classical performers. Ethel Waters was Black Swan's biggest star, but the label also featured Lucille Hegamin, James P. Johnson, and Alberta Hunter. Louis Armstrong, Lucille Bogan, Blind Blake, Blind Lemon Jefferson, and Charlie Patton also recorded for Black Swan.

Success proved hard to sustain, though, as bigger labels began producing "race records" of

2289 7th Ave.

their own and poached some of the Black Swan artists. In total, Black Swan released more than 180 records but declared bankruptcy by 1923, when it was absorbed by the Paramount label.

SMALL'S PARADISE

2294 7th Ave. (a.k.a. Adam Clayton Powell Blvd.)
Originally opened in 1925 by Ed Smalls, the Paradise was the only one of Harlem's jazz-era clubs to be both black-owned and integrated. Malcolm Little (later Malcolm X) waited tables here from 1942 to 1943. In 1955 the club was sold to the unrelated Tommy "Dr. Jive" Smalls, a popular DJ with WWRL. In the early '60s it was owned for a time by basketball great Wilt Chamberlain and renamed Big Wilt's Small's Paradise. Ray Charles played Small's many times, as did King Curtis, who recorded a live album here in 1966. The Commodores played here in 1968 prior to signing with Motown. The club continued in various guises featuring R&B, rock & roll, jazz, and disco before finally closing in 1986. The building stood vacant for several years before being refurbished as the Thurgood Marshall Academy in 2004.

SAVOY BALLROOM ⊘

596 Lenox Ave.
Known as "The Home of Happy Feet," the Savoy was the largest ballroom in Harlem, accommodating up to 4,000 people. It was envisioned as an uptown counterpart to the Roseland Ballroom, but the Savoy took on an identity all its own. It was large enough to house

Commemorative plaque marking the former location of the Savoy

two full bands, leading to frequent musical battles of the bands. One such legendary contest in 1937 pitted house band Chick Webb's Orchestra against Benny Goodman's, with Webb finishing on top. Many of the greats of the big band era, including Count Basie, Fletcher Henderson, and Jimmie Lunceford, played here, too.

Unusual for its day, the Savoy also maintained a no-discrimination policy. Blacks and whites were both welcome to take the dance floor, something with which authorities were not always comfortable. In 1943 the Savoy was forced to close for a few months due to alleged prostitution and the spread of venereal disease. The NAACP strongly objected in a letter to Mayor LaGuardia, and eventually the Savoy was reopened, but it confined its advertising to black newspapers and rarely brought in white musicians again.

A succession of popular dance crazes passed through the Savoy, but one became its signature dance. The Lindy Hop, with its explosive twists, flips, and throws, became one of the biggest exemplars of the swing era, and an enormous draw. Lindy Hoppers became dance floor celebrities, and many went on to professional careers.

By the 1950s, the big bands had largely been displaced by smaller combos playing a less elaborate form of dance music known as boogie-woogie, jump blues, or rhythm & blues, and the jitterbug emerged as the popular dance. Artists such as Meade Lux Lewis, Albert Ammons, and Pete Johnson were beginning to point the way toward R&B and rock & roll.

In 1958 the Savoy closed, and it was eventually demolished and replaced by public housing.

GOLDEN GATE BALLROOM ⊘
640 Lenox Ave.
The Golden Gate Ballroom was an enormous venue that, for a time in the 1940s, was a popular big band destination. It also hosted popular gospel events where groups of singers from different churches competed against one another. It was here that the Mount Lebanon Singers, featuring a young Clyde McPhatter, rose to prominence as the best in New York. McPhatter was a recent arrival from North Carolina, but his distinctively smooth tenor and movie-star good looks made him an instant star in Harlem. He had ambitions beyond the choir, however, and won an amateur night at the Apollo in 1950. He joined Billy Ward and his Dominoes and later formed the original Drifters at Atlantic Records.

THE 400 TAVERN
400 W. 148th St.
Immediately after the Second World War, two recently transplanted southerners, Jimmy Ricks and Warren Suttles, formed a vocal harmony group that helped pave the way for generations of rhythm and blues performers.

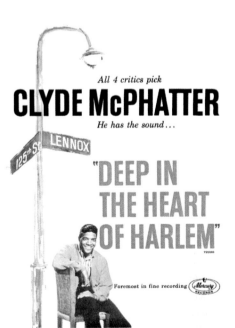

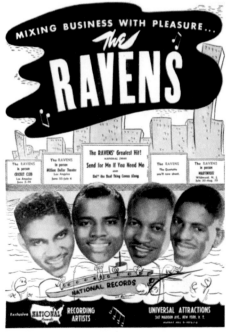

THE RONETTES

The Ronettes didn't look like the typical girl group of the early 1960s. Being of mixed race, they couldn't be neatly categorized as either black or white. They often wore tight dresses and swirled their long hair into enormous gravity-defying beehives. Their eyes were creatively and copiously lined. They also produced some of the best and most endearing hits of the era, most notably "Be My Baby" in collaboration with producer Phil Spector. Sisters Ronnie Bennett and Estelle Bennett, who lived at 405 W. 149th St., and their cousin Nedra Talley, who lived nearby, had been singing together since childhood. By the time they were students at **George Washington High School (549 Audubon Ave.)**, they were taking singing lessons and playing Bar Mitzvahs, sock hops, and other gigs around the neighborhood. By 1961 they were gigging as the Darling Sisters, and then Ronnie & the Relatives when they landed a deal with Colpix Records. They recorded a few singles, but

George Washington High School

Left to right: Estelle Bennett, Ronnie Bennett, Nedra Talley

none made any impact. By the following year they were working as dancers at the **Peppermint Lounge (128 W. 45th St.)**, accompanying Joey Dee & the Starlighters. When the owners opened a new lounge in Miami, the girls flew down for the opening festivities, where they were spotted by Murray the K, one of the biggest DJs in New York. By then they were calling themselves the Ronettes. Murray offered them a job with his Rock & Roll Revue at the **Brooklyn Fox (20 Flatbush Ave., Brooklyn)**, one of the most popular shows in town, where they would typically dance between acts and clown around with him.

The Ronettes became frustrated with Colpix, whom they hadn't heard from in months. They were determined to find a producer who would know what to do with them, so in early 1963 they resolved to present themselves to the hottest

producer in the business, Phil Spector. Still in his early twenties, Spector had already put together an impressive string of hits on his own Philles label.

One afternoon, Estelle called information to get the office number for **Philles Records (440 E. 62nd St.)** and rang them up. Incredibly, she was put through to Spector, who agreed to meet with her and the girls the next evening at the **Mira Sound Studios (145 W. 47th St.)**. After they sang a few songs, Spector knew he had something special. First, however, was the matter of their parents' approval and that pesky Colpix contract. Spector came to dinner at the 149th St. apartment and helped concoct a story to extract them from the arrangement. The mothers contacted the label and made it clear that the girls were done with show business and would be going to secretarial school. The plan worked and they duly signed with Philles. Spector rehearsed them for three months before he brought them to Los Angeles to record. They were on the road that August in Wildwood, New Jersey, when they first heard "Be My Baby" on *Dick Clark's American Bandstand*. The record, written by Jeff Barry and Ellie Greenwich with Spector, hit number two and went on to sell more than two million copies that year.

Spector eventually produced an entire Ronettes album, something he rarely did in an era when singles reigned supreme. The group even toured with the Rolling Stones and the Beatles. More hits followed, including "Baby I Love You" and "Walking in the Rain."

Success didn't last, however. Spector had begun a relationship with Ronnie—the couple would marry in 1969—and made decisions that frustrated the group. His "Wall of Sound"

405 W. 149th St.

was also becoming somewhat passé as music evolved in the '60s. In early 1967 the Ronettes called it quits. After leaving Spector in 1972, Ronnie attempted a comeback as a solo artist, releasing four albums. In 1988 the original Ronettes sued Phil Spector for back royalties (the case didn't resolve until 2002).

Spector, a member of the Rock & Roll Hall of Fame's Board of Governors, had long kept the group out of consideration for induction, but his arrest for murder in 2003 took him out of the equation. On March 12, 2007, Ronnie, Estelle, and Nedra reunited at the **Waldorf Astoria (301 Park Ave.)**, where they were introduced by Keith Richards. Estelle, already in poor health, was unable to perform with the others, and passed away two years later.

FRANKIE LYMON'S HOME
470 W. 165th St.

Fourteen-year old Frankie Lymon and his group, the Teenagers, were a black and Puerto Rican vocal group that hit it big in 1956 with "Why Do Fools Fall in Love," but after a few fairly successful follow-up singles, they never recaptured the enormous success of their debut. Lymon struck out solo in 1957, but neither he nor the remaining members ever met with much commercial success again. Lymon spent time in the army and struggled with drug abuse, to which he succumbed, dying of a heroin overdose in 1968. At the time of his death, he was staying with his grandmother in the same West 165th Street home where he grew up.

After Diana Ross made "Why Do Fools Fall in Love" a hit again in 1981, Lymon's three ex-wives all sued for a share of the royalties. A much-protracted legal battle to determine who, in fact, was legally Lymon's widow and who actually wrote the song ensued and wasn't resolved until 1992.

Ricks, while waiting tables at The 400, worked occasional gigs with the Melodeers, a vocal group led by Herb Kenny, whose brother Bill sang lead for the Ink Spots. When Herb Kenny broke up the Melodeers to join his brother, Ricks partnered with Suttles, a fellow waiter. The pair assembled the Ravens and would soon be playing the top venues in Harlem, such as **Club Baron (437 Lenox Ave.), Club Baby Grand (319 W. 125th St.)**, and the **Apollo (253 W. 125th St.)**.

The Ravens were distinguished by Ricks' rich bass and innovative arrangements that produced several hits on multiple labels into the early '50s, such as "Write Me a Letter" and "Count Every Star." They influenced legions of younger vocalists and informed what came to be known as doo-wop, as well as popular R&B stylists like the Temptations in the '60s.

Today The 400 Tavern sits shuttered and largely invisible, if not for the faded and rusted sign hanging overhead.

470 W. 165th St.

AUDUBON BALLROOM
3940 Broadway

Built originally as a theater in 1912, the Aububon Ballroom was used as a vaudeville house, movie theater, synagogue, union hall, and many other community uses over the years. Unfortunately, the Audubon is probably best known as the site of Malcolm X's assassination in February 1965. Malcolm X had founded the Organization of Afro-American Unity (OAAU), which held its weekly meetings here. For a time in the late '60s and '70s the ballroom was known as the **San Juan Theater**. By the late '70s, it became a Mecca for the first generation of hip-hop artists, including Grandmaster Flash & the Furious Five, DJ Hollywood, Cold Crush Brothers, and Grand Wizzard Theodore. The Ballroom closed in 1980 and remained empty until 1989, when after a protracted battle between preservationists and the city, the site was extensively redeveloped. Most of the original facade facing Broadway was preserved and restored, and a museum honoring Malcolm X was created inside.

RUTH BROWN'S HOME
600 W. 165th St.

Ruth "Miss Rhythm" Brown had been Atlantic Records's first big star in the 1950s. In fact, the label was often referred to as "The House that

Ruth Built." A decade or so later her star had faded; she married and moved to Long Island to be a mother and housewife. She returned to Harlem in the '70s, and in the '80s joined with other former Atlantic stars such as Clovers and Big Joe Turner to fight her old label, long since acquired by Warner Bros., for back royalties. In 1988 Atlantic agreed to pay Ruth and 35 other artists 20 years of retroactive royalties and contributed $2 million to help establish the Rhythm & Blues Foundation to help older musicians in need. Brown had a successful second act to her illustrious career. She won a Grammy in 1989 for her album *Blues on Broadway* and a Tony award for her performance in the musical *Black and Blue* the same year. She was inducted into the Rock & Roll Hall of Fame in 1993 and worked steadily until her death in 2006.

UNITED PALACE
4140 Broadway

First built in 1930 as an enormous, elaborately decorated movie theater, the United Palace was purchased by TV evangelist Reverend Ike in 1969 and transformed into a church, which it remains. It houses the United Palace House of Inspiration, as well as the United Palace of Cultural Arts. Beginning in 2007, the 3,000-seat theater became a concert venue and has presented a wide array of performers, including Bob Dylan, Bjork, Neil Young, Sonic Youth, and Arcade Fire.

JIM CARROLL'S HOME
585 Isham St.

Probably best known today for his 1978 memoir *The Basketball Diaries* and the subsequent film it inspired, Jim Carroll was also a highly regarded poet and a prime contributor to the downtown Manhattan scene of the 1970s. He later fronted his own band and recorded several albums into the late '90s. An Irish bartender's son, Carroll spent his earliest years on the Lower East Side but moved with his family to Inwood when he entered the sixth grade.

He attended the Good Shepherd School (620 Isham St.) and later earned a scholarship to the exclusive Trinity School (131 W. 91st St.).

An outstanding student and gifted basketball player, he became a heroin addict who supported his habit by hustling gay men.

He published his first book of poetry at age 16 and began to draw acclaim as an important new literary voice. He briefly attended Wagner College and **Columbia University** before making his way downtown to the burgeoning creative scene centered on the Hotel Chelsea (222 W. 23rd St.), **Max's Kansas City (213 Park Ave. South)**, and the East Village. He worked with Andy Warhol and lived for a time with Patti Smith, whom he knew from the Poetry Project at St. Mark's Church (131 E. 10th St.). In addition to *The Basketball Diaries*, Carroll published another memoir, *Forced Entries* (1987), and four more books of poetry in his lifetime. He formed a band, debuting with the album *Catholic Boy* in 1980, which produced the hit "People Who Died." Carroll battled a variety of health issues, and he returned to his street-level childhood home on Isham Street in 2008. He was finishing a novel, *The Petting Zoo*, when he died there at the age of 60 in 2009.

HURRAH ⊘
36 W. 62nd St.

Known for being the venue where Sid Vicious got into a fight with Patti Smith's brother in late 1978 (earning himself nearly two months detox at Rikers Island), Hurrah was also a rock venue owned by Robert Boykin and managed by Jim Fouratt open between 1976 and 1980. The first New York City gig by New Order took place at Hurrah, when the group opened for fellow Mancunians A Certain Ratio. Other artists playing the venue included Suicide, the Cure, Ultravox, Liquid Liquid, Klaus Nomi, the Specials, Bauhaus, the Feelies, and others. Hurrah, sometimes known as Hurrah's, can still be seen in the video for David Bowie's 1980 single "Fashion."

LINCOLN CENTER
10 Lincoln Center Plaza

New York's preeminent performing arts complex contains several venues that have featured many significant rock and rock–related performers since its completion in the '60s.

David Geffen Hall, originally opened as Philharmonic Hall in 1962 and known as Avery Fisher Hall for many years, has featured a variety of artists over time, including Bob Dylan, Simon & Garfunkel, the Supremes, Patti Smith, Aretha Franklin, Ray Charles, the Roots, and Elvis Costello. The Dylan and Simon & Garfunkel performances were both released as live albums. The hall has also hosted the VH1 Hip-Hop Honors.

The hall's namesake, Brooklyn native David Geffen, has had a long and important presence in the music industry as a talent agent, manager, and record executive, founding Asylum Records, Geffen Records, and DGC Records. He was also a co-founder of Dreamworks. Joni Mitchell's "Free Man in Paris" was written about Geffen in 1973. The hall was renamed in his honor in 2015.

The Metropolitan Opera House opened in 1969 and hosted a performance of *Tommy* by the Who on June 7, 1970. It has also hosted MTV's Video Music Awards twice, in 1999 and 2001.

Damrosch Park, immediately adjacent to the Opera House, has hosted many outdoor concerts featuring a wide array of performers spanning multiple musical genres, including Patti Smith, Darlene Love, and Nick Lowe. On

Lee Ranaldo and Jesse Malin perform at Damrosch Park in 2016.

David Geffen Hall

July 30, 2016, a daylong celebration of Lou Reed featured Laurie Anderson, David Johansen, Lenny Kaye, Garland Jeffreys, Nona Hendryx, and John Zorn. Reed's personal archives are housed at the New York Public Library for the Performing Arts (40 Lincoln Center Plaza).

ST. NICHOLAS ARENA ⊘
69 W. 66th St.

Known primarily as a venue for boxing and indoor ice skating, the Arena was the site of WINS DJ Alan Freed's first big live event in New York—the Rock 'n' Roll Jubilee Ball on January 14 and 15, 1955. Among the performers were Big Joe Turner, Fats Domino, Red Prysock, the Moonglows, Buddy Johnson, local favorites the Harptones, and the Drifters, in what would be Clyde McPhatter's final performance with the group.

PYTHIAN TEMPLE
135 W. 70th St.

Originally built as a men's club for the Knights of Pythias in 1927, the Pythian Temple contained a large auditorium that was frequently leased to Decca Records for use as a recording studio. Over the years it was used by a variety of recording artists, including Bill Haley & His Comets, who recorded "Rock Around the Clock" here, and Buddy Holly. It was for many years a hotel before eventually being converted to luxury residences.

Facade detail of the Pythian Temple

UNGANO'S
210 W. 70th St.

The Allman Brothers Band and MC5 may not have a lot in common on the surface, but both made their New York City debuts at Ungano's. A bootleg of the Stooges playing the club on August 17, 1970, recorded by their then-manager Danny Fields, has since been officially released by Rhino Records as *Have Some Fun: Live at Ungano's*. The performance is largely comprised of the band playing songs off their recently released sophomore album, *Fun House*, and the packed house reportedly included Miles Davis and Johnny Winter. Led Zeppelin held a press conference at Ungano's in 1969.

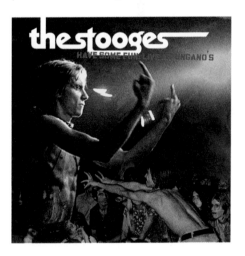

BEACON THEATRE
2124 Broadway

The Beacon Theatre spent over forty years as a first-run movie theater before it began showing live rock shows in the early 1970s. Early performers in the nearly 3,000-person-capacity venue included the Grateful Dead, Rush, Santana, Fleetwood Mac, the Kinks, Bob Marley & the Wailers, and Queen. The Allman Brothers Band famously played extensive residencies in the venue over many years. Duran Duran performed there in August 1987 at the end

Beacon Theatre

of an extensive world tour for the Association to Benefit Children, with a special guest appearance by Lou Reed on a cover of "Sweet Jane" by the Velvet Underground.

In 2006, Martin Scorsese shot the *Shine a Light* concert film around a pair of dates by the Rolling Stones at the Beacon, with guest appearances by Jack White, Buddy Guy, and Staten Island–native Christina Aguilera.

After a renovation, the Beacon is still going strong today, hosting shows by Blondie, Garbage, Nick Cave & the Bad Seeds, Wilco, Ryan Adams, and many others in 2017.

THE LANGHAM
135 Central Park West
Carly Simon and James Taylor lived and raised their children in the Langham between the years 1972 and 1983, when they divorced.

THE PARK BELVEDERE
101 W. 79th St.
For a period in the mid-1980s, the 27th floor of the Park Belvedere was a plush bacchanalia, as both Duran Duran's John Taylor and Culture Club's Boy George succumbed to era-appropriate excess in apartments next to each other.

312 W. 77th St.

MILES DAVIS'S HOME
312 W. 77th St.
Miles Davis is one of the most popular and influential jazz musicians of all time, and he used to live here at 312 W. 77th St. In the late '60s he began to embrace the emerging sounds of R&B, funk, and soul and integrated them into his groundbreaking album *Bitches Brew* in 1970. This merger of influences would create ripples throughout the rock world as well, and give rise to jazz-rock, or fusion.

Davis toured his new sound before rock audiences, including shows at the **Fillmore East (105 2nd Ave.)**. His successive albums, including *A Tribute to Jack Johnson* and *Live-Evil*, cemented his position as a figure whose influence spanned multiple forms of music.

THE DEATH OF KING CURTIS
50 W. 86th St.

Curtis Ousley, better known as King Curtis, was one of R&B's great sax men, and he had an illustrious career as a bandleader, session musician, sideman, and solo artist from the '50s until his death in 1971 at the age of 37.

Curtis had worked with the Coasters, Buddy Holly, Aretha Franklin, John Lennon, and LaVern Baker, among others. He had solo instrumental hits with Soul Twist and Soul Serenade.

Curtis, who lived at 150 W. 96th St., was visiting this 86th Street address, a property he owned, and had an altercation with a man who was seated on the stoop around midnight. A fight ensued and Curtis was fatally stabbed. Before his assailant escaped, though, Curtis was able to take the knife and wound him before collapsing. The killer was later captured. Curtis's funeral was administered by Jesse Jackson and attended by music royalty, including Aretha Franklin, Stevie Wonder, Duane Allman, and Curtis's band the Kingpins.

DING DONG LOUNGE
929 Columbus Ave.
Open from 2002 to 2014, Ding Dong Lounge was a punk dive bar and venue appealing to Columbia University students and locals in search of a cheap drink in an authentically gritty atmosphere. The rest of Vampire Weekend reportedly asked Chris Baio to join the group as its bass guitarist over beers at the Ding Dong Lounge.

THE VELVET UNDERGROUND

The Velvet Underground & Nico in 1967

The Velvet Underground merged primal rock & roll, art, and intellectualism with gritty tales straight from the streets of New York City. The group's influence far outstripped their record sales, and there are few artists who more perfectly evoked the feel of the city.

The unusual was nothing unusual for the Velvet Underground. On January 13, 1966, the then-fledgling band performed live at the Delmonico Hotel for the first time with Nico, a steely German chanteuse. Not only is this performance noteworthy for giving the public its first look at the group that would go on to record a debut album that was bought by almost no one, yet seemingly went on to influence almost everyone, the audience for that show was also remarkable. Not because it was comprised of fellow outsider musicians, artists, and scenesters, but because this first group of people who saw the Velvet Underground with Nico was a vast hall full of psychiatrists.

The **Delmonico Hotel (502 Park Ave.)** was the scene for the forty-third annual dinner of the New York Society for Clinical Psychiatry, and Andy Warhol, the Velvet Underground's primary artistic benefactor and manager, was guest speaker. As he did with almost everything that caught his attention, Warhol chose to turn the night into an event, showing a pair of his films, encouraging the hip cognoscenti who frequently

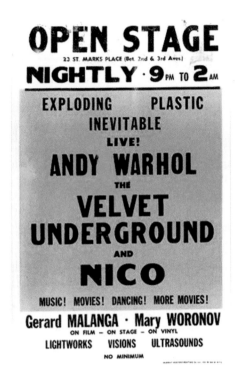

OPEN STAGE
23 ST. MARKS PLACE (Bet. 2nd & 3rd Aves.)
NIGHTLY · 9PM TO **2**AM

EXPLODING   PLASTIC
INEVITABLE
LIVE!

ANDY WARHOL
THE
VELVET
UNDERGROUND
AND
NICO

MUSIC! MOVIES! DANCING! MORE MOVIES!

Gerard MALANGA · Mary WORONOV
ON FILM — ON STAGE — ON VINYL
LIGHTWORKS   VISIONS   ULTRASOUNDS
NO MINIMUM

hung out at his studio and nerve center, the Factory, to ask deliberately confrontational questions of the guests. According to fellow Velvets founder John Cale, it also provided frontman Lou Reed an opportunity to exact revenge for teenage shock treatment by showcasing the group.

The performance at the Delmonico wasn't the first Velvet Underground show in New York City, and it wouldn't be the last. But as it was the debut of the group with Nico, it may have been one of the most important gigs of the early stages of their all-too-short career.

Warhol had come into the picture a month earlier when, at the behest of filmmaker Barbara Rubin, he and Factory figures Paul Morrissey, Edie Sedgwick, and Gerard Malanga attended a Velvet Underground performance on December 16, 1965, at **Cafe Bizarre (106 W. 3rd St.)**⊘, a gig in the middle of a residency arranged by Al Aronowitz. This run marked the first shows the band had performed in New York

City with drummer Maureen "Moe" Tucker, who'd been enlisted after founding member Angus MacLise left the band. Tucker wasn't allowed to play drums in the club and was relegated to tambourine instead.

According to guitarist Sterling Morrison, the band's uniform desire not to play Cafe Bizarre that New Year's Eve led the Velvet Underground to loudly and deliberately cause the termination of their residency by playing "Black Angel's Death Song" after being explicitly asked not to by the club's manager.

Instead, the group traveled much farther uptown, where they were part of a Factory field trip to witness a James Brown show at the **Apollo Theater (253 W. 125th St.)**.

But even before heading to Harlem, the Velvets watched the *CBS Evening News with Walter Cronkite*, which ran a report that night about underground film. Almost two months earlier, a network news crew had filmed the Velvet Underground performing "Heroin." Reed, Cale, and Morrison appeared shirtless, pale, and painted in the film. Tucker played the grim role of a mourning bride complete with dour face obscured by a veil.

The CBS News report was shot in the apartment of filmmaker **Piero Heliczer (450 Grand St., Apt. 5E)**⊘, a dwelling that for a time was also the home of Reed and Morrison. The apartment was also the location where, in July 1965, the band recorded rudimentary demos of a handful of songs, including "Venus in Furs," "Heroin," "I'm Waiting for the Man," and "All Tomorrow's Parties." Years later Cale discovered a copy of the tape, which was cleaned up and officially released as part of the band's box set, *Peel Slowly and See*.

Morrison told a reporter in 1983 that fans of the Velvet Underground's albums were only getting part of the picture, as their live shows were a much more fully immersive experience. The band's New York City shows over the span of their short career were mostly performed in Manhattan, with a number of residencies and return engagements both during and after their relationship with Warhol.

Like much of the country around this time, the East Village was in a constant state of evolution. Over a five-year period, the Velvet Underground technically played three different venues on the same street, though that was largely because of name and ownership changes in the same block of buildings.

It began in April 1966 with what has commonly been referenced as a month-long residency at the Dom. In actuality, the Velvet Underground performed with Warhol's multimedia showcase, the Exploding Plastic Inevitable, in an upstairs venue, the **Open Stage (23 St. Marks Pl.)**. By the time Warhol's revue returned for a run of dates spread out from September to October of the same year,

Sokol Hall, a.k.a. The Gymnasium

the venue was partly renamed the Balloon Farm to suit the then-contemporary trend toward the psychedelic surreal.

The Velvet Underground and Nico performed with the Exploding Plastic Inevitable for one more weeklong run at the Balloon Farm in mid-March of 1967, the same year Warhol opened the **Electric Circus (19-25 St. Marks Pl.)**, a venue that took up considerably more space.

The Electric Circus remained open for four years, the last of which saw one of the final incarnations of the Velvet Underground perform on January 29 and 30, 1971. By that time, Reed

· · **JAN. 2** THRU **JAN. 14** · ·

· · · · · IN PERSON · · · ·

ANDY WARHOL'S
VELVET UNDERGROUND
& NICO
VERVE RECORDING ARTISTS

· · · · · · · · ·

The STEVE PAUL & ANDY WARHOL
UNDERGROUND
AMATEUR HOUR

· · · · IN PERSON · · · ·

STARS of "The CHELSEA GIRLS"
ANDY WARHOL
gurus · creative people · pop celebrities
society submergers · super spatials · swamis · me

TWO GENUINELY GREAT GROUPS NIGHTLY

· · · · · · · · · · · · · ·

STEVE PAUL'S
THE SCENE

301 W. 46 ST. at 8 AVE. - NYC - JU 2-5760

56 Ludlow St.

had already left the band, playing his last shows as a member of the Velvets the previous summer.

Reed's departure from the Velvet Underground occurred near the end of a two-month residency at **Max's Kansas City (213 Park Ave. South)** on August 23, 1970, a show that was recorded by Warhol associate Brigid Polk and officially released two years later as Live at Max's Kansas City.

The Max's residency began on July 23 and ran through August 28. Tucker didn't perform during this run, as she was pregnant. Instead, bass guitarist and Doug Yule's teenage brother Billy sat in on drums, introducing a more traditional backbeat to the Velvet's sometimes simplistically tribal rhythms.

It was at Max's on October 1, 1968, that Doug Yule met up with Reed and then-manager Steve Sesnick after driving directly from Boston. The conversation led to Yule joining the Velvets as a replacement for the recently departed Cale. After just two days of rehearsals, Yule took the stage as a member of the band for the first time in Cleveland. For some, the group continuing

49 Bond St.

without the avant-garde contributions of Cale was tantamount to treason, but for others the Velvet's best work was yet to come.

52 Ludlow St.

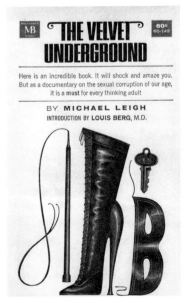

The book that inspired the band

MORE OF THE VELVET UNDERGROUND

NOTEWORTHY LIVE PERFORMANCES

Cafe Wha? (115 MacDougal St.): According to Cale, the band performed here as the Falling Spikes in the spring of 1965.

Art D'Lugoff's Village Gate (160 Bleecker St.): Dick Gregory is overheard calling the Velvets "trash" at the April Fool's Dance and Model's Ball show with the Fugs on March 31, 1966.

Broadway Central Hotel (673 Broadway)⊘: The Falling Spikes played here on August 11, 1965.

The Pocket Theater (100 3rd Ave.): Eric Satie's "Vexations," an 80-second composition written in 1920, was played 840 times in a row in September 1963 by 10 pianists during an event organized by John Cage and including John Cale.

Film-Makers' Cinematheque (125 W. 41st St.) ⊘: The Velvet Underground and Nico performed as part of Andy Warhol Up-Tight from February 8 to 13, 1966, and at the NY Relief Fun Glitter Acidheadspeed Ball & Parade in February 1967.

Steve Paul's the Scene (301 W. 46th St.)⊘: From January 2 to 14, 1967, the Velvet Underground and Nico played the Steve Paul & Andy Warhol Underground Amateur Hour. That May the Velvets performed without Nico for the final show of the Exploding Plastic Inevitable.

Cheetah (Broadway & West 53rd)⊘: The Velvet Underground and Nico performed alongside Tiny Tim on April 11, 1967, at An Imperial Happening, a benefit for radio station WBAI.

Lincoln Center (70 Lincoln Center Plaza): The Velvet Underground performed at a fundraiser for WNET/Channel 13 on November 13, 1967.

Paraphernalia (795 Madison Avenue): In March 1966, the Velvets performed at the opening party of a mod clothing store. In-house designer Betsey Johnson and Cale would marry the following year.

The Gymnasium (424 E. 71st St.): The Exploding Plastic Inevitable featuring the Velvet Underground and Nico performed each weekend of April 1967.

The Southampton East Gallery (145 E. 72nd St.): The Velvets performed alongside Andy Warhol at Pop Sounds, a press-only event, on March 22, 1966.

Central Park SummerStage: The Velvet Underground performed a free show as part of a blood drive in the summer of 1970.

Brooklyn Academy of Music (30 Lafayette Ave., Brooklyn): The Velvets performed at BAM on May 15, 1968, with a semi-reunion on December 3, 1989, when Tucker joined Reed and Cale on stage, playing "Pale Blue Eyes."

NOTEWORTHY RECORDING LOCATIONS

Mayfair Studios (701 7th Ave.)⊘: "Sunday Morning," the second single by the Velvet Underground and Nico, was recorded at Mayfair in November 1966. Later recorded here was the second Velvets album, *White Light/White Heat*, and Nico's *Chelsea Girl*.

Record Plant (321 W. 44th St.): Demos for the band's aborted fourth album were sporadically recorded between May and October of 1969; many would later appear on *VU* and *Another View*.

A&R Studios (112 W. 48th St.): The group recorded "Temptation Inside Your Heart" and "Stephanie Says" at Phil Ramone's A&R Studios over a two-day period in mid-February 1968.

Scepter Studio (254 W. 54th St.): The Velvet Underground recorded nine songs during a session that ran from April 18 to 23, 1966.

Atlantic Studios (157 W. 57th St.) Ⓞ**:** The band's fourth album proper, *Loaded,* was recorded at Atlantic Studios in 1970.

Pickwick Studios (8-16 43rd Ave., Queens) Ⓞ **:** Reed, an in-house songwriter for Pickwick Records, played on many of the label's releases. Reed and Cale also recorded demos in the studio on May 11, 1965, including two takes each of "Heroin" and "Why Don't You Smile Now."

OTHER NOTEWORTHY LOCATIONS

The corner of Essex and Delancey: Morrison and Cale bumped into MacLise and Heliczer sometime during the spring of 1965, leading to the formation of the Velvet Underground.

Film-Makers' Cinematheque (Colonnade Row, 418 to 426 Lafayette St.): Reed, Cale, Morrison, and MacLise first performed here as part of Heliczer's Launching the Dream Weapon, a multimedia event in the spring of 1965.

52 Ludlow St.: Early photo of the group taken on the stoop of this building in 1965.

56 Ludlow St.: Cale, Reed, MacLise, and Heliczer all lived here at various times. Five Velvets demos were recorded in the building in December 1965, including "Here She Comes Now."

49 Bond St.: A pre-VU rehearsal by the Primitives was recorded in a loft here in December 1964. The band was Reed and Cale's first together.

Riviera Cafe (225 W. 4th St.): Reed summoned Morrison and Tucker here in September 1968 to let them know he wanted Cale out of the group. Doug Yule took Cale's place.

The Waldorf Astoria (301 Park Ave.): Reed, Cale, and Tucker performed at the group's induction ceremony into the Rock & Roll Hall of Fame in honor of the late Morrison on January 17, 1996.

New York Public Library (476 5th Ave.): Reed, Tucker, and Yule celebrated the book release of *The Velvet Underground: New York Art,* with a Q&A session led by critic David Fricke in the Celeste Bartos Forum in December 2009.

Times Square Subway Station: Maclise said he bought a copy of S&M paperback *The Velvet Underground* from a newsstand here.

MGM Records (1540 Broadway) Ⓞ**:** The Velvet Underground, including Christa Paffgen ("p.k.a., Nico") signed a record contract with MGM on July 16, 1966.

The Factory (231 E. 47th St., 5th floor) Ⓞ**:** The Velvets first rehearsed with Nico at this location of Andy Warhol's Factory on January 3, 1966, running through a handful of originals, jams, and brief forays into covers.

16 E. 63rd St.: John Cale's brief affair with Warhol Superstar Edie Sedgwick resulted in his moving into her apartment in December 1965.

Glenn Horowitz Bookseller and Art Gallery (50½ E. 64th St.): Reed, Tucker, and Yule appeared with Morrison's widow, Martha, for the opening of the c/o The Velvet Underground, New York, NY exhibition in April 2007.

City College of New York (160 Convent Ave.): Sterling Morrison spent about two weeks at City College.

Beth El Hospital (Linden Boulevard and Rockaway Parkway, Brooklyn): Lewis Allan Reed was born here on March 2, 1942. It is now known as the Brookdale University Hospital and Medical Center.

Forest Hills High School (67-01 110th St., Queens): MacLise and Heliczer met here during high school. The founding members of the Ramones later attended this school.

COPACABANA
10 E. 60th St.

In its heyday, the Copa was considered the best and classiest nightclub in New York, boasting top acts, including Frank Sinatra, Tony Bennett, Nat King Cole, Sammy Davis Jr., Peggy Lee, Billy Eckstine, and Dean Martin and Jerry Lewis. For many years it had a strict whites-only policy, but that changed in 1957. Many key acts of the rock era played there, and several issued live albums, including Sam Cooke, Bobby Darin, the Supremes, the Temptations, and Marvin Gaye.

The Pierre Hotel

PHIL SPECTOR'S OFFICE AND RESIDENCE
440 E. 62nd St.

In the 1960s, Phil Spector kept his Philles New York office here and maintained a penthouse apartment above.

PIERRE HOTEL
2 E. 61st St.

Led Zeppelin stayed at the Pierre in 1974, later returning to host a post-screening party for their documentary *The Song Remains the Same* in 1976. John Lennon decamped here with May Pang during his Lost Weekend in the mid-'70s, writing some of the songs that appeared on *Walls & Bridges.*

BILLY JOEL'S HOME
49 E. 67th St.

Billy Joel lived at 49 E. 67th St. in the late 1970s, a period during which he recorded his 1978 album *52nd Street,* named after the location of the **A&R Recording Studio** ⊘ **(799 7th Ave. at 52nd St.),** where he'd also cut his previous album, 1977's *The Stranger.*

HUNTER COLLEGE
695 Park Ave.

The Doors, Jefferson Airplane, Chuck Berry, Canned Heat, and Eric Burdon and the Animals were among the notable musicians playing shows on campus at Hunter College in the late '60s. Janis Joplin's final New York City show with Big Brother & the Holding Company took place here on November 15, 1968.

Notable musical alumni include Bobby Darin and Nick Valensi and Nikolai Fraiture, guitarist and bassist for the Strokes, respectively.

JUNCO STUDIOS
157 E. 69th St.

When the producers of Elvis Presley's first movie, *Love Me Tender*, saw the completed film, they realized they'd made a mistake by killing off the hero at the end. The film opened in November 1956, and they had little time to spare, so when Elvis was in New York to appear on the *Ed Sullivan Show* in October, he quickly made a trip to Junco Studios to film his spectral coda scene

singing the title song on October 29 before heading back to Memphis the following day.

The former Junco Studios

CRAMPS H.Q.
322 E. 73rd St.

After coming to New York in September 1975, Lux Interior and Poison Ivy of the Cramps found an apartment on the fourth floor at 322 E. 73rd St.

The Carlyle Hotel

322 E. 73rd St.

THE CARLYLE HOTEL
35 E. 76th St.

Perhaps most famous for President John F. Kennedy's maintaining a residence on the 34th floor for a decade, the Carlyle has also played host to well-heeled rock stars over the years. Mick Jagger kept a residence there for some time, and both John and Andy Taylor of Duran Duran stayed in the hotel during the expensive creation of their self-titled *Power Station* album in the mid-'80s.

REGIS HIGH SCHOOL
55 E. 84th St.

Though she attended high school at nearby sister school Convent of the Sacred Heart, Stefani "Lady Gaga" Germanotta appeared in plays at Regis High School, tackling the role of Adelaide in *Guys and Dolls*, and Philia in *A Funny Thing Happened on the Way to the Forum.*

KENNY'S CASTAWAYS
211 E. 84th St./157 Bleecker St.

Though closed now, Kenny's Castaways was a rare live music venue that actually thrived after moving. Originally opened by Pat Kenny at 211 E. 84th St., Kenny's Castaways early years included some of Bruce Springsteen's earliest shows, as well as appearances by the New York Dolls. In 1976 Kenny's relocated to 157 Bleecker St., picking up steam in the Greenwich Village music scene and remaining under its original ownership until Kenny's death in 2002. The venue remained open until 2012, taking with it a long legacy of live music with performances by Patti Smith, Jeff Buckley, the Fugees, and many others.

BARNEY GOOGLE'S ⊘
225 E. 86th St.

The brief mid-'70s run for Barney Google's included soul-oriented shows by David Ruffin, the post–Smokey Robinson Miracles, and Sam & Dave. The *New York Times* reported issues with the then-new club in February 1975, claiming an $8 door charge and two-drink minimum, brusque security, a loud pre-show sound system, and late entry and short set by the Miracles meant for a disappointing night out.

CONVENT OF THE SACRED HEART
1 E. 91st St.

Stefani Germanotta, later known around the world as Lady Gaga, went to Convent of the Sacred Heart, an independent Roman Catholic girls' school, from elementary through high school. One of her first public appearances was a piano recital at Sacred Heart when she was 8 years old.

JOHN HAMMOND'S HOME
9 E. 91st St.

It's hard to imagine American music in the 20th century without John Hammond's influence. He grew up in a house at 9 E. 91st St. as the product of a wealthy family, developing a deep appreciation for African-American music at a young age and becoming one of its most important advocates. For many years, beginning

in the early 1930s he connected performers with audiences and record companies. He is credited with playing a crucial role in advancing the careers of Billie Holiday, Benny Goodman, Count Basie, Bessie Smith, and many others in the jazz age. In 1938 and 1939 he organized a pair of concerts at **Carnegie Hall (881 7th Ave.)** titled From Spirituals to Swing that introduced white audiences to important black artists, including Count Basie, Meade Lux Lewis, Big Joe Turner, Sister Rosetta Tharpe, James P. Johnson, and Big Bill Broonzy. Benny Goodman performed with his pioneering integrated sextet, which included Charlie Christian, Lionel Hampton, and Fletcher Henderson. Hammond had tried to include blues legend Robert Johnson in the event, only to discover he had recently died. He would later collect Johnson's recordings and issue them on Columbia, with whom he had a close association for many years.

He also helped book talent for **Cafe Society (1 Sheridan Sq.)**, one of the very first integrated clubs south of 125th Street that showcased black talent. Billie Holiday, Lena Horne, Ruth

9 E. 91st St.

Brown, Sarah Vaughan, and Big Joe Turner all played here during the 1940s.

Hammond also signed Bob Dylan, Aretha Franklin, and Bruce Springsteen to Columbia before his retirement in the 1970s.

In addition to his musical contributions, Hammond was also a staunch civil rights advocate, serving on the board of directors of the NAACP. His son, also named John Hammond, has had a long and successful career as an accomplished blues performer.

PS 109

215 E. 99th St.

One of the earliest successful girl groups formed as the Harlem Queens in the glee club at PS 109 in 1955. Each of the girls came from the adjoining Washington Houses. Consisting of Emma Pought, Jannie Pought, Laura Webb, Helen Gathers, and Reather Dixon, they spent the next couple of years appearing at various amateur shows, including the **Apollo**, and were eventually approached by manager James Dailey. Dailey felt the Harlem Queens sounded like a female biker gang, so he strongly suggested a name change. They chose

Bobbettes, after Laura's new baby sister. Dailey brought them to Atlantic Records in 1957, where they presented a song they'd written themselves about a despised fifth-grade teacher named Mr. Lee. Atlantic liked the tune but insisted they change the derogatory lyrics. When the cleaned-up version of "Mr. Lee" was released in June, it reached Number 6 and remained on the charts for nearly six months. The following singles went nowhere, so the group penned and cut a sequel, "I Shot Mr. Lee" in 1959, which Atlantic refused to release. They left the label and released it on Triple X, where it was moderately successful. They continued to tour and changed labels several times over the years. One of their most notable recordings was "Love That Bomb" for the *Dr. Strangelove* soundtrack in 1964. They continued to record into the early '80s.

THE BEATLES

Alamy

The Beatles arrive at John F. Kennedy International Airport on Feb. 7, 1964.

The Beatles arrived at John F. Kennedy International Airport on February 7, 1964, on Pan Am flight 101 out of Heathrow Airport in London. They'd left behind what had by then become a familiar scene in their homeland, thousands of screaming fans seeing them off on their journey. What they didn't expect to find in America was much the same reaction. As they taxied down the runway, John, Paul, George, and Ringo were surprised to realize that the crowds of thousands in Queens weren't there to see someone else, perhaps President Lyndon Johnson. Beatlemania had already gripped the US, and for much of the next week it was focused on New York City.

Following a typically goofy press conference during which the Beatles charmed reporters with their quick wit, the group was whisked off to the **Plaza Hotel (768 5th Ave.),** where they were met by further scenes of mayhem as thousands of fans were thwarted in their efforts to get close to the Fab Four by police barricades and over a dozen mounted policemen. The Beatles stayed in the 12th-floor Presidential

"What do you think of Beethoven?" —PRESS QUESTION
"Great. Especially his poems." —RINGO STARR

Plaza Hotel

THEATRE THREE PRODUCTIONS

PRESENT

THE FIRST NEW YORK APPEARANCE OF THE

BEATLES

CARNEGIE HALL
WED. FEB. 12

2 SHOWS 7PM & 8·30PM

PRICES $4·00 $4·50 $5·00   TICKETS GO
ON SALE AT CARNGIE HALL FROM JAN 27

Suite, where they entertained guests such as the Ronettes, George Harrison's sister Louise, and Murray the K, a popular NYC DJ who'd dubbed himself the "Fifth Beatle."

On February 8 the Beatles held a press conference in the hotel's Baroque Room, after which George retired to his bed with a sore throat. The rest of the group went on a sightseeing walk through Central Park, trailed by a fleet of news photographers and a few hundred teenage girls. The trio then went to the

SID BERNSTEIN

PRESENTS THE

BEATLES

IN PERSON

PLUS **ALL STAR SHOW**

SHEA STADIUM
TUES. 7:30 P.M. AUG. 23

ALL SEATS RESERVED: $4.50, 5.00, 5.75 phone **265-2280** FOR INFORMATION
TICKETS NOW AT
SINGER SHOP, RECORD DEP'T. Rockefeller Center Promenade, 49th-50th Sts. on Fifth Ave.

CBS Studios (**1697 Broadway**), today officially called the Ed Sullivan Theater, for a sound check and run through of the following day's *Ed Sullivan Show* program. The group's assistant and friend Neil Aspinall stood in for George during the camera checks.

That evening, John, Paul, and Ringo were joined by their record producer George Martin at **21 Club (21 W. 52nd St.)** for a dinner hosted by executives with Capitol Records.

Much of February 9 was spent back at CBS Studios, where the Beatles taped performances before a live audience that didn't appear until the February 23 episode of the *Ed Sullivan Show*. They played "Twist & Shout," "Please Please Me" and "I Want to Hold Your Hand" to a different, but no less enthusiastic audience than the crowd there for the actual live broadcast later in the evening.

For the 8 p.m. live broadcast, before an audience of 728 in the deceptively tiny theater

The Delmonico Hotel

181 E. 73rd St.

and an estimated 73 million watching on television across the country, the Beatles opened the *Ed Sullivan Show* with "All My Loving," "Till There Was You," and "She Loves You." Later in the episode, they returned to play "I Saw Her Standing There" and "I Want to Hold Your Hand."

Also on the episode that night was magician Fred Kaps, comedian Frank Gorshin, Welsh entertainer Tessie O'Shea, comedy outfit McCall & Brill, and the cast of *Oliver!*, a then-current Broadway production that included future Monkee Davy Jones in the role of the Artful Dodger.

After stopping by the **Playboy Club (5 E. 59th St.)** with Murray the K, the Beatles walked to the nearby **Paul Taubman's Penthouse Club (30 Central Park South)** for dinner. They closed out the night dancing at the **Peppermint Lounge (128 W. 45th St.)**.

Much of February 10 was split between press interviews and industry awards presentations for the group's recent and quite sudden success in America. With snowfall blanketing the northeast, the Beatles boarded a train at **Pennsylvania Station (7th and 8th Avenues between 31st and 33rd Streets)** the following morning for the journey to Washington, D.C., where they performed at Washington Coliseum. They returned the following day, Abraham Lincoln's birthday, to an estimated 10,000 kids at Penn Station. After a quick shower and shave at the Plaza, the group set out for **Carnegie Hall (881 7th Ave.)**, where they performed a pair of shows that evening. Demand for tickets was so high, a few rows of extra seats were set up on the stage.

The next morning, Beatlemania headed south on National Airlines Flight 11 to Miami. When the Beatles returned to New York City later in the year, the shock waves of their initial British Invasion were still being felt across all five boroughs by young kids growing their hair long, picking up guitars, and starting their own groups.

MORE OF THE BEATLES

NOTEWORTHY LIVE PERFORMANCES

Paramount Theater (1501 Broadway): On the final date of their first North American tour, the Beatles performed at a charity event for the United Cerebral Palsy Fund on September 20, 1964.

Forest Hills Tennis Stadium (1 Tennis Pl., Queens): The Beatles performed as part of the Forest Hills Music Festival's 1964 season on August 28 and 29.

Shea Stadium (126-01 Roosevelt Ave., Queens) ⊘: The Beatles made history when they played before an audience of nearly 56,000 fans at Shea Stadium on August 15, 1965. They returned to play Shea on August 23, 1965.

OTHER NOTEWORTHY LOCATIONS

NBC Studios 6B (30 Rockefeller Plaza): John and Paul appeared on *The Tonight Show* on May 14, 1968, to promote Apple Records and Apple Corps.

St. Regis Hotel (2 E. 55th St.): John and Paul spent most of May 13, 1968, in a suite at the St. Regis conducting interviews about Apple Records and Apple Corps.

Americana of New York (811 7th Ave.): On May 14, 1968, John and Paul held a press conference at the Americana Hotel during their brief Apple press blitz.

181 E. 73rd St.: In town to promote Apple Records and Apple Corps between May 11 and 15, 1968, John and Paul stayed at the home of their lawyer, Nat Weiss.

Hans Christian Andersen **(Central Park, just west of Conservatory Lake):** John and Paul were photographed leaning on the bronze statue of this Danish fairy-tale author in May 1968.

Plaza Hotel (768 5th Ave.): Half of the Beatles returned to the Plaza on December 19, 1974, when Paul and George signed paperwork to legally end the group's partnership.

Downtown Manhattan Heliport (Pier 6): For their 1964 shows at the Forest Hills Tennis Stadium, the Beatles flew to Queens from this Wall Street heliport to avoid getting stuck in traffic.

Delmonico Hotel: (502 Park Ave.): The Beatles stayed at the Delmonico in late August 1964. Bob Dylan introduced the Fab Four to marijuana for the first time there. Previously, the group's manager Brian Epstein met Ed Sullivan at the Delmonico in November 1963 to negotiate contracts for the Beatles' appearances on Sullivan's show the following year.

Warwick Hotel (65 W. 54th St.): The Beatles took up the entire 33rd floor of the Warwick Hotel between August 13 and 17, 1965.

Empire State Building (350 5th Ave.): A photograph of George was taken by his brother Peter on the observation deck of the Empire State Building during a pre–British Invasion visit in September 1963.

Fillmore East (105 2nd Ave.): The Beatles' film *Magical Mystery Tour* was screened here on August 11, 1968, as a benefit for the Liberation News Service. No one from the group was in attendance.

Riviera Idlewild Hotel (151-20 Baisley Blvd., Queens): The Beatles spent the night here after their show at the **Paramount Theater** on September 20, 1964, before flying home from JFK International Airport the following morning.

JOHN & YOKO

Yoko Ono and John Lennon at the Hit Factory, August 1980

"If I'd lived in Roman times, I'd have lived in Rome. Where else? Today, America is the Roman Empire, and New York is Rome itself."—JOHN LENNON

John Lennon and Yoko Ono came to New York City in 1971 in part to escape the negativity of the British press, but also because New York City is New York City. The couple's first stop was the **St. Regis Hotel (2 E. 55th St.)**, opened in 1904 by John Jacob Astor IV. The couple rented four suites on the 17th floor of the St. Regis for around three months, during which they shot footage for a promotional film with celebrities such as Dick Cavett, Fred Astaire, Jack Palance, and former Beatle George Harrison.

By the end of the year, they'd decamped to a decidedly less lush, but significantly more bohemian two-room loft in the West Village at 105 Bank St., which they rented from Joe Butler of the Lovin' Spoonful in October 1971. In a back bedroom beneath a skylight, much of John and Yoko's time at home was spent in a large bed in front of a large television. Immersed in the city's counterculture and inspired to act after forging friendships with, among others, Chicago Seven members Jerry Rubin and Abbie

The Dakota

105 Bank St.

Hoffman, the couple marched and performed at several high-profile benefit concerts and channeled their political rage into *Some Time in New York City*, a confrontational album released in 1972 and credited to John & Yoko/Plastic Ono Band with Elephant's Memory and Invisible Strings. The album was a critical and commercial disappointment, with its sleeve including a doctored image of Richard Nixon and Mao Zedong dancing in the nude that didn't help Lennon's reputation with the US government. The couple lived on Bank Street for around sixteen months, leaving after the loft was robbed.

The Dakota (1 W. 72nd St.) is John and Yoko's most widely known residence. In February 1973, seeking privacy and security, the couple moved to the seventh floor of The Dakota, a formidable co-op along Central Park West that by then had already been designated a New York City Landmark and was listed on the National Register of Historic Places. By 1976 it was also cited as a National Historic Landmark. John and Yoko's first few years in The Dakota were

marked by a rocky period in their relationship that resulted in a protracted separation. Though Ono remained at The Dakota during this period, Lennon left for Los Angeles with the couple's personal assistant, May Pang. He began a creative period marked by notorious nights on the town with the Hollywood Vampires, a celebrity drinking posse formed by Alice Cooper, which counted among its members Ringo Starr, Harry Nilsson, Keith Moon, and Micky Dolenz.

By early 1975, Lennon and Ono were reunited at The Dakota, and when the couple's son Sean was born on John's 35th birthday that October, the former Beatle largely retreated from the public eye to focus on fatherhood. The next

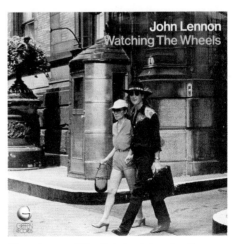

The entrance of The Dakota pictured on the sleeve of "Watching the Wheels"

434 E. 52nd St.

few years were spent in relative domestic bliss, with Yoko handling the couple's business affairs and John baking bread and spending time with Sean. But by the end of the decade, the couple was recording music again, resulting in *Double Fantasy*, and its lead single, "(Just Like) Starting Over"/"Kiss Kiss Kiss." *Double Fantasy*

was released on November 17, 1980, and was initially a modest worldwide hit. Within three weeks, everything changed.

On December 8, 1980, photographer Annie Leibovitz visited John and Yoko at The Dakota to photograph the couple for *Rolling Stone*. An iconic shot of Lennon, fully nude and kissing a clothed Ono, his leg draped over her, was taken during the session.

Late in the afternoon, John and Yoko took a limousine to the **Record Plant (321 W. 44th St.)** to mix Ono's "Walking on Thin Ice," which featured a scathing guitar line by Lennon. The couple returned home shortly before 11 p.m., and as they exited their limousine and walked through the 72nd Street entrance to The Dakota, Lennon was shot in the back by Mark David Chapman.

As the news of Lennon's death spread across the world, fans converged on The Dakota to hold a vigil, singing and grieving throughout the night.

John Lennon memorial in Central Park near The Dakota

1 White St.

MORE JOHN & YOKO

NOTEWORTHY LIVE PERFORMANCES

Fillmore East (105 2nd Ave.): John and Yoko performed here with Frank Zappa & the Mothers of Invention on June 6, 1971.

Madison Square Garden (4 Pennsylvania Plaza): John and Yoko headlined the One to One concert here on August 30, 1972, alongside Stevie Wonder, Roberta Flack, and Sha Na Na.

Duffy Square (7th Ave. and West 47th St.): John and Yoko addressed the crowd and played an impromptu version of "Give Peace a Chance" following a peace rally.

Waldorf Astoria (301 Park Ave.): John Lennon's final live performance took place at the Waldorf Astoria on April 18, 1975, as part of a celebrity-heavy television tribute to British media mogul Lew Grade.

Apollo Theater (253 W. 125th St.): On December 17, 1971, John and Yoko performed at the Apollo Theater for a benefit following the deadly riot at Attica Correctional Facility three months earlier.

NOTEWORTHY RECORDING LOCATIONS

Record Plant (321 W. 44th St.): John's first solo recordings in New York were made here in July 1971, when he recut some tracks for *Imagine*. He returned frequently over the years.

Right Track Recording (168 W. 48th St.): Yoko recorded *Starpeace* with Bill Laswell in 1985.

Sear Sound Recording (353 W. 48th St. #6): *Yokokimthurston*, an experimental collaboration between Yoko Ono and then–Sonic Youth members Kim Gordon and Thurston Moore, was recorded at Sear Sound.

Hit Factory (421 W. 54th St.): The pair recorded *Double Fantasy* here in 1980. Yoko returned to record the cathartic *Season of Glass*, released in June 1981.

Quad Recording Studios (723 7th Ave. #10): Yoko Ono and IMA recorded *Rising* in 1995 and produced *Blueprint for a Sunrise* here in 2001.

OTHER NOTEWORTHY LOCATIONS

Strawberry Fields (Central Park West between 71st and 74th Streets): Living memorial and meditative spot dedicated to John Lennon. It was dedicated on October 9, 1985, what would have been Lennon's 45th birthday.

Tavern on the Green (Central Park West & 67th Street): John and Sean Lennon reportedly celebrated their shared birthdays at Tavern on the Green on October 9, 1979 and 1980. In the latter year, Yoko Ono had "Happy Birthday John and Sean" written in the sky above Central Park.

West Side Pharmacy (255 Columbus): Lennon's local pharmacy while he lived at The Dakota.

Cafe La Fortuna (69 W. 71st St.): A favorite spot of Lennon's for cappuccino and conversation.

92nd Street Y (1395 Lexington Ave.): John used to take Sean for swimming lessons at the 92nd Street Y.

Pierre Hotel (2 E. 61st St.): Lennon decamped here with May Pang after returning from Los Angeles following his Lost Weekend, writing some of the songs that appeared on *Walls & Bridges*.

434 E. 52nd St.: John and May Pang rented a penthouse apartment here in 1974 during his separation from Yoko Ono.

Mr. Chow (324 E. 57th St.): Feeling good about their work with Lennon on *Double Fantasy*, Ono

and the musicians who'd performed agreed here over a jubilant toast in November 1980 that they would tour together the following year. The tour would never happen.

1700 Broadway: Former Beatles manager Allen Klein's offices, where Lennon and Ono met May Pang; headquarters of Beatles' company Apple Corps, Ltd.

Berlitz Language Center (40 W. 51st St.): Lennon studied Japanese here with tutor Tamiko Steinberg in advance of a 1977 visit to Japan.

New York City Bar Association (42 W. 44th St.): In the midst of Lennon's deportation fight, the couple and their attorney, Leon Wildes, held a press conference in the Stimson Room on April Fool's Day, 1973.

Flux-Hall (359 Canal St.): Exhibitions by John and Yoko appeared in Fluxfest, April 11 through 17, 1970, with further weekly installments running through June 12.

1 White St.: The fictional embassy address of John and Yoko's "conceptual country," Nutopia.

SPUR ROCK IN HECKSCHER PLAYGROUND

The cover photo of the Lovin' Spoonful's 1966 single "Daydream" was shot here. John Sebastian, wearing a fur coat, is the felled prey, while the rest of the band stands above him. Zal Yanofsky holds a rifle and has his foot on Sebastian, with the entire group giving off the air of scruffy landed gentry.

concerts in the rink that lasted through 1976. During those years, artists such as the Jimi Hendrix Experience, the Who, Traffic, Jerry Lee Lewis, Led Zeppelin, Sam & Dave, Ray Charles, the Four Tops, the Byrds, the Band, Little Richard, Peter Frampton, Bob Marley & the Wailers, the Bee Gees, and Patti Smith performed there.

Dr. Pepper took over sponsorship of the series in 1977, with Ronnie Spector, Hall & Oates, Bonnie Raitt, Dion, Odetta, Richie Havens, Patti Smith, the Kinks, Muddy Waters, Blondie, the Ramones, the B-52s, Peter Tosh, the Cars, Devo, Talking Heads, the Pretenders, and many other playing before the festival was moved to **Pier 84** along the Hudson River following the 1980 season.

GAPSTOW BRIDGE

Dion & the Belmonts shot the photo for the cover of their 1966 album *Together Again* while standing in the middle of this bridge.

WOLLMAN RINK

Originally opened in 1949 as a skating rink, Wollman Rink went on to host jazz concerts with artists such as Billie Holiday, the Dave Brubeck Quartet, Dizzy Gillespie and others performing there.

In the mid-'60s, the Rheingold Music Festival, which became the Schaefer Music Festival in 1968, began a series of summer

BETHESDA ARCADE

The Young Rascals shot the photo for their 1966 single "You Better Run" at the top of the Bethesda Arcade steps, with its iconic carved patterns seen just behind the group's heads. The cover photo for *The Beau Brummels, Volume 2*, a 1965 album by the San Francisco–based Beau Brummels, was shot just inside the arcade.

NAUMBURG BANDSHELL

The cover photo of 1965's *The Best of Herman's Hermits* was shot at the bottom of the steps on the right side of the band shell, with the group looking relaxed and casual and not nearly as peppy as their music. Many artists, including Grateful Dead and Jefferson Airplane, played the band shell in the '60s. BritPop icons Oasis shot clips for their "Live Forever" video in Central Park, including a mimed performance of the single at the Naumburg Bandshell on July 22, 1994.

ALICE IN WONDERLAND

Dedicated in 1959, the bronze statue of *Alice in Wonderland* and her storybook friends was

commissioned by George Delacorte and created by sculptor José de Creeft. Engraved around the statue are lines from Lewis Carroll's nonsense poem "Jabberwocky." Separated by nearly two decades, the Jimi Hendrix Experience and Sonic Youth both posed on the *Alice in Wonderland* sculpture alongside small children.

THE GREAT LAWN

Central Park

Central Park's Great Lawn, a 55-acre pasture located roughly between 79th and 85th Streets, has been the site of many large summertime concerts, including:

- Elton John, September 13, 1980
- Simon & Garfunkel (Reunion Concert), September 19, 1981
- Diana Ross, July 21, 1983
- Paul Simon, August 15, 1991
- Garth Brooks, August 7, 1991
- Dave Matthews, September 25, 2003
- Bon Jovi, July 12, 2008

DIANA ROSS PLAYGROUND

Central Park West and W. 81st Street

Diana Ross donated the money to open a playground bearing her name with some of the proceeds from her concert on the Great Lawn in 1983. Found at the base of Summit Rock, the playground features a sprawling wooden play structure, bucket swings, and a sprinkler used on hot summer days.

PATTI SMITH

For the casual fan of the era that would come to define "Punk," it may come as something of a surprise to learn that the first musical figure to emerge from that gritty downtown scene and have a significant national impact has her creative roots in the visual arts and poetry.

Patricia Lee Smith was born in Chicago but grew up in and around Philadelphia and its southern New Jersey environs. From an early age, Patti developed an acute interest in the arts and reading, and she would go through a series of restlessly creative phases that would propel her into poetry, prose, art, photography, and music throughout her life.

In 1964, as the Beatles, the Rolling Stones, and Bob Dylan were transforming the landscape of popular music, Patti graduated from Deptford Township High School intending to go to art college, but instead she attended Glassboro State Teachers College for two years, leaving in frustration. She had a harrowing experience in the ensuing workplace (as recounted in the 1974 single "Piss Factory") and an accidental pregnancy, which caused her to live with another family for a few months before giving the baby up for adoption. She knew where her destiny awaited, though, and at age 21, with barely enough to cover the bus fare, she fled to New York City, armed with her love of Arthur Rimbaud, Dylan, the Stones, and an unflinching self-confidence.

Patti Smith arrived in New York on July 3, 1967, via the decidedly unscenic **Port Authority Bus Terminal (625 8th Ave.)**, where she immediately transferred to the subway and headed for Brooklyn. She hoped to connect with a friend who was enrolled at the nearby Pratt

Bob Gruen

Patti Smith onstage at the Schaefer Music Festival in Central Park on July 9, 1976

Institute, an Engineering and Arts college in Clinton Hill. Unfortunately, it was summer break and her friend had moved to a new apartment. One of the current residents knew where her friend could be found, though, and offered to direct her there. This would be her first fleeting encounter with Robert Mapplethorpe, a young Pratt art student, and the man who would ultimately become her closest companion for the next few years. Alas, her friend was not at the said address, so Patti would sleep rough for the next several days, on porches, and in Central Park close to the statue of *Alice in Wonderland*. Like many young newcomers, she would wander the streets of Greenwich Village and spend hours observing the people in Washington Square Park, an active gathering place for artists, folkies, activists, and people of every stripe imaginable. She explored **St. Marks Place** and the East Village, then a fairly ragged but colorful neighborhood of immigrants, hippies, artists, and the poor, always dragging her plaid suitcase along with her. One day she and a street friend found a little money and treated themselves to a hot meal at the **Waverly Diner (385 6th Ave.)**, but otherwise she ate day-old bread and handouts. The rest of the time she was desperately looking for work, and after a disastrous single shift waiting tables at a Times Square restaurant, she found work at the midtown flagship location of **Brentano's (586 5th Ave.)**, a venerable bookstore near Rockefeller Center. She still had no place to stay, though, and often surreptitiously slept in the store overnight, only to emerge from the bathroom in the morning as the others readied the store. One day she ran into Mapplethorpe again in the bookstore. He, coincidentally, worked at the downtown branch of **Brentano's (20 University Pl.)** in the Village. Not long afterwards, in the midst of an uncomfortable date with an older bookstore patron, Patti spotted Mapplethorpe in Tompkins Square Park, where he happily rescued her by posing as her boyfriend. The two shared an egg cream at **Gem Spa (131 2nd Ave.)** while commiserating. The pair would become inseparable. He brought her to stay at his place, an attic room in the home of some friends on Waverly Avenue in Brooklyn. After several weeks, the two had enough money saved for their own place nearby at **160 Hall St.** on the second floor for $80 per month. This would become their headquarters for well over a year.

By winter, both Patti and Robert had lost their jobs at Brentano's but found seasonal employment at **FAO Schwarz (745 5th Ave.)**, the gigantic toy shop. Robert decorated windows,

160 Hall St., Brooklyn

but Patti was stuck at the cash register. Afterward, she worked briefly at **Argosy Books (116 E. 59th St.)** before settling at **Scribner's Book Store (597 5th Ave.)**. Scribner's would be her steady job for the next couple of years. Robert, meanwhile, went through a succession of jobs, one of which was as an usher at the **Fillmore East (105 2nd Ave.)**, where he was able to get Patti in to see The Doors. Jim Morrison was to have a lasting influence on her.

By early 1969 Patti had moved out of the Hall Street apartment and into the arms of a new boyfriend nearby. Robert, distraught, threatened to turn gay. Shortly thereafter, he moved to San Francisco. Patti took a leave of absence from Scribner's and spent three months in Paris with her sister Linda. After returning to New York in July, she decided to reconcile with Robert and found him house-sitting on Delancey Street, having just broken up with a boyfriend. Additionally, he had neglected his health and had become seriously ill. They both stayed for a short time until a neighbor was murdered, then decided to go elsewhere, ending up at the

Allerton Hotel (302 W. 22nd St.) in Chelsea, a decrepit fleabag for transients, junkies, and hookers. Patti eventually got them into the **Hotel Chelsea (222 W. 23rd St.)**, legendary home of artists and writers from Bob Dylan to Dylan Thomas. This was no small feat. Though relatively inexpensive, applicants had to gain approval from the manager, Stanley Bard, who could be extremely choosy about his tenants. Thankfully, the Chelsea had a tradition of catering to struggling artists, and Patti and Robert passed inspection and moved into the smallest room in the sprawling building, #1017, at $55 per week. Living at the Chelsea would change their lives and social circles dramatically. William Burroughs, Allen Ginsberg, Gregory Corso, and an unending variety of musicians, poets, filmmakers, and other colorful characters would become part of their daily routine.

One of the Chelsea denizens Patti befriended was Harry Smith in room 705. He is remembered today primarily for his multi-

The former Allerton Hotel

volume *Anthology of American Folk Music*, originally released in 1952 and enormously influential to the folk revival of the 1950s and '60s. He frequently accompanied Patti to **Samuel Weiser's (734 Broadway)**, a specialty occult book shop, where she enjoyed flipping through vintage editions and once bought a deck of tarot cards.

Another good friend at the Chelsea was Sandy Daly, a photographer and filmmaker. She made the self-explanatory *Robert Having His Nipple Pierced* in 1970 with Patti providing vocal commentary. Later, when Patti had a lightning bolt tattooed on her knee, Daly filmed that, too.

Sandy also brought Robert and Patti to **Max's Kansas City (213 Park Ave. South)** for the first time. Robert idolized Andy Warhol, and this had been his virtual living room. Ostensibly a bar, restaurant, and musical venue, Max's was the hippest headquarters for the downtown cultural cognoscenti. By 1969, however, Warhol was absent, having narrowly survived a shooting at his new Factory only the year before. Many of his friends and acolytes were present, however, and making it to the round table in the back room where he once held court was still considered a high plateau of cool. Going to Max's would become a nightly ritual for Patti and Robert, though it would take quite some time for the regulars to take to the scruffy pair. In time, though, they were accepted and became part of the scene.

In May 1970 Patti appeared in a production of Jackie Curtis's *Femme Fatale: The Three Faces of Gloria* at **LaMama Experimental Theater (74 E. 4th St.)** with Penny Arcade and Mary Woronov, directed by Tony Ingrassia. It was one of her first experiences performing for an audience. She later appeared in Ingrassia's production of *Island* with Arcade and Wayne County. These productions were not the bright lights of Broadway, but they were seen and appreciated by an influential crowd. Andy Warhol, for example, came to see *Island* multiple times.

Bobby Neuwirth was another Chelsea habitué and friend of Bob Dylan's who saw potential in Patti and encouraged her writing. He also brought her to different music venues and introduced her to a variety of artists, including the Velvet Underground at Max's. In the summer of 1970, Neuwirth brought Patti to see Janis Joplin at the **Forest Hills Tennis Stadium (1 Tennis Place, Queens)**. The show was rained out, but she returned with Bobby, Janis, and her posse to the Chelsea to spend the evening and witnessed Kris Kristofferson teaching Janis her future hit "Me and Bobby McGee." The show was held the following evening and was a huge success. Afterward the gang got together at **Remington's (11 Waverly Pl)**, one of Janis's favorite watering holes in the Village. By the wee hours of the morning, Janis was heartbroken after striking out with some guy, so Patti, as recounted in her memoir *Just Kids*, brought her back to her room at the Chelsea and sang a song she had written for her. Unfortunately, Janis would never sing it, dying tragically of a drug overdose in Los Angeles two months later.

In August, Jimi Hendrix opened **Electric Lady Studios (52 W. 8th St.)** on the site of the former Generations Club. Patti was among the faithful invited to the opening celebration but was too intimidated to go inside. Luckily for her, Jimi was taking a powder from his own bash and quietly chatted with her on the sidewalk out front. Patti would later record her first single and first album here.

By this time Patti was supplementing her income with record reviews, then selling the gratis records for additional cash. Impressed by an article she read about a capella groups, she sought out the author, Lenny Kaye, and discovered he worked at **Village Oldies (149 Bleecker St.)**, a used-record store. Kaye was a

prolific music journalist, having published in *Crawdaddy, Fusion, Jazz & Pop*, and *Cavalier*. He had his own group, the Zoo, and had even released a single, "Crazy Like a Fox," under the name Link Cromwell in 1966. They soon established a friendship that was to last for the next three decades. In 1972 Kaye assembled the *Nuggets* double LP for Elektra Records. Subtitled *Original Artyfacts From the First Psychedelic Era*, it proved to be a major inspiration for punk musicians just as Harry Smith's compilation had done for folkies.

In 1970 Patti and Robert, stifled by their cramped quarters in the Chelsea, rented a small loft on the second floor of **206 W. 23rd St.** just down the block. They ultimately exited the Chelsea and took over the entire second floor; Robert in the back and Patti in the front room facing the street.

Gregory Corso introduced Patti to the **Poetry Project at St. Mark's Church (131 E. 10th**

St. Mark's in the Bowery

St.). Led by Anne Waldman, the Poetry Project had become an important and influential literary venue. It offered free readings and workshops that featured contributors such as Allen Ginsberg, John Ashbery, Lou Reed, and Jim Carroll. Patti became a regular spectator at their readings as her confidence in her own work grew. In February 1971 she secured a spot opening for Gerard Malanga that attracted a large audience, primarily due to Malanga's Warhol connections, but also because Patti by this time had a few followers of her own. With Lenny Kaye as accompanist on electric guitar, Patti opened with an irreverent rendition of "Mack the Knife," then declared, "This reading is dedicated to crime."

What followed was an energetic rapid-fire performance of poetry and song that electrified the audience. It contained several notable literary and entertainment figures, including Lou Reed Terry Ork, Danny Fields, Lisa Robinson, Steve Paul, Johnny & Edgar Winter, and Sam Shepard. Considering the specialized reach of a poetry reading, it had a dramatic impact. Many have described it as one of the transformative events where the 1960s became the 1970s in terms of style and delivery. Patti's use of literary allusion mated with a rock & roll street sensibility wasn't completely unprecedented, but it was fresh, and the fact that it was being presented by a woman was somewhat revolutionary. Patti would return to St. Mark's many times over the years in support of the Poetry Project.

From this point forward, Patti's star was on the rise, at least among the New York arts crowd. She was offered a record deal by impresario Steve Paul for his new Blue Sky label, which she turned down. Patti would leave her job at Scribner's, though, and work as Paul's assistant.

Sam Shepard was someone who entered Patti's life via his alternate identity as drummer Slim Shadow with the Holy Modal Rounders. Shepard had written several well-received plays with Theatre Genesis at **St. Mark's Church** and the screenplay for Michaelangelo Antonioni's *Zabriskie Point*. The two had a brief relationship and jointly wrote an autobiographical one-act play entitled *Cowboy Mouth*. The title is from a lyric in Bob Dylan's "Sad-Eyed Lady of the Lowlands." It premiered on a double bill with Shepard's "Back Bog Beast Bait," which starred his wife O-Lan, at the **American Place Theater** on April 29, 1971, at **St. Clement's Episcopal Church (423 W. 46th St)**. Shepard and Smith performed *Cowboy Mouth* as Slim Shadow and Johnny Guitar. The production lasted all of three nights before Shepard left with his family for France. It has since been revived in various forms over the years. She would later perform another Shepard play, *Blue Bitch*, at St. Mark's Church in 1973.

In 1971 Patti began a relationship with Allen Lanier, keyboard player for the emerging group Soft White Underbelly, soon to be known as Blue Öyster Cult. Lanier moved into Patti's half of the loft on 23rd Street, but the couple soon moved to their own apartment in the Village, initially on E. 10th Street, but later at 107 MacDougal Street. This would be their home for the next five years.

In late 1971 Telegraph Books, at the suggestion of Gerard Malanga, offered to publish a book of Patti's poetry. Established by Andrew Wylie, Victor Bockris, and Aram Saroyan, Telegraph created a collection of small paperback poetry editions, similar in format to the City Lights Pocket Poets series and operated out of a bookstore at 32 Jones St. *Seventh Heaven* was published in the spring of 1972 and was dedicated to Mickey Spillane and Anita Pallenberg. Despite its relatively low circulation, the book did create something of a stir, thanks to Patti's contacts in the music press. Another

107 MacDougal St.

ROCK 'N' RIMBAUD

On November 4 and 10, 1973 (the anniversary of Arthur Rimbaud's death), Patti launched the first of her Rock 'n' Rimbaud events at the Hotel Diplomat's disco **Le Jardin (108 W. 43rd St.)**. It consisted of several poems and a variety of rock & roll tunes, all loosely collected around themes in Rimbaud's work with backing by Lenny Kaye and pianist Bill Elliott. She would repeat the R 'n' R events for the next two years on November 10 at other locations:

- October 27, 1974: Riverside Plaza Hotel (253 W. 73rd St.)
- November 10, 1974: Hotel Roosevelt's Blue Hawaii Discotheque (45 E. 45th St.)
- November 15, 1975 (Two Shows): Larry Richardson's Dance Gallery (242 E. 14th St.)

small chapbook of her poetry, *kodak*, would be published later that year by Middle Earth Press in Philadelphia.

Patti also began an association with the **Gotham Book Mart (41 W. 47th St.)**. Gotham's Andreas Brown had been in the audience for her performance at St. Mark's, and he was impressed enough to produce *A Useless Death*, a three-page chapbook, and in 1973 *Witt*, her second volume of poetry. Gotham had a long and illustrious history supporting both writers and artists, including e.e. cummings, William Burroughs, and Edward Gorey. In later years, Gotham would display Patti's drawings and publish another chapbook, *Ha! Ha! Houdini!* in 1977.

Around this time Patti also worked for a short while in the basement at the **Strand Bookstore (828 Broadway)**, her last regular job. Things began to move quickly for Patti in late 1972 and into 1973. New manager Jane Friedman booked her first at the **West End Bar (2909 Broadway)** near Columbia University with Lenny Kaye, then as an opening act for Teenage Lust, Ruby & the Rednecks, and, most notably, the New York Dolls at the **Mercer Arts Center (240 Mercer St.)** Ø, where she often dealt with hostile crowds not especially interested in her kind of performance art. She gave as good as she got, however, and soon won over at least part of the crowd. It was here that she first presented "Piss Factory," her brutal homage to her former working life.

Continued engagements into 1974 led Patti and Lenny to add a regular keyboard player. Richard Sohl came to the audition wearing a sailor suit and was quickly dubbed DNV

Known as the Riverside Plaza Hotel when Patti performed there, it is today The Level Club, a luxury residence.

after the character Tadzio in the Visconti film of *Death in Venice*. Many intense rehearsals took place at the office of their manager, Jane Friedman, within the old **Victoria Theater (1547 Broadway)** Ø before the trio would be ready to play live together, but they were inexorably moving closer to full-fledged band status. On April 14, 1974, Lenny and Patti went to see the band Television at **CBGB (315 Bowery)** for the first time. Patti knew Richard Hell, a fellow poet, from that scene, but hadn't experienced the club or the band before, and it would prove to have an enormous impact. This was the early pre-recorded edition of Television that included both Hell and Tom Verlaine, whom Patti fell for immediately.

On June 5, she and the group, along with Tom Verlaine, went into **Electric Lady Studios** to record her first single on the privately issued Mer label. The A-side featured "Hey Joe," a song based loosely on the Jimi Hendrix version but influenced by the then-ongoing Patti Hearst saga. "Piss Factory," which Patti had been performing live for some time, was on the B-side. The 45 was distributed via **Village Oldies**, Gotham Book Mart, and an assortment of other local book and music shops.

Most of Smith's remaining live performances through 1974 were at **Max's Kansas City**, initially with the trio as an opening act for groups such as Elephant's Memory, but by fall she was headlining with Television as her supporting act. In November she made her first trip to the West Coast, playing LA and Berkeley. Shortly after returning to New York, the trio added Ivan Kral, a Czechoslovakian guitar player with a wealth of experience who had lately been playing with an early edition of Blondie.

In February, March, and April of 1975, the now foursome played exclusively at **CBGB**, primarily on a joint bill with Television. This long residency would prove to be the clincher, as Patti would sign with Clive Davis's **Arista**

Records by early May for a reported $750,000 for seven albums.

Jay Dee Daugherty worked initially as the group's sound engineer but was eased in as the regular drummer in May and June of 1975.

Patti's first album, *Horses*, was recorded at **Electric Lady Studios** in August and September of 1975. John Cale, veteran of the Velvet Underground, prolific solo artist, and producer for the Stooges and Modern Lovers, was called

Patti Smith Horses/Horses

in to produce. The relationship between Cale and Smith was a contentious one, but it produced an album that many still consider her signature achievement. The release was almost universally acclaimed by American critics, and it regularly appears on lists of the greatest albums of the rock era. The iconic photo for the album cover was shot by Robert Mapplethorpe in the penthouse apartment of his partner and patron Sam Wagstaff, at 1 5th Ave. Clive Davis reportedly hated it, but Patti persisted. It was very much against the then-contemporary sexy '70's rock chick look, and many weren't sure what to make of the stark black and white photo. Camille Paglia has described it as "an anorexic Frank Sinatra . . . one of the greatest pictures ever taken of a woman." Shortly after *Horses'* completion, Patti performed at an event hosted by Arista Records at **City Center (131 W. 55th St.)**. Ostensibly a showcase for the fledgling label, Patti shared a bill with Barry Manilow, Loudon Wainwright III, and Gil Scott-Heron, among others.

1 Fifth Ave., viewed through the Washington Square arch

On March 9, 1976 at a reception in Detroit, Patti met Fred "Sonic" Smith, formerly of the MC5, with whom she would begin a long-distance relationship.

On November 29, 1976, Patti was banned from WNEW for using offensive language with Harry Chapin on the air during a broadcast for world hunger. Her show at the **Palladium (126 E.14th St.)** on December 31 was originally to be broadcast live on WNEW, but that was cancelled due to her ban the previous month. The performance included special guests John Cale, Dee Dee Ramone, Richard Lloyd, and Tom Verlaine.

While opening for Bob Seger in Tampa, Florida, on January 23, 1977, Patti fell from the stage and was badly injured. She suffered two cracked vertebrae in her neck, broken bones in her face, and required 22 stitches. After two days in a Tampa hospital, she returned to New York to recuperate. The rest of the tour was cancelled, but Patti vowed to return by Easter.

Patti would spend most of the next few months recovering in the new apartment she shared with Allen Lanier at 1 Fifth Ave., the very same building where her *Horses* cover photo was shot. When she wasn't engaged in strenuous physical therapy, she hosted several regular visitors, including Richard Hell, Bruce Springsteen, journalist Lisa Robinson, and *Punk Magazine*'s Legs McNeil. She also organized an exhibition of her drawings at Gotham Book Mart and produced a new volume of poetry entitled *Babel*, which included older material plus new work dictated to her assistant Andi Ostrowe.

True to her word, Patti returned to the stage at **CBGB** on Easter Sunday, April 10, 1977, dramatically tearing off her neck brace midway through the show. William Burroughs was in attendance. She would perform several more dates into June at CBGB and in July at the **Village Gate (160 Bleecker St.)** and **Elgin Theater (175 8th Ave.).** In September she did a joint book signing with William Burroughs and Allen Ginsberg at the **Gotham Book Mart**, and in November a benefit for the American Museum of Natural History at the **Hayden Planetarium (200 Central Park West)**. At the planetarium gig she unveiled "Till Victory," which would appear on her next album, *Easter*.

Easter proved to be her commercial breakthrough, spearheaded by "Because the Night," the single she co-wrote with Bruce Springsteen. Accounts vary, but both Bruce and Patti were at the Record Plant working on their respective albums when the collaboration took place. Springsteen, because of a legal issue with his prior manager, had been unable to record for nearly three years and had a plethora of first-rate material for what would ultimately become *Darkness on the Edge of Town*. He had a tune and a chorus, and Patti provided the rest of the lyrics. Jimmy Iovine worked on both albums, as producer for *Easter* and engineer for *Darkness*. Patti would premiere the new song at a December 30 gig at **CBGB's 2nd Avenue Theatre (66 2nd Ave.)**, accompanied by Springsteen on guitar.

Shortly before *Easter*'s release, Patti would leave Allen Lanier and New York and go to live with Fred "Sonic" Smith in Detroit. Patti spent most of the next few months on the road, but she did return to New York for two television appearances in February. The *Stanley Siegel Show* was broadcast live on WABC-TV at 9 a.m. from the **Café des Artistes (1 W. 67th St.)**. Siegel was notorious for antagonizing his guests, but Patti seemed to enjoy the experience and read several poems. She enjoyed her appearance on NBC's *Today Show* **(30 Rockefeller Plaza)** less, where she performed "Lullaby (I Was Working Real Hard)" with Ivan Kral as accompanist.

Her other New York shows that year included performances in May at Max's and the **Palladium**, and in August, **Central Park's Wollman Rink** and **Hurrah (36 W. 62nd St.)**. On November 30 through December 2, Patti participated in the three-day Nova Festival at the **Entermedia Theater (189 2nd Ave.)**, an expansive celebration of the work of William Burroughs. In addition to the writer himself, other notable artists included Frank Zappa, Philip Glass, Laurie Anderson, the B-52s, plus Debbie Harry and Chris Stein of Blondie.

Earlier in June, Patti and Robert Mapplethorpe opened their joint show Films and Stills at the **Robert Miller Gallery (41 E. 57th St.)**.

After her world tour for *Easter*, Patti retreated to her new life with Fred in Detroit. She and the band would reconvene that winter in Bearsville, New York, to work with producer Todd Rundgren on what would become her fourth album, *Wave*. What was kept secret, even from the group, was that this would be Patti's last album and that after the ensuing tour, she planned to retire. The album was released in

May to mixed reviews. She would play her New York shows in May at the Palladium and CBGB.

One of the more unusual appearances Patti made was on the children's TV show *Kids Are People Too* **(WABC TV, 7 Lincoln Square)**, where she answered questions from the studio audience and sang the Debby Boone hit "You Light Up My Life," accompanied by the tune's composer Joe Brooks. She would perform the song several more times, both on television and in concert.

On August 11, Patti would perform once again at **Central Park's Wollman Rink**, and later that evening at CBGB. They would be her last New York appearances for more than 10 years.

The retirement was from music, of course, not life. Her son Jackson was born in 1982, and her daughter Jesse in 1987. She and Fred had, in starts and stops, been putting together material for a new album, and in 1987 they checked in to the **Hit Factory (421 W. 54th St.)**. Richard Sohl and Jay Dee Daugherty were brought back to play on the record, but not Ivan Kral or Lenny Kaye. The result was *Dream of Life*, which was released in June 1988. Once again, Robert Mapplethorpe provided the cover photo. The single "People Have the Power" got airplay, but Patti had no interest in touring and the album tanked.

In March 1989, Robert Mapplethorpe died of AIDS-related complications at age 42. It would be the first in a series of tragedies to friends and loved ones Patti would live through. The following year, Richard Sohl died at 37 of a heart attack.

Patti would make a fleeting appearance at a 1990 Arista Records celebration at **Radio City Music Hall (1260 6th Ave.)**, and then hold a true concert as part of Central Park's SummerStage program at **Rumsey Playfield (near 5th Avenue and 71st Street)** on July 8, 1993. By all accounts she loved the experience

Cathedral of St. John the Divine

of performing live again, but no true comeback was forthcoming.

On November 4, 1994, her husband Fred died at age 46. A month later her brother Todd died as well.

On January 1, 1995, Patti participated in the annual Poetry Project reading at **St. Mark's Church**, as she often had over the years.

Accompanied by Lenny Kaye, she recited a spoken version of "People Have the Power" and "Ghost Dance."

Beginning in February of that year Smith began to perform in the Detroit area, and then at a club in Toronto. By July 27 she was back in New York at SummerStage, and the following day she made an unannounced appearance at the Lollapalooza Festival at **Randall's Island**. Joined by Lenny Kaye and Jay Dee Daugherty but not Ivan Kral, a true comeback was finally in the offing.

Smith would make a handful of other appearances in New York that year, including a November 19 memorial service for William Kunstler at the **Cathedral of St. John the Divine (1047 Amsterdam Ave.)** and a "secret" warm-up gig on December 4 at the **Nightingale Lounge (213 2nd Ave.)**, to which she would return the following year. On December 11 and 14 she opened for Bob Dylan at the **Beacon Theatre (2124 Broadway)** and joined him during his set for "Dark Eyes."

By now Patti had returned to New York and was working on a new album at Electric Lady Studios. The resulting album, *Gone Again,* would be released in June 1996.

MORE PATTI SMITH

NOTEWORTHY LIVE PERFORMANCES

Reno Sweeney's Paradise Room (126 W. 13th St.): Beginning April 2, 1973, Patti and Lenny Kaye opened for drag queen Holly Woodlawn at the venue that would become a center of cabaret culture. Joey Ramone is said to have first seen Patti here.

Kenny's Castaways (211 E. 84th St.): In April and May of 1973, Patti played several gigs here and premiered "Redondo Beach" and "Rape." A reviewer from the *Village Voice* described her as a "lank, pouting, frou-frou weirdo, but very entertaining and surprisingly affecting."

Max's Kansas City (213 Park Ave. South): Patti and Lenny ended 1973 with six gigs between Christmas and New Year supporting folk singer Phil Ochs at Max's, in what must have been a somewhat startling combination.

The Metro (188 W. 4th St.): Four January shows at and another return engagement in April 1974 at Reno Sweeney would prove to be the last appearances of Patti and Lenny as a duo.

Sheep Meadow, Central Park: Patti performed at the massive War Is Over concert on May 11, 1975. Other performers included Paul Simon, Joan Baez, Phil Ochs, and Richie Havens.

WBAI Free Music Store (359 E. 62nd St.) ⊘ : A benefit radio show for the left-leaning public radio station took place in the former Bethesda Covenant Church on May 28, 1975. On recordings Patti can be heard pleading for a drummer. Her pleas would soon be answered.

The Other End (147 Bleecker St.): Patti performed shows between July 25 and 29, 1975, here. The July 26 gig is notable as the night

Patti met Bob Dylan for the first time. He was in the audience and introduced himself after the late set, with cameras capturing the moment. He was assembling his supporting cast for the forthcoming Rolling Thunder Revue and hoped to recruit Patti. He later invited her to **Gerde's Folk City (130 W. 3rd St.)**, where she would join Eric Anderson in an impromptu performance. She ultimately declined Dylan's invitation, but the pair forged a lifelong friendship. The Other End, as it was known briefly in the mid-'70's, is now known as the Bitter End.

Bottom Line (15 W. 4th St.): Patti played three nights at this classic venue from December 26 to 29, 1975, before embarking on her first national tour to support *Horses*. After a lengthy European tour the following year, Patti returned home for a weeklong residency between November 22 and 28, 1976. On November 26, Bruce Springsteen and John Cale joined her for a few numbers onstage.

Avery Fisher Hall, Lincoln Center (10 Lincoln Center Plaza): Patti performed here on March 24 and 31, 1976.

Wollman Rink, Central Park: Patti played here as part of the annual Schaefer Music Festival on July 9, 1976.

Lower Manhattan Ocean Club (121 Chambers St.): Patti joined John Cale, Lou Reed, David Byrne, Mick Ronson, Allen Lanier, and Chris Spedding for a couple of impromptu sets here on July 20 and 27, 1976. She would play her own gig on August 31.

Palladium (126 E.14th St.): Patti joined Bruce Springsteen onstage for "Rosalita" and "Land" on October 30, 1976.

Carnegie Hall (881 7th Ave.): Patti appeared at the sixth annual Tibet House benefit on February 19, 1996. She would continue to perform at this event for many years to come.

CBGB (315 Bowery): Patti played here between October 28 and 31, 1997.

Bowery Ballroom (6 Delancey St.): Patti would make this a regular venue after her July 28 through 31, 1998, shows, often on New Year's Eve.

The Village Vanguard (178 7th Ave. South): Patti played three nights at this classic jazz venue between June 5 and 7, 2001.

Damrosch Park (Lincoln Center 165 W. 65th St.): Patti first played this outdoor space on August 18, 2001, returning again in 2016.

Warsaw (261 Driggs Ave., Brooklyn): Patti played here for the first time on March 2, 2002.

NOTEWORTHY RECORDING SESSIONS

Record Plant (321 W. 44th St.): In July 1976, Patti returned to this studio to record her second album, *Radio Ethiopia*, with Jack Douglas producing. The album was credited to the Patti Smith Group, as her band had been billed for some time.

OTHER NOTEWORTHY LOCATIONS

36 Greene St.: On July 13, 1973, Patti participated in a poetic tribute to Jim Morrison on the roof of experimental filmmaker Jack Smith's loft here.

Cafe Wha? (115 MacDougal St.): On May 5, 1974, Patti and Lenny performed on *The Underground Tonight Show* for local cable TV here.

Barnard Hall, Columbia University (3009 Broadway): Smith read at a poetry reading here on April 3, 1975.

NBC Studios (30 Rockefeller Plaza, Studio 8H): Patti's first national television appearance on *Saturday Night Live* on April 17, 1976, was most of America's first look at contemporary punk culture. She performed "Gloria" and "My Generation," both sides of her first Arista single.

Waldorf Astoria (301 Park Ave.): Patti inducted the Velvet Underground into the Rock & Roll Hall of Fame on January 17, 1996. She would also induct Clive Davis in 2000.

Ed Sullivan Theater (1695 Broadway): The first of several appearances on *Late Night with David Letterman* happened on June 19, 1996.

Sony Studios (460 W. 54th St.)⃠: Smith taped a live show here on July 23, 1997, which aired that September.

NBC Studios (30 Rockefeller Plaza): Patti appeared on *Late Night with Conan O'Brien* on November 14, 1997.

Cathedral of St. John the Divine (1047 Amsterdam Ave.): Patti attended the Buddhist cremation ceremony of Allen Ginsberg on May 14, 1998.

Cooper Union's Great Hall (30 Cooper Square): To help kick off National Poetry month, Patti participated in the People's Poetry Gathering on April 1, 2001. She would perform later that day at Washington Irving High School (40 Irving Place).

World Financial Center Plaza: Patti performed an outdoor show on July 8, 2003, where she sang, among other things, "Free Money."

ESSEX HOUSE/HOTEL
160 Central Park South

Soul singer Donny Hathaway was working on the *Roberta Flack Featuring Donny Hathaway* album when he fell out of a window on the 15th floor on January 13, 1979. His death was ruled a suicide, though friends and family maintained it was an accident. Hathaway had completed vocals for just two tracks on the album, which was released in November 1980.

In happier times, both David Bowie and Liam Gallagher of Oasis have owned apartments here.

Bowie and his wife Iman owned Apartment 915, a three-bedroom unit with views of Central Park. Bowie purchased the unit under his original name—David R. Jones—for $1 million in 1991, and the couple sold it in 2002. The apartment was sold again in 2004, and it was most recently listed in early 2017 for $6.5 million. A Yamaha piano that once belonged to Bowie remained, as did a dressing room off the master bedroom that was designed to Iman's specifications. A panic room added by the couple has since been removed.

In the summer of 2012, Gallagher paid $2.5 million for Apartment 1709, a two-bedroom condo that reportedly came with a 40-bottle wine cooler in the kitchen and an option with the hotel to rent it out to cover costs whenever the singer was out of town. Gallagher put the unit back on the market two years later, but not before undertaking an extensive interior makeover, which included the addition of leopard-skin wallpaper in the master bedroom and dark paint on the walls elsewhere. Union

Jack curtains in the smaller bedroom provided a link to home. After initially listing the property in the summer of 2014 for $4 million, Gallagher finally unloaded it in December 2016 for $2 million.

GREAT NORTHERN HOTEL ⊘
118 W. 57th St.

The Doors stayed at the Great Northern Hotel for over two weeks during their residency at **Steve Paul's the Scene** ⊘ **(301 W. 46th St.)** in June 1967. The building has since been torn down, with luxury hotel Le Parker Meridien going up in its place. The lobby entrance to Le Parker Meridien is actually on W. 56th; a smaller guests-only entrance is located where the Great Northern used to stand. The Great Northern during the Doors' stay boasted a narrow tower with a 24-hour beauty salon, though it's unknown whether Jim Morrison ever stopped by to get his flowing locks trimmed.

FONTANA DI TREVI ⊘
151 W. 57th St.

Billy Joel acknowledged in a 2008 interview that this was the eatery that inspired his song "Scenes From an Italian Restaurant." Evidently he enjoyed dining here before his pair of shows at **Carnegie Hall (881 7th Ave.)** across the street in June 1977. The song was recorded the following month at **A&R Studios** ⊘ **(799 7th Ave.)** and released that fall on *The Stranger*. Sadly, both the restaurant and the building that housed it are now gone.

CARNEGIE HALL
881 7th Ave.
Since 1891 Carnegie Hall has been world-renowned as one of the great venues for classical music, but it has hosted a wide variety of performers since its inception. Many legendary jazz, folk, pop, country, and rock artists have performed and recorded live at Carnegie. Its Rose Museum displays numerous artifacts and is not to be missed.

In 1938 and 1939 producer John Hammond organized the From Spirituals to Swing concerts, which introduced many African-American performers to a mainstream white audience for the first time. These artists greatly influenced rock & roll. Along with jazz greats Count Basie and Benny Goodman were blues and gospel artists such as Big Bill Broonzy, Big Joe Turner, Pete Johnson, and Sister Rosetta Tharpe.

On November 4, 1961, Bob Dylan made one of his very first New York appearances north of Greenwich Village when he performed before a tiny crowd at Carnegie's Chapter Hall, a small space once located above today's Weill Recital Hall. Dylan would later play the main hall on September 22, 1962, as part of a Pete Seeger Hootenanny. He had solo appearances on October 26, 1963, and October 1, 1965, the first electric tour. Dylan made his last—so far—appearance on January 20, 1968, with the Band as part of a Woody Guthrie Memorial concert.

The Beatles may have played the *Ed Sullivan Show* a few days earlier, but their first two proper New York concerts took place at Carnegie Hall on February 12, 1964. Paul McCartney returned to Carnegie on November 19, 1997, for a performance of his neo-classical composition *Standing Stone*. In the wake of the Fab Four's success came a plethora of British Invaders, most notably the Rolling Stones. Their first New York gig included two shows on June 20, 1964, at Carnegie to a packed house of primarily screaming teenage girls. The hall thereafter banned rock acts for the next five years.

Carnegie Hall reopened its doors to rock when Led Zeppelin played two shows on October 17, 1969. Many other top acts were to follow well into the '70s and beyond. Notable performers to rock the hall include Bill Haley & His Comets, Chuck Berry, Ray Charles, Neil Young, T.Rex, Frank Zappa, Billy Joel, Elton John, and Bruce Springsteen.

Rock & roll is infrequently scheduled today in Carnegie Hall, though there are exceptions. Philip Glass's Tibet House Benefit Concert has attracted many contemporary performers, including Iggy Pop, Patti Smith, the Flaming Lips, Lou Reed, David Bowie, Brian Wilson, and Vampire Weekend.

HARD ROCK CAFE
221 W. 57th St. ⊘**/1501 Broadway**
Opened in the 1980s as an offshoot of the original London location, the Hard Rock on W. 57th Street moved to a more tourist-friendly location on Broadway in August 2005. The idea is still the same as it is in the chain's many restaurants, hotels, and casinos around the world: rock memorabilia and ephemera, autographs, instruments, and outfits. If you're wary of visiting the Times Square area, there's a satellite location at Yankee Stadium (Gate 6 at the corner of 161st St. and River Ave.).

PROFILE RECORDS
250 W. 57th St./740 Broadway
From 1981 to 1985, Profile Records operated out of an office at 250 W. 57th St., with their artists at the time including Run-DMC, who were signed to the label after the group's manager Russell Simmons sent Profile a demo. In addition to numerous hip-hop artists, Profile also released records by punk groups the Plasmatics, Cro-Mags, and Murphy's Law; and others. Profile's headquarters moved to 740 Broadway in 1985.

ATLANTIC RECORDS
234 W. 56th St.
After the death of their father, the Turkish ambassador, Ahmet and Nesuhi Ertegun chose to remain behind in the US. They had amassed a collection of American rhythm and blues and jazz recordings and wanted to start a record company of their own. In 1947 they partnered with industry veteran Herb Abramson and established Atlantic in New York. After borrowing some money from the family dentist, they briefly set up shop in the old **Ritz-Carlton Hotel (Madison Avenue & 46th Street)** ⊘ , before moving to the **Jefferson Hotel (208 W. 56th St.)** ⊘, which was condemned soon afterward. They then moved to 301 W. 54th St. for a brief time. Ahmet and Herb spent much of the early years scouting talent and acquiring artists and had their first hit in 1949 with Stick McGhee's "Drinkin' Wine Spo-Dee-O-Dee," which reached number two on the R&B charts. Beyond that it was an eclectic roster of jazz, blues, and R&B artists, but little of it sold. In 1949 Ahmet signed Ruth Brown while she lay in a hospital bed in Chester, Pennsylvania, after a serious car accident. He would pay her bill and get her to New York, where the effort would pay off. Brown would become Atlantic's first major star, with hits "So Long," "Teardrops in My Eyes," and "I'll Wait For You" in 1949 and '50. In the early '50s Ruth "Miss Rhythm" Brown would be their most consistent hit maker, and Atlantic was often referred to as "The House that Ruth built." Some of her other important hits include "Mama He Treats Your Daughter Mean," and "Oh, What a Dream."

By June 1951 they had secured the top floor at 234 W. 56th St., which would prove to be a pivotal time in their history. By day it was an office, with all the furniture on wheels. By night it became a studio where they could record their own artists. Soon after they also acquired the services of Jerry Wexler, another industry

234 W. 56th St.

veteran who had coined the term rhythm and blues while writing for *Billboard*. Wexler, also an obsessive enthusiast of the music Atlantic wanted to record, would play a crucial role in both recruiting and producing talent.

The roster of legendary artists that recorded in the makeshift studio included the Clovers, Big Joe Turner, Ivory Joe Hunter, Ruth Brown, LaVern Baker, Clyde McPhatter, and Ray Charles. Charles had been a popular artist on a tiny label, Swing Time. When they folded, Ahmet

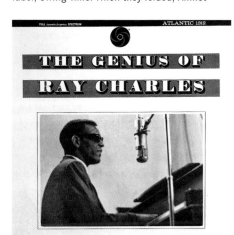

Ertegun signed him and ushered in a classic era of R&B. Charles would be hailed as "The Genius" and have a great run of success at Atlantic, producing classics such as "Come Back Baby," "I Got a Woman," "What'd I Say," and "Lonely Avenue" before his departure in 1959. Clyde McPhatter had emerged from Harlem's gospel Mount Lebanon Singers before joining Billy Ward & his Dominoes. His high tenor made the Dominoes one of the most successful R&B acts of the early '50s, but he chafed under the domineering leadership of Ward. In 1953 Ertegun and Wexler went to see him perform with the Dominoes at **Birdland (1678 Broadway)**, only to discover he had quit the group. In desperation Ertegun phoned every McPhatter in the phone book until he found him. He was invited to form his own group at Atlantic, which he did. McPhatter and his new group, the Drifters, would be big stars, producing such hits as "Money Honey," "Such a Night," and "White Christmas." After a term in the army, Clyde decided to go solo and the hits continued, most notably "A Lover's Question" in 1958. He would leave Atlantic not long after and never enjoy that level of success again. The Drifters would go through multiple personnel changes and identities after he left them. By 1958 manager George Treadwell essentially fired the group and hired a new one, the Five Crowns, to become the new Drifters. This edition of the group, with lead singer Ben E. King, would reach even greater heights of success under the guidance of the songwriting and production team of Jerry Leiber and Mike Stoller. They would produce many hits, including "Dance With Me," "This Magic Moment," and "Save the Last Dance For Me." King would leave the group a couple of years later, but the hits continued, including "Up on the Roof" and "Under the Boardwalk."

As Atlantic grew, so did their need for space, and in 1956 they moved the studio to **157 W. 57th St.** ⊘ The entire company would relocate two years later to **1841 Broadway**, where they would remain until a move to **75 Rockefeller Plaza** in the '70s. They are currently headquartered at 1633 Broadway.

In the ensuing years Atlantic would record legendary artists such as John Coltrane, Wilson Pickett, Otis Redding, and Aretha Franklin. Franklin had floundered at Columbia for a few years before but established herself as the Queen of Soul at Atlantic. The label would expand into the rock market with Buffalo Springfield; Crosby, Stills, Nash, & Young; Cream; and Led Zeppelin. In 1967 Atlantic was sold to Warner Bros, and Wexler moved on shortly thereafter. When the Rolling Stones left Decca in 1971 they too joined the Atlantic roster of artists.

The original group that had founded and managed the business since its inception had all left by the early '70s, except Ahmet Ertegun, who managed to keep some semblance of autonomy in Warner's shifting corporate firmament. He would continue to work closely with the company until his death in 2006.

QUINTANO'S SCHOOL FOR YOUNG PROFESSIONALS
156 W. 56th St. ⊘/17-21 W. 60th St./322 W. 45th St.
Founded in 1951 by Leonard S. Quintano, affectionately known to students as Dr. Q, Quintano's School for Young Professionals had a reputation for taking in talented kids who'd been kicked out of other schools, as well as a lackadaisical view on attendance and other golden rules. Tales abound of kids drinking and smoking in the halls, and sometimes in the classroom.

"The school had been around a long time," said Jesse Malin, founding member of Heart Attack and D Generation, and celebrated singer-songwriter. "It was kind of like a real free-for-all. It was just these little rooms that were not even classroom size. People would smoke in the class and drink, and your friends could visit

you. This kid who was in a band called Reagan Youth, Andy Apathy, he said to me, 'You know, there's a school that's very cheap. It's a private school, but it's for artists, and if you want to go on tour and do these different things they set it up and you just let them know.' I said, 'I don't know.' I had this grandmother in the Bronx who had a little bit of money tucked away, and I called her up and said, 'It's a school like Julliard!' Of course it was not. It was $1,600 for the year, which I guess was cheap even then."

Quintano's in the '80s was reportedly the center of a male prostitution ring.

"I would watch these guys in suits come in and point at some of the kids in biology class, and the kids would leave," Malin recalled. "I'd say, 'Where are they going? I want to get out of here.' I'd look out the window down into the street and it was Town Cars. Andy Apathy said to me one day, who I think always wanted to be Dee Dee Ramone, being from Forest Hills, but he was his own special person . . . He said, 'Jesse, I see you've got a Japanese guitar. Do you want to get a real Gibson?' I said, 'Hell yeah!' He said, 'Well, you should get in the car with us, go down to Atlantic City. These rich women will pay lots of money while their husbands are playing blackjack to suck on your balls for hours . . . And once in a while you've got to be with a man.' I said, 'I think I'll stay in biology class.'"

Quintano's was first located on W. 56th Street before moving to the same building as High Times in the '80s. Among its musical alumni are Aerosmith's Steven Tyler, Blondie's Chris Stein, Mary Weiss of the Shangri-Las, Frankie Lymon, Brenda K. Starr, Waddy Wachtel, and Tony Sales. Johnny Thunders, Sylvain Sylvain, and Billy Murcia—three-fifths of the New York Dolls—went to Quintano's in the late '60s. Other well-known alumni include Sal Mineo, Patty Duke, Diane Lane, Bernadette Peters, and Valerie Harper.

STUDIO 54
254 W. 54th St.

Opened by Steve Rubell and Ian Schrager in a former CBS television and radio studio in 1977, Studio 54 quickly became one of the world's most famous—and infamous—nightclubs, a decadent discotheque where glamour and excess were celebrated by an elite clientele. Frequent guests at Studio 54 during its disco days included Mick Jagger, Andy Warhol, Elizabeth Taylor, Halston, and many others. The club also featured live performances in the late '70s by artists such as Grace Jones, Stevie Wonder, Donna Summer, Gloria Gaynor, James Brown, and Klaus Nomi.

The Ed Sullivan Theater during its Letterman era

The end of the glory days for Studio 54 roughly coincided with the end of disco, and after a closing party in February 1980, Rubell and Schrager spent over a year in prison for tax evasion.

Studio 54 reopened in September 1981, with many famous faces returning, and live appearances by some of the new decade's shining stars, including Culture Club, Spandau Ballet, Cyndi Lauper, Menudo, and others. Duran Duran, appropriately, held a midnight screening of their video album at Studio 54 on April 29, 1983.

On April 3, 1985, metal bands Slayer, Venom, and Exodus played Studio 54, billed as the Ultimate Revenge for Disco. It was among the final live shows in the fabled discotheque.

From 1988 to 1993, the former Studio 54 was the home of the Ritz. Studio 54 is currently a Broadway theater.

ED SULLIVAN THEATER
1697 Broadway

The building now named for the iconic television host has had many identities over the years, but will forever be associated with the numerous performers who made an impact on popular culture from its stage.

Originally opened in 1927 as Hammerstein's Theater, it changed names and ownership a few times until it was acquired by CBS Radio in 1936; it remains a CBS facility to this day. Radio shows ultimately gave way to television in 1950 when it was renamed **CBS Studio 50**. The theater hosted a wide variety of television programs throughout the '50s and '60s, including the *Jackie Gleason Show, What's My Line?* and the *Merv Griffin Show*. But it was the *Ed Sullivan Show* for which it is best remembered.

Television and rock & roll hit it off almost immediately, and in a pre-cable era when upwards of 60 million Americans regularly tuned in to Sullivan, an appearance could make a career.

The first rock & roll act to appear on the *Ed Sullivan Show* was Bill Haley & His Comets in August 1955, but that was presented from a theater in Stratford, Connecticut. On November 20 of the same year, Bo Diddley made his first nationally televised performance, specially introduced by DJ Tommy "Dr. Jive" Smalls. Due to a misunderstanding with Sullivan over song selection—a recurring Sullivan theme in coming years—Diddley was never asked back.

Elvis Presley's first national television appearance was produced in the theater, though not for Ed Sullivan. On January 28, 1956, Presley performed on Tommy & Jimmy Dorsey's *Stage Show* at Studio 50. The show was produced by Jackie Gleason and preceded Gleason's own program on Saturday nights. Elvis was such a success that he was quickly booked for five more appearances during February and March of 1956. Sullivan initially resisted hiring Presley, feeling Elvis's act wasn't suited for his family audience. After two hugely successful appearances on the *Milton Berle Show*, and the now-notorious "Hound Dog" performance on Steve Allen at the nearby **Hudson Theater**, Sullivan caved, signing Presley for three performances at $50,000, then the highest sum ever paid for a performer to appear on TV. The King finally debuted on Sullivan's show on September 9, 1956. The second appearance was on October 28, and the third on January 6, 1957. The rest, as they say, is history.

After Presley's enormous success, other rock & rollers followed. Bill Haley made a second appearance on April 28, 1957, and Buddy Holly & the Crickets made two appearances, on December 1, 1957, and January 26, 1958. Sullivan was reportedly irked with Holly's decision to perform his hit "Oh Boy," thinking it too raucous. Holly would ultimately make a home in New York a few months before his death in February 1959.

Often cited as one of the most culturally significant events in television history, the Beatles' *Ed Sullivan Show* appearance on February 9, 1964, attracted an unprecedented 73 million viewers, nearly half the nation, and propelled the cultural phenomenon known as Beatlemania. They had the top single in the country with "I Want to Hold Your Hand," but something else, something unique was happening. Fans had laid siege to the Plaza Hotel, where they had arrived only days before, and CBS received 50,000 requests for the 700-seat Studio 50. The Beatles actually played two shows on February 9. The first was taped before their live appearance and was broadcast on February 23. On February 14 they had performed for Sullivan from Miami Beach. The Fab Four appeared just once more on *Ed Sullivan*, in a performance taped on August 14, 1965, and broadcast September 12. By then they had established themselves as the most successful musicians on the planet. Civilization would never be quite the same again.

As the music of the '60s grew in cultural influence, the *Ed Sullivan Show* continued to be a huge opportunity for both established and newly emerging musical acts. Sometimes, though, performers were asked to drop songs or alter lyrics to placate Sullivan or his conservative sponsors' tender sensibilities. In 1964 Bob Dylan walked out rather than drop his tune "Talkin' John Birch Society Blues." Other performers dealt with Sullivan's rules in different ways.

Like the Beatles before them, the Rolling Stones enjoyed a mutually fruitful relationship with Sullivan and appeared on the show several times. Notoriously, at Sullivan's insistence, the Stones agreed to change the lyrics of "Let's Spend the Night Together" to "Let's Spend Some Time Together" for a 1967 appearance, despite the song already being a huge hit under its original title. Also in 1967, the Doors were told to drop references to getting high in "Light My Fire," but Jim Morrison sang them anyway, much to Sullivan's ire.

Motown artists were also particular favorites on the show. The Supremes, the Temptations, the Miracles, the Four Tops, Gladys Knight & the Pips, Marvin Gaye, Stevie Wonder, and the Jackson 5 all appeared on the program in the '60s.

After the demise of *The Ed Sullivan Show* in 1971, the building was used to film game shows, sitcoms, and assorted TV specials. In 1993 CBS renovated the then-derelict facility to host the *Late Show with David Letterman,* where it once again became an extremely popular and coveted venue for musicians. With succeeding host Stephen Colbert, it continues to serve in that capacity today.

CHEETAH ⊘
Broadway and 53rd Street
A discotheque as grand in stature as design, the Cheetah was an expansive venue with thousands of glittering lights that seemed to travel infinitely as they reflected off aluminum sheets. Open from 1966 to 1972, the Cheetah was host to a run of 45 performances of the musical *Hair* between December 1967 and January 1968 prior to its moving to Broadway three months later for a successful run of 1,750 performances at the **Biltmore Theater (261 W. 47th St.)**.

LLOYD PRICE'S TURNTABLE/
LLOYD PRICE'S CRAWDADDY
1674 Broadway
Soul legend Lloyd Price ("Lawdy Miss Clawdy") bought the former **Birdland** in the late '60s as a means of giving the Lloyd Price Orchestra a place to call home. He briefly renamed the club after buying an interest in *Crawdaddy* magazine. Soul legends the Coasters, Wilson Pickett, and Jean Wells all reportedly played here while it was still the Turntable. After switching its focus to rock, the venue featured such groups as Suicide, Zoot Sims, and the Pox, a pre–New York Dolls group started by Sylvain Sylvain and Billy Murcia.

ROSELAND BALLROOM ⊘
239 W. 52nd St.
The history of the Roseland Ballroom doesn't just stretch back in time, but to another city entirely. Founded in Philadelphia in 1917, Roseland moved to 1658 Broadway in Manhattan two years later in search of less restrictive blue laws. It opened as an all-white

Roseland's 53rd St. wall prior to demolition

ballroom on New Year's Eve 1919, integrating over the next two decades as hot jazz played by African-American groups became increasingly popular. Roseland thrived in the age of the big band, and many performances of the era were broadcast over the radio live from Roseland.

That building was demolished in 1956, with Roseland moving to 239 W. 52nd St. in a former roller rink. In the '70s and early '80s, Roseland hosted disco nights, eventually dropping them in the wake of spates of violence, which included the death of Robert Dudley, a Staten Island teenager who was shot on the dance floor in November 1984.

For many years, Roseland also served as a live music venue, with shows over the years by Nirvana, AC/DC, My Bloody Valentine, Beyoncé, Phil Collins, Duran Duran, Portishead, and many others. After selling out the spacious venue in 1984, Metallica, Anthrax, and Raven all signed major label deals.

Roseland was demolished for redevelopment of the site after seven sold-out shows by Lady Gaga in the spring of 2014.

WINTER GARDEN THEATRE
1634 Broadway
Beginning October 5, 1972, Neil Diamond played 20 shows here, the first time a pop star had done a one-man show on Broadway since Al

Jolson. He would take a four-year break from live performance afterwards.

BRILL BUILDING
1619 & 1650 Broadway

While the Brill Building at 1619 Broadway is indeed an actual building, it should be noted that the term **Brill Building** has come to represent more than just the building itself. It represents the pop music industry of a particular time period, much as the term Hollywood represents the film industry, or Wall Street the financial industry. New York had been the center of the music publishing industry for several decades, originally centered on West 28th Street, known as "Tin Pan Alley." As the entertainment industry moved uptown and centered around Times Square, the music business moved with it, and by the 1930s many of those publishers were headquartered in 1619 Broadway, in what was originally built as the Lefcourt Building and renamed for a haberdasher who once occupied the street level. Other buildings nearby, particularly 1650 Broadway, but also 1674 and 1697 Broadway atop what's now known as the **Ed Sullivan Theater**, were similarly filled with music industry people. Songwriters, publishers, arrangers, and often musicians occupied the various offices while creating the pop hits of the day. By the '50s, as rock & roll stormed the charts, that establishment was under siege, as a new kind of performer began its ascension to the mainstream. Many in the industry transitioned to meet that demand for material, often hiring young songwriters best equipped to produce songs that would most appeal to America's youth and the galaxy of relatively small independent labels that catered to them. The songs they wrote and the records that resulted would dominate the pop charts for the next several years, and introduce many new recording stars. Initially 1619 Broadway

tended to house the more established writers and publishers who represented the pre–rock & roll old guard of pop music, while 1650 favored the younger, more inclusive companies who produced rock & roll, pop, country, R&B, and Latin. Elvis Presley's music-publishing business, and its star songwriter, Brooklyn-born Otis Blackwell, worked here. Blackwell penned legendary hits "Don't Be Cruel," "Return to Sender," and "All Shook Up" for Presley, as well as "Great Balls of Fire" and "Breathless" for Jerry Lee Lewis.

Aldon Music, created in 1958 by Don Kirshner and Al Nevins, employed some of the top young songwriters of the era, including the teams of Carole King and Gerry Goffin, Ellie Greenwich and Jeff Barry, Cynthia Weil and Barry Mann, and Neil Sedaka and Howard Greenfield. They produced numerous memorable hits spanning the '60s, including "One Fine Day" by the Chiffons (Goffin/King), "You've Lost That Lovin' Feeling" by the Righteous Brothers (Mann/Weil/Spector), "Be My Baby" by the Ronettes (Barry/Greenwich/Spector),

and Neil Sedaka's own "Breaking Up Is Hard To Do" (Sedaka/Greenfield). Also in 1650 was the team of Doc Pomus and Mort Shuman, who produced hits for Elvis, Dion & the Belmonts, and the Drifters, among many others. When they achieved a measure of success, they would move over to the top floor of 1619.

Burt Bacharach and Hal David's partnership began in the late '50s at 1619, but they would hit their stride in the '60s, particularly when partnered with Dionne Warwick, who had initially been hired to sing demo recordings. Florence Greenberg of Scepter Records, then based at 1674 Broadway, would release a string of hits produced by the trio, including "Walk on By" and "Anyone Who Had a Heart." Scepter would also record the Shirelles, who struck gold with the Goffin/King classic "Will You Love Me Tomorrow," among other hits.

Jerry Leiber and Mike Stoller had been working together since the early '50s in Los Angeles, producing hits for the Coasters ("Young Blood") and Big Mama Thornton

("Hound Dog"), among others, when they were brought to New York by both Atlantic Records and RCA. Elvis Presley had a huge hit covering "Hound Dog," and Leiber and Stoller were to produce several other smashes for the King, including "Jailhouse Rock" and "King Creole." For Atlantic, they wrote, arranged, and produced several hits for the Drifters ("On Broadway") and Ben E. King ("Stand by Me"). They would later create their own label, Red Bird, with impresario George Goldner. Red Bird is most notable for having recorded Queens natives the Shangri-Las. They teamed with producer George "Shadow" Morton to record several memorable hits, including "Remember" and "Leader of the Pack," written with Barry and Greenwich.

DJ Alan Freed, sometimes cited as the man who coined the term rock & roll, kept an office at 1619 Broadway, as did his business partner Morris Levy, one of the heavyweights in the independent record business. Levy owned Roulette Records as well as the club Birdland. Freed would later be ruined in the payola scandal of 1959 for allegedly taking bribes to play records, and Levy, after many years of accusations, was finally convicted of extortion in 1990.

The popular narrative is that the Brill Building sound was effectively silenced by the Beatles and Bob Dylan, recording artists who wrote their own material. That may be partly true, but the Lennon and McCartney songwriting partnership may never have existed without it. In fact, the Beatles covered many Brill Building songs early in their career and were clearly influenced by the tunes of Goffin and King, et al. The artists and the music created here endure.

BOND INTERNATIONAL CASINO
1530 Broadway

Bond International Casino wasn't a casino, and save for a brief period in the early '80s, it was barely a music venue. But its importance in NYC rock & roll history is undeniable thanks to a few weeks in May and June 1981.

Looking for a venue where they could make a splash, the Clash settled on Bond International Casino, a former Times Square department store with its second floor converted into a 1,750-person-capacity venue. Eight shows were booked and scheduled, but promoters reportedly double-sold each show, leading to overcrowding and, just a few gigs into the residency, the cancellation of a show by the New York City Fire Department. Devoted to their fans, the Clash added enough dates to accommodate all ticket holders, extending their run to 17 shows.

The Clash brought in a variety of different support acts befitting their expansive musical taste, including the Fall, the Dead Kennedys, Bad Brains, Lee "Scratch" Perry, Grandmaster Flash and the Furious Five, and others. The hip-hop artists in particular caught plenty of flak from the more narrow-minded fans in attendance, with the Clash's Joe Strummer expressing his displeasure with how the band's choices were treated.

Either in spite or because of the various controversies, the Clash's Bond residency has become the stuff of legend, and music recorded during the shows have been heavily bootlegged, and at least partially officially released.

Other artists playing Bond International Casino in the early '80s include Blue Oyster Cult, Grace Jones, and New Edition.

THE PEPPERMINT LOUNGE ⊘
128 W. 45th St./100 5th Ave.

The original Peppermint Lounge opened at 128 W. 45th St. in 1958, with its peak coming a few years later when the success of "Peppermint Twist" by Joey Dee & the Starliters turned the nightclub into an overnight sensation. It was

during this period that celebrities such as Truman Capote, Marilyn Monroe, Judy Garland, Frank Sinatra, Greta Garbo, and Jackie Kennedy frequented the club. The Beatles visited the Peppermint Lounge during their first whirlwind visit to New York City in February 1964, and performers included the Ronettes, the Crystals, the Isley Brothers, the Four Seasons, and Chubby Checker, who started the whole dance craze with his 1960 hit single, "The Twist."

The Peppermint Lounge closed in December 1965 when it lost its liquor license. By 1980, the venue had become both Hollywood and G.G. Barnum's Room, gay-friendly spaces, with the latter including trapeze artists and male go-go dancers. In November 1980, the Peppermint Lounge was revived at its original 128 W. 45th St. location, booking modern acts like the Cramps, the Go-Gos, Joan Jett, Grandmaster Flash & the Furious Five, Afrika Bambaataa, and X. VIPs such as Mick Jagger and David Bowie began turning up, and the club's popularity was once again on the rise.

The Peppermint Lounge moved to 100 5th Ave. in 1982, staying open at its new location for another three years before closing for good.

According to Jesse Malin of Heart Attack and D Generation, a Black Flag show at the original location in March 1981 was a key moment for the developing New York City hardcore scene.

"I went and met all these kids from D.C. who had been out west," Malin said. "They had the creepy-crawl dance style, they went on the dance floor and wrecked all the New Yorkers, because we used to just like pogo and knock from side to side. And at Max's [Kansas City] at a Stimulators gig it would be fun to knock all the tables over and pile them up. But it was female friendly, male friendly, gay friendly. It wasn't like this other thing. I liked the creepy crawl, the way Ian [MacKaye] and Henry [Rollins] had it, because it was kind of crazy when they started to hit us with it. That was a big night where New York changed."

TOWNHOUSE THEATRE
120 W. 44th St.
Among the groups who played this Broadway-area theater during its brief mid-'70s run as a live music venue were Suicide, Television, and the Fast.

HUDSON THEATER
141 W. 44th St.
In the '50s the Hudson Theater was the home of the *Steve Allen Show*, where Elvis Presley was infamously compelled to perform his hit "Hound Dog" in formal wear to a basset hound on July 1, 1956. Elvis's previous performances on the *Milton Berle Show* for NBC were huge ratings successes, and the network wanted to keep the ball rolling. Allen was less than thrilled, however, and chose to undermine his guest by making him look ridiculous. Presley performed with good humor but was privately furious and swore never to do the show again.

HOTEL DIPLOMAT ⊘
108 W. 43rd St.
Perhaps best known as the site of early shows by groups such as the New York Dolls in the early '70s, Hotel Diplomat was still semi-active by the mid-'80s, when fledgling Def Jam impresario and NYU freshman Rick Rubin organized a concert here. Dubbed "Uptown Meets Downtown," the eclectic lineup included hip-hop (the Treacherous Three), No Wave (Liquid Liquid), and hardcore (Heart Attack).

ACADEMY
234 W. 43rd St.
A concert hall, which has since returned to the Great White Way as part of the Lyric Theatre, this mid-'90s incarnation as the Academy was a rare rock & roll blip, with shows from Smashing Pumpkins, Sonic Youth, Pavement, Blur, Pulp, Living Colour, Pearl Jam, Duran Duran, and Iggy Pop.

RAMA RECORDS
143 W. 41st St./220 W. 42nd St.
In 1948 George Goldner owned a chain of dance halls and wanted to capitalize on the increasing popularity of Latin music, so he established Tico Records at 143 W. 41st St. Tico recorded Tito Puente, Joe Loco, and Tito Rodriguez and rapidly became the most important Latin specialty label. By 1953 he saw an opportunity to record and commercialize the many popular black vocal harmony groups and created Rama Records. One of the first acts he signed was the Harlem group the Crows. Their first few singles went nowhere, but their third single "Gee," released in May, began to rapidly climb both the R&B and pop charts. It would eventually reach number 14 on the pop charts, a remarkable accomplishment for a small R&B label at that time. No one quite knew it yet, but it was the first pangs of an

143 W. 41st St.

220 W. 42nd St.

emerging teen culture that wasn't about to obey the traditional racial barriers of the music industry. By the end of the year, Goldner had moved his operation to larger digs at 220 W. 42nd St. He continued to sign and record new acts, including the Cleftones from Jamaica, Queens. He would even create the subsidiary label Gee, as DJs would typically play only a limited number of tunes from one label. In 1955 Goldner struck gold when Frankie Lymon & the Teenagers auditioned. They would record "Why Do Fools Fall in Love" in 1955, by far Rama's biggest hit. Not long after, Goldner began a business relationship with nightclub owner Morris Levy, and they established Roulette Records. Unfortunately for Goldner, he compiled gambling debts and would have to sell his interests in both Tico and Rama to Levy. He would start again with End and Gone Records,

where he would have more success with Little Anthony & the Imperials, the Chantels, and the Flamingos. More debt, however, forced him to sell that enterprise to Levy as well. A few years later Goldner would team up with Jerry Leiber and Mike Stoller to form Red Bird, which produced several hits with the Shangri-Las, Dixie Cups, and Ad-Libs in the '60s. Leiber and Stoller would eventually bail out of that arrangement, and Goldner's continued gambling problems caused Red Bird to fall into the hands of the Mafia. He tried his hand once more in 1970 with Firebird, but died of a heart attack soon after its creation.

GOOD VIBRATIONS
1440 Broadway

In December 1974, at the behest of Island Records, Television recorded demos with Brian Eno at Good Vibrations. Songs included "Marquee Moon," "Venus de Milo," "Prove It," "Friction," and "Double Exposure." The group wasn't keen on the results, and neither were Island Records, who didn't make them an offer. The group signed with Elektra Records two years later, resurrecting all the songs they'd demoed at Good Vibrations with the exception of "Double Exposure" for their debut album, *Marquee Moon*.

FUNKADELIC STUDIOS
209 W. 40th St., 5th floor
Twenty-first-century post-punk band Interpol began coalescing in a fifth-floor rehearsal room at Funkadelic Studios when fellow NYU students Daniel Kessler and Carlos Dengler booked time to jam together.

MUSIC BUILDING
584 8th Ave.
The Music Building opened in 1979 with 69 rehearsal studios available by lease to musicians. Among the well-known artists who've honed their sound in the building are the Patti Smith Group, Joey Ramone, Madonna, the Strokes, Television, Billy Idol, and Interpol. They Might Be Giants, the Magnetic Fields, and Joseph Arthur have all recorded in their rehearsal spaces. The Music Building is still open, with perhaps your next favorite group making noise behind closed doors.

HAMMERSTEIN BALLROOM
311 W. 34th St.
Built in 1906 by Oscar Hammerstein as the Manhattan Opera House, the Hammerstein Ballroom has been used for a variety of purposes over the years, including a Freemason's temple, trade shows, and a union headquarters. After falling into disrepair, the building in which it resides was renamed the Manhattan Center Studios in 1986, with the primary theater becoming the Hammerstein Ballroom after an extensive renovation in 1997.

Hammerstein Ballroom is an ornate 12,000-square-foot space with a pair of balconies and six opera boxes. Pixies, the Strokes, the Black Crowes, Portishead, Iron Maiden, Beck, and many others have played shows in the large venue.

Manhattan Center also includes the equally opulent Grand Ballroom, which holds around 1,200 and has hosted shows by the Grateful Dead, Procol Harum, Fleet Foxes, Animal Collective, Elvis Costello, and Sting.

STEVE PAUL'S THE SCENE ⊘
301 W. 46th St.
Though only open between 1964 and 1970, Steve Paul's the Scene served as a key live venue of the era, with many of the most significant artists of the time performing on its tiny basement-level stage. It was also a

well-known musicians' hangout for post-gig peacocking and jamming.

In 1967, the Doors played a lengthy engagement in the club, running from June 12 through July 1. Curiously, the Scene shut its doors for the weekend of June 15 through 17 out of respect for the Monterey Pop Festival, held on the other side of the country. The Doors headed out to Long Island and Philadelphia for performances during the weekend, returning to continue their residency on Monday, June 18.

The building that housed the Scene prior to its demolition

had Hendrix not also jammed wherever and whenever possible.

Led Zeppelin was due to perform four nights at the club in early February 1969, but after a pair of dates at the **Fillmore East** and a quick jaunt up to Toronto, the Scene shows were cancelled when drummer John Bonham had to return to England to look after his son, who had taken ill. The gigs were never rescheduled.

Everyone from the Seeds to the Flying Burrito Brothers played Steve Paul's the Scene, and one of the day's great luminaries, Tiny Tim, was a more-than-regular attraction.

ALICIA KEYS' HOME
Manhattan Plaza (400 W. 43rd St.)

Multi-platinum and award-winning artist Alicia Keys grew up in **Manhattan Plaza (400 W. 43rd St.)**, a high-rise development that catered to the performing arts community in a pre-gentrified Hell's Kitchen. It would also house other show business notables such as Terrence Howard and Larry David.

Keys attended the **Professional Performing Arts School (320 W. 48th St.)** before briefly attending **Columbia University**, when her career took off. Her 2001 debut, *Songs in A Minor*, established her as a major star. She would later live with husband Swizz Beatz in a luxury pad at **30 Crosby St.**, purchased from Lenny Kravitz.

Earlier that year, the Velvet Underground and Nico performed during a residency between January 2 and 14. Billed as The Steve Paul & Andy Warhol Underground Amateur Hour, the predictably wild events featured "gurus, creative people, pop celebrities, society submergers, super spatials," and "swamis" on the bill, as well as stars of Warhol's film *Chelsea Girls*.

On July 3 and 4, 1967, the Jimi Hendrix Experience made its New York debut with a pair of gigs at the Scene, with Hendrix returning frequently over the next two years for impromptu jam sessions; this might seem more noteworthy

Manhattan Plaza

In 2009 she would release, in collaboration with Brooklynite Jay-Z, the single "Empire State of Mind," an urban love ode to the city that has become a modern anthem, and in October 2016 she would fill **Times Square** to debut material from her latest album, *New*. The show featured guest stars Jay-Z, Nas, Q Tip, Questlove, and John Mayer and was broadcast on BET.

Professional Performing Arts School

WASHINGTON JEFFERSON HOTEL
318 W. 51st St.
In Lizzy Goodman's *Meet Me in the Bathroom*, Caleb and Nathan Followill of Kings of Leon

talk about staying in a room at the Washington Jefferson Hotel that was so small Caleb could flush the toilet from his bed.

REEVES TELTAPE STUDIOS ⊘
851 9th Ave.
After having two months of shows cancelled in the wake of a disastrous show at the Dinner Key Arena in Miami in early March 1969, the Doors spent April 28 and 29 of that year in a television studio at 851 9th Ave., where they performed live and were interviewed by Richard Goldstein of the *Village Voice* for a PBS program called *Critique*. Morrison, wearing sunglasses and a beard, shared a vision of the future of electronic music that was surprisingly prescient. The group performed a few older numbers, as well as songs from their forthcoming album, *The Soft Parade*.

HIT FACTORY
421 W. 54th St./237 W. 54th St. ⊘/130 W. 42nd St.
The Hit Factory was purchased in 1975 by producer Edward Germano, becoming one of the city's favored recording studios for many of rock's biggest stars. During its heyday, there were multiple hit factories, with the central studio, Hit Factory Mastering, located at 421 W. 54th St., starting in 1992. Hit Factory Broadway was nearby at 237 W. 54th St., and Hit Factory Times Square was at 130 W. 42nd St.

Hit Factory Mastering occupied five floors, with five recording studios and private lounges, offices, production rooms, and assorted other areas dedicated to the studio's operations. In 2002, Hit Factory Broadway closed, and the main facility expanded to seven in-house studios.

Stevie Wonder's 1976 epic *Songs in the Key of Life* was one of the first albums recorded at the Hit Factory, though he'd already completed much of the work in studios on the West Coast before spending six weeks in New York.

John Lennon and Yoko Ono (*Double Fantasy*, 1980), Paul Simon (*Graceland*, 1986), Bruce Springsteen (*Born in the USA*, 1984) and Patti Smith (*Dream of Life*, 1986) all recorded key albums at the Hit Factory, as did the Rolling Stones, U2, Michael Jackson, Mariah Carey, Beyoncé, and the Chemical Brothers. The Hit Factory closed in 2005, moving its headquarters to its Miami location.

The facility at 237 W. 54th st. was previously Bell Sound Studios, where countless classic recordings were cut in the '50s and '60s by artists such as the Teenagers, Bill Haley & His Comets, Lloyd Price, Frankie Avalon, the Drifters, Dionne Warwick, the Shirelles, Wilson Pickett, Ike & Tina Turner, and the Stooges. Bell Sound also occupied studio space at 135 W. 54th St.

POWER STATION/AVATAR STUDIOS
441 W. 53rd St.
Originally built for Con Edison, this building served as a television studio for several years before being converted by Tony Bongiovi into the recording studio called the Power Station in 1977. Many classic albums were recorded here, including Bruce Springsteen's *Born in the USA*, Madonna's *Like a Virgin*, Bob Dylan's *Infidels*, the Kinks' *Low Budget*, Blondie's *Eat to the Beat*, and David Bowie's *Scary Monsters. The Power Station*, a 1985 album by a super group of the same name featuring singer Robert Palmer, former Chic drummer Tony Thompson, and Andy

and John Taylor of Duran Duran was fittingly recorded here. In 1996 the Power Station was rescued from bankruptcy and renamed Avatar Studios, where it has hosted such luminaries as Paul McCartney, Kings of Leon, Norah Jones, and My Morning Jacket.

TERMINAL 5
610 W. 56th St.
For over a decade, the 3,000-person-capacity Terminal 5 has been a go-to venue for bands too big for club shows but perhaps not quite ready to play Madison Square Garden. The large hall features a main floor, two balconies, an outdoor lounge, and a very busy calendar. Though it's a bit of a trek from the subway, that hasn't stopped Terminal 5 from hosting key live shows from My Bloody Valentine, the National, St. Vincent, the Black Keys, Iggy Pop & the Stooges, Nine Inch Nails, and others. LCD Soundsystem played a run of warm-up shows at Terminal 5 in March 2011 ahead of their then-farewell gig at Madison Square Garden.

PIER 84
12th Ave. and 45th St.
After years of hosting outdoor music in Central Park, the Dr. Pepper Music Festival moved to Pier 84 in 1982, opening the season with a show by Duran Duran and Split Enz on June 25. Other shows that season included the Clash, Iggy Pop, Bonnie Raitt, Miles Davis, Gang of Four, the Waitresses, and Haircut 100.

BEASTIE BOYS

Bob Gruen

Beastie Boys in 1987

It's somehow fitting that the last Beastie Boys concert in New York City was a benefit show. On March 4, 2008, Adam "MCA" Yauch, Michael "Mike D" Diamond," and Adam "Ad-Rock" Horovitz played a full set at **Terminal 5 (610 W. 56th St.)** in support of the Bronx-based Institute for Music and Neurologic Function, a nonprofit organization that studies the impact of music therapy on people who have suffered strokes, Alzheimer's, Parkinson's, dementia, and other trauma. For many years, the Beasties used their music to bring attention to various causes, a career turn that might have seemed implausible to anyone who didn't actually know them back in the mid-'80s, when their live shows were more likely to result in someone being doused

in a spray of Budweiser than a plea for Tibetan independence.

But while *Licensed to Ill*, the group's chart-topping 1986 debut album, was a petulant, offensive classic, the group was by then already accustomed to benefit shows. Before transitioning to hip-hop, the Beastie Boys were part of Manhattan's downtown hardcore scene, a style of music to which they'd regularly return with short, fast, and very loud blasts cropping up in the middle of albums like *Check Your Head* (1992) and *Ill Communication* (1994). The group's first benefit show took place at the New York Theatre Experience (62 E. 4th St.) on December 1, 1981, when they shared the bill with Bad Brains, Heart Attack, Reagan Youth,

A 1983 ad for a gig at Great Gildersleeve's

62 E. 4th St.

and the Mob on the third and final night of the A7 Unity Benefit, held in a historic dance and catering hall opened in the late 19th century that's now known as the **Duo Multicultural Arts**

Center. Performers on previous nights of the benefit included Richard Hell, the Stimulators, and 3 Teens Kill 4.

2641 Broadway

The former site of Chung King Recording Studios, 170 Varick St.

262 Mott St.

A benefit for **Rat Cage Records (171 Avenue A, later 307 E. 9th St.)**, which released the group's debut EP, *Polly Wog Stew*, was held at **CBGB (315 Bowery)** on November 20, 1982.

The cover of *Paul's Boutique*

Beastie Boys played the first day of the two-day matinee festival alongside Reagan Youth and the Young and the Useless, which at the time included Horovitz on guitar, and who played the Rat Cage benefit with Diamond sitting in on drums. Beastie Boys would play CBGB numerous times, including a memorial show for the late Patrick Mack of the Stimulators. On a 19-band bill, the group was joined by Sonic Youth, Swans, and Murphy's Law.

Beastie Boys played with Reagan Youth at the **Taller Latinoamericano Loft (19 W. 21st St.)** on March 5, 1983, at a benefit for NY-CARD (Coalition Against Registration & Draft), a show produced by Rock Against Racism.

At the **Academy (234 W. 43rd St.)** on May 27, 1994, the Beastie Boys played alongside Luscious Jackson, a group featuring former Beasties drummer Kate Schellenbach, on May 27, 1994, a concert in conjunction with the Milarepa Fund in support of Artists for Tibet. Along the same socially conscious lines, the group's annual Tibetan Freedom Concert took place at **Downing Stadium** from June 7 to 8, 1997, the only year it took place in New York. Also on the bill were Patti Smith, Radiohead, Sonic Youth, U2, Foo Fighters, De La Soul, Blur, Noel Gallagher of Oasis, and many more.

59 Chrystie St.

Adam Yauch Park, Brooklyn

On October 28 and 29, 2001, Beastie Boys hosted and headlined a two-night fundraiser at the **Hammerstein Ballroom (311 W. 34th St.)** for New Yorkers Against Violence, raising more than $125,000 with guest appearances by the Strokes, Yoko Ono, the B-52s, Mos Def, Moby, Michael Stipe, and Bono.

Beastie Boys played an intimate set in the former **Hiro Ballroom, Maritime Hotel (371 W. 16th St.)** on October 4, 2006, in support of Gimme Shelter: Rock & Rescue NYC, which celebrated animal rescue and no-kill shelters. Also on the bill were Blue Öyster Cult, Marshall Crenshaw, Sic Fucks, Nellie McKay, and Debbie Harry.

Though they didn't plan for the 2008 show at Terminal 5 to be their last in NYC, it's retroactively appropriate for a group that, no matter how far they traveled, has always been connected to the city's myriad rhythms and rhymes.

MORE BEASTIE BOYS

NOTEWORTHY LIVE PERFORMANCES

John Berry's Loft (2641 Broadway): The first-ever Beastie Boys show took place during a party at the home of their guitarist, John Berry, a loft at the northwest corner of Broadway and 100th Street.

Max's Kansas City (213 Park Ave. South): On December 11, 1981, the final night of live music at the venerable Max's Kansas City featured a headlining set by Bad Brains with support from both Beastie Boys and the Influence.

Danceteria (30 W. 21st St.): Beastie Boys played Danceteria for the first time, coming on an hour before Rat at Rat R, on August 25, 1983.

Great Gildersleeves (331 Bowery): Beastie Boys played Great Gildersleeves, sometimes simply Gildersleeves, on April 24, 1983, sharing the bill with Reagan Youth, the Blessed, Artless, and You Suck.

The World (254 E. 2nd St.) ⊘: Beastie Boys played a handful of shows at The World between December 13, 1985, and April 24, 1986. The April 19, 1986, show took place after the group played the Apollo Theater supporting Run-DMC earlier in the evening.

The Roxy (515 W. 18th St.): Beastie Boys played the Roxy on September 21, 1984, the same year the epic breakdance battle from the movie *Beat Street* was filmed in the club.

The Kitchen (484 Broome St.): Beastie Boys shared the bill at the Kitchen with Ordinaries and Mofungo on December 30, 1982. They returned—with a "Cooky Puss"–themed flyer designed by Ad-Rock and Kate Schellenbach—on December 12, 1983.

The Reggae Lounge (285 West Broadway): Beastie Boys played at the Reggae Lounge with Dead Kennedys, Heart Attack, and Reagan Youth on July 6, 1983.

Studio 54 (254 W. 54th St.): Beastie Boys played Band Wars at Studio 54 on March 7, 1984, on a bill with Bop Apocalypse and the Screamin' Honkers.

Apollo Theater (253 W. 125th St.): Beastie Boys headed uptown to support Def Jam label mates Run-DMC at the legendary Apollo Theater on April 19, 1986.

White Columns (325 Spring St.): Beastie Boys headlined the fourth of the five-night Speed Trials at White Columns on May 7, 1983, playing with Swans and other groups.

Irving Plaza (17 Irving Place): Beastie Boys played a warm-up for the Washington, D.C., iteration of the Tibetan Freedom Concert at Irving Plaza on June 11, 1998. It was just their second show with Mix Master Mike as DJ.

The Ritz (119 E. 11th St.): Beastie Boys played the Ritz—originally and now again Webster Hall—on October 22, 1984, sharing the bill with Urban Blight. On December 26, 1986, the *Licensed to Ill* Tour kicked off from the Ritz, with support from Murphy's Law.

30 Rockefeller Plaza: Beastie Boys were the musical guest on *Saturday Night Live* on December 10, 1994; November 21, 1998; and September 25, 1999; where they played a few bars of "Sabotage" before being mock-interrupted by Elvis Costello and launching into "Radio Radio."

Radio City Music Hall (1260 6th Ave.): Madonna's *Like a Virgin* Tour with support from Beastie Boys finally rolled into New York City in early June 1985, where they played Radio City Music Hall from the 6th through the 8th.

Madison Square Garden (4 Pennsylvania Plaza): The first time the Beastie Boys played Madison Square Garden on June 10 and 11, 1985, it was as the opening act for Madonna, a job that primarily involved them antagonizing the mothers and daughters in the crowd by being as vulgar as humanly possible. They would return to play there several times, including an October 9, 2004, show that yielded *Awesome; I Fuckin' Shot That,* a live concert film culled from footage recorded by 50 fans who were given camcorders.

Central Park SummerStage: Beastie Boys played the annual Central Park SummerStage on August 7, 2007, while touring in support of *The Mix-Up,* an all-instrumental album.

Building (51 W. 26th St.): For their first New York City gig in more than four years, Beastie Boys played a low-key set at Building, the former site of **Area**, on November 2, 1989. Making their live debut that night was Luscious Jackson, which included former Beastie Boys drummer Kate Schellenbach.

Roseland Ballroom (239 W. 52nd St.): Beastie Boys first played Roseland on the *Skills to Pay the Bills* Tour on May 23, 1992, with support from fIREHOSE and Basehead.

Cat Club (76 E. 13th St.): After opening the second of two nights for Madonna at Madison Square Garden on June 11, 1985, the Beastie Boys played a set at the Cat Club.

Hammerstein Ballroom (311 W. 34th St.): On December 31, 1986, Beastie Boys were the odd group out at the MTV Nero's Eve Rock 'n' Roll Ball, sharing the bill with Dave Edmunds, Lone Justice, the Georgia Satellites, and former Duran Duran guitarist Andy Taylor.

Coney Island High (15 St. Marks Pl.): Beastie Boys, as hardcore alter-egos Quasar, played Coney Island High on November 22, 1995. Their set included classic, hardcore-era tracks, as well as more recent stabs at the genre, "Heart Attack Man" and "Time for Livin'."

McCarren Park Pool (776 Lorimer St., Brooklyn): On August 9, 2007, Beastie Boys played McCarren Park Pool, a short-lived live performance space that has since been reopened as a community pool.

Encore Club (89-25 Merrick Ave. Ave., Queens) ⊘: Beastie Boys played Encore, a hip-hop club in Queens, on September 28, 1984. They were at the bottom of a bill that included Kurtis Blow, Spyder D, and T La Rock.

NOTEWORTHY RECORDING LOCATIONS

Rat Cage Records (171 Avenue A): *Polly Wog Stew,* the Beastie Boys' first EP as a hardcore band, was recorded and released by Dave Parsons of Rat Cage Records in 1982.

Chung King Recording Studios (170 Varick St.): Dubbed Chung King House of Metal by Rick Rubin, the studio was housed in a former Chinese restaurant and was where the Beastie Boys recorded much of their 1986 debut album, *Licensed to Ill.*

262 Mott St.: Beastie Boys had a basement rehearsal space and recording studio at 262 Mott St., where they recorded much of their 1998 album *Hello Nasty.* A live in-studio version of "Three MCs and One DJ" with Mix-Master Mike was shot on video there.

Oscilloscope Laboratories (511 Canal St.): Starting with *To the 5 Boroughs,* the Beastie Boys began recording at Oscilloscope, a Canal

St. studio that became the headquarters of Adam Yauch and David Fenkel's Oscilloscope film company in 2008. Oscilloscope has since relocated to 140 Havemeyer St. in Brooklyn.

Celebration Studios (56 W. 45th St.): The Beastie Boys' first foray into hip-hop, a prank phone call over a simple beat and fuzz guitar riff, was produced at Celebration Studios in early 1983. "Cooky Puss" paid juvenile tribute to a signature frozen cake created by Carvel in the 1970s.

OTHER NOTEWORTHY LOCATIONS

New York University, Weinstein Hall (5 University Place, Room 712): Producer and label impresario Rick Rubin famously founded and ran Def Jam Records from his dorm room at NYU's Weinstein Hall.

59 Chrystie St.: Chinatown loft that Beastie Boys rented in the mid-'80s after winning their settlement with British Airways over the use of an unlicensed sample in an ad.

182 Spring Street: Horovitz lived in a 2,560-square-foot town house at 182 Spring St. from 2000 to 2012, then sold it for $5.5 million. Horovitz and his wife, singer and activist Kathleen Hanna, most recently of the Julie Ruin, were married in 2006.

Paul's Boutique (Rivington and Ludlow): Though the sample on the album indicates a Brooklyn location, the panoramic cover of the Beastie Boys' 1989 album *Paul's Boutique* was shot at the intersection of Rivington and Ludlow Streets on the Lower East Side of Manhattan.

Friends Seminary (222 E. 16th St.): Yauch attended high school at Friends Seminary, a Quaker day school in Manhattan that also counted among its famous alumni John Sebastian of the Lovin' Spoonful and former US President Theodore Roosevelt. Yauch also attended **Edward R. Murrow High School (1600 Ave. L, Brooklyn)**, where he caught grief for being a punk.

City-As-School High School (16 Clarkson St.): Horovitz was reportedly still a student at City-As-School, which encouraged experience as well as traditional study, when the Beastie Boys toured with Madonna in 1985.

El Dorado (300 Central Park West): Diamond grew up in the El Dorado, an apartment building at 300 Central Park West.

Saint Ann's School (129 Pierrepont St., Brooklyn): Diamond went to high school at Saint Ann's, a private school with a progressive non-grading pedagogy.

Adam Yauch Park (27 State St., Brooklyn): Dedicated in honor of the late Beastie Boys MC, filmmaker, and activist, the former Palmetto Playground was renamed Adam Yauch Park in a May 2013 ceremony.

148 Baltic St., Brooklyn: Cobble Hill town house once owned and meticulously restored by Diamond and his then wife, filmmaker Tamra Davis, which the couple sold in 2015.

242 Pacific St., Brooklyn: Formerly a lot for an auto repair business, this black brick and ipe wood town house was co-designed by Diamond; his then wife, filmmaker Tamra Davis; and architects Jill and John Bouratoglou.

THE WARWICK HOTEL
65 W. 54th St.

Built by William Randolph Hearst in 1926, the 36-story Warwick Hotel was a vital New York City nerve center for Elvis Presley in 1956 and '57. This was when the King came to town to appear on the *Dorsey Brothers' Stage Show*, the *Steve Allen Show*, and the *Ed Sullivan Show*. Presley was famously photographed by Alfred Wertheimer in a moody portrait on the sidewalk along West 54th Street in front of the hotel.

Like their hero before them, the Beatles also stayed at the Warwick, giving press conferences there in August of both 1965 and 1966. The first year, the Fab Four was touting their upcoming show at Shea Stadium, by their next visit they were opening up about the Vietnam War.

In July 1967 the Pre-Fab Four once again followed in the footsteps of the Beatles, when the Monkees gave a press conference in the same lattice-lined conference room as Liverpool's finest had one year earlier.

The Warwick remains one of the Big Apple's finest hotels, catering to the elite traveler.

THE DRAKE HOTEL ⊘
440 Park Ave.

While in town for a run of sold-out shows at Madison Square Garden in July 1973, Led Zeppelin stayed at the Drake Hotel, where a safe deposit box containing $180,000 of the group's tour proceeds was robbed. Discovered by tour manager Richard Cole, the theft was reported to the police, but a subsequent investigation came up empty. To date, the money has never been recovered and those involved have not been caught. The incident was covered in *The Song Remains the Same,* a documentary film released in 1976.

RKO 58TH STREET THEATRE ⊘
154 E. 58th St.

Murray the K's 1967 Easter Extravaganza, a.k.a. Music in the Fifth Dimension, took place at the RKO 58th Street Theatre. The run featured five shows a day and included the American debuts of the Who and Cream. Also on the bill were Simon & Garfunkel, the Blues Project, and Wilson Pickett.

The opulent theater, first opened in 1928, featured tunnel-esque lobbies that connected to the Grand Foyer, a vast balcony that held nearly as many seats as the main floor of the theater. The RKO 58th Street Theatre closed in 1967, with Murray the K's Easter Extravaganza being one of the final events held there.

ONDINE
308 E. 59th St.

Ondine, an early Hard Day's Night–esque discotheque, opened for business on New Year's Eve 1965, with its peak era happening over the next few years. The Doors played extensive residencies at Ondine in November 1966 and January 1967, and the Buffalo Springfield stayed for a similar six-nights-a-week run between March 13 and April 2, 1967. Andy Warhol's Factory crowd hung out at Ondine, in part, Warhol wrote in his diary, because the club shared a name with one of his Superstars, whom he'd met at an orgy in the early '60s.

In his Pop Eye column from March 23, 1967, the *Village Voice*'s Richard Goldstein called Ondine, "that Queensboro Bridge of the soul, vast enough to encompass local beasts of prey, an occasional Rolling Stone on holiday, and a generation of post-pubic passion flowers who come to be seen and—knock on Formica—felt."

THE EXCELSIOR
303 E. 57th St.

In the '80s, Billy Joel and Christie Brinkley lived in a two-bedroom apartment on the 44th floor of The Excelsior.

P.J. CLARKE'S
915 Third Ave.

In early 1958 Buddy Holly was visiting his music publisher, **Peer-South (810 7th Ave.)**, when he was smitten with the receptionist, Maria Elena Santiago. He asked her to lunch and she demurred, so he asked her to dinner. Holly picked her up that evening in a limo and brought her to P.J. Clarke's, where they reportedly spent five hours. At the end of the meal he proposed. She said yes, and the couple wed that April in Holly's hometown of Lubbock, Texas, before returning to live in New York in September.

The former Ondine

THE PHONE BOOTH ⊘
152 E. 55th St.

Originally dubbed "New York's Only Drinker's Paradise" in the mid-'60s, The Phone Booth's "All You Can Drink" policy included dinner, dancing, and a show for just $5.95 ($6.95 on Friday and Saturday), but the nightclub also had a no cover, no minimum for live performances by hit makers such as the Turtles, the Rascals, and Sam the Sham & the Pharaohs.

SNIFFEN COURT
150-158 E. 36th St.

Photographer Joel Brodsky shot the Fellini-inspired cover of *Strange Days*, the 1967 sophomore album by the Doors, in this charming private alley. The Doors themselves only appear in a poster in the right of the image, while the

Sniffen Court

street itself bursts with circus performers and musicians.

THE MARK TWAIN RIVERBOAT
Empire State Building, 350 5th Ave.

Former Monkees Micky Dolenz and Davy Jones performed short runs at the Riverboat, a nightclub located on the ground floor of the Empire State Building, first in April 1976 as part of a tour with songwriters Tommy Boyce and Bobby Hart, and then again the following year. Other mid-'70s performers at the Riverboat included Mary Wells, Gary Lewis & the Playboys, and Sam the Sham & the Pharaohs. For $11.95 plus a $2.50 music surcharge, patrons could enjoy an all-you-can-drink bar, steak dinner, and spirited runs through tunes such as "Last Train to Clarksville" and "I Wanna Be Free" by the guys who sang 'em and the guys who wrote 'em.

THE IROQUOIS
49 W. 44th St.

The Iroquois is perhaps best associated with the late actor James Dean, who lived in the hotel for two years and now has a suite named in his honor, though it has also at times been a popular destination for visiting rock stars. On their first visit to NYC in the early '80s, New Order stayed at the Iroquois, where they ran into frequent guests the Clash, and, according to the former's bass guitarist Peter Hook in his memoir *Substance*, scrapped over the free hors d'oeuvres in the bar. Some of the Clash's breakthrough hit "Rock the Casbah" was reportedly written at the Iroquois.

OKEH RECORDS
24 W. 45th St.

Founded in 1918 by Otto K. Heinemann, Okeh (pronounced O.K.) dabbled almost from the first with material not well served by the major labels of the time, particularly different varieties

a black artist, "Crazy Blues" by Mamie Smith & Her Jazz Hounds. The record proved to be a smash, reportedly selling more than 75,000 units in the first two months alone. Smith would become a major star and pave the way for an entire generation of black performers. So-called "race records" were quickly established as a fundamental component of the recording industry and were to make an incalculable impact on American culture. Heinemann sold Okeh to Columbia in 1926, and it continued as a jazz and rhythm and blues label into the 1960s before being deactivated. It was revived in the 1990s before being retired yet again in 2000, but is currently active once again as a jazz label.

PALEY CENTER FOR MEDIA
25 W. 52nd St.
See and hear classic television and radio broadcasts featuring classic rock & roll performances here. Formerly the Museum of Television & Radio, and the Museum of Broadcasting.

of American ethnic music in a multitude of languages including German, Polish, and Yiddish. It was here in August 1920 that Okeh recorded what most musicologists consider the first commercially issued blues recording by

MADONNA

Madonna with dancers on the Danceteria rooftop, July 1983

For most of her life, Madonna has been famous. A world-renowned singer, actress, style icon, and entrepreneur. It's rare when Madonna isn't the most recognizable face in the room no matter which room she happens to be in. But that was the case in October 1982, when she started a brief relationship with neo-expressionist Jean-Michel Basquiat, who along with Keith Haring would come to personify an '80s visual aesthetic.

Basquiat lived and worked in a loft at 101 Crosby St. for the three or four months he and Madonna were dating, a time during which she effectively moved in while she was recording her eponymous debut album at Sigma Sound Studios (1697 Broadway), a celebrated studio above what's now known as the **Ed Sullivan Theater**.

There's been some question as to whether the loft was on the fourth floor, as was the assertion in a notorious listing on Airbnb; or on the second, as indicated by Marc H. Miller, who joined Paul Tschinkel to record an interview with Basquiat in the loft in November 1982 for a video series on contemporary art called *Art/new york*.

Whether she was bounding down one flight of stairs or three on her way to the studio,

232 E. 4th St.

Former Star Hotel, 303 W. 30th St.

Yeshiva of Congregation Tifereth Israel

Terrace on the Park, Queens

Madonna's confidence, even in the early stages of her recording career, was limitless. Outside the art world, anyway, she was soon to eclipse Basquiat's celebrity. And from there on, pretty much everyone else's, too.

MORE MADONNA

NOTEWORTHY LIVE PERFORMANCES

Danceteria (30 W. 21st St.): Already signed to Sire Records, Madonna would go on to perform live for the first time as part of Haoui Montaug's No Entiendes cabaret revue on December 18, 1982, on the second-floor stage at Danceteria.

FunHouse (526 W. 26th St.): In an event organized by producer and then-fiancé Jellybean Benitez and hosted by hip-hop legend Kurtis Blow, Madonna performed "Physical Attraction" at FunHouse on May 13, 1983.

Red Parrot Club (617 W. 57th St.) ⊘: Madonna's early performances were largely brief promotional appearances where she sang along to backing tracks at various clubs. Such was the case when she brought "Everybody" to the Red Parrot Club on January 26, 1983.

Studio 54 (254 W. 54th St.): Madonna's pre-album release promotional tour included a stop at Studio 54 on June 4, 1983, where she performed "Holiday" live for the first time.

Paradise Garage (84 King St.): Madonna performed "Dress You Up" at a belated birthday party for artist Keith Haring at Paradise Garage on May 16, 1984.

Washington Square Park: Madonna performed an impromptu half-hour concert in Washington Square Park on November 7, 2016, that she promoted on social media in support of Democratic presidential candidate Hillary Clinton.

Radio City Music Hall (1260 Avenue of the Americas): On September 14, 1984, Madonna performed "Like a Virgin" during the MTV Video Music Awards, held at Radio City Music Hall. Madonna would return to Radio City Music Hall for three nights on the Virgin Tour between June 6 and 8, 1985.

Madison Square Garden (4 Pennsylvania Plaza): The last two dates on Madonna's Virgin Tour took place at Madison Square Garden on June 10 and 11, 1985. She would return to the venue numerous times over the years.

Yankee Stadium (1 E. 161st St.): Madonna brought her MDNA World Tour to Yankee Stadium for a pair of shows on September 6 & 8, 2012.

NOTEWORTHY RECORDING LOCATIONS

Power Station (441 W. 53rd St.): For her second album, *Like a Virgin*, Madonna chose to work with former Chic guitarist Nile Rodgers, who'd

recently had success working with artists such as David Bowie and Duran Duran.

D&D Studios (320 W. 37th St., 4th floor): Madonna recorded some of her fourth studio album, 1989's *Like a Prayer*, at D&D Studios, which would go on to become a key location for many iconic hip-hop productions in the '90s.

OTHER NOTEWORTHY LOCATIONS

232 E. 4th St.: Madonna's first apartment of her own was a fourth-floor walkup at 232 E. 4th St. between Avenues A and B, with two small rooms, a single futon, and a radiator that hissed like a snake.

Music Building (584 8th Ave.): During her pre-Sire years, Madonna rehearsed in, and for a period illegally lived in, room 604 at the Music Building, a 12-floor facility that opened in 1979.

58 Ave. B: Locals may remember this as the location of longtime vegetarian diner Kate's Joint, but when Madonna was living around the corner this was a coffee shop where she used to hang out.

Star Hotel (303 W. 30th): After she began working with early manager Camille Barbone in 1981, Madonna found a room on the third floor

of the Star Hotel, where she briefly lived until a break-in.

The Russian Tea Room (150 W. 57th St.): To make ends meet during her early days in New York, Madonna took a series of odd jobs, including working as a coat-check girl at the famed Russian Tea Room.

65 Central Park West: Madonna and Sean Penn lived at 65 Central Park West in the mid- to late-'80s while they were married. They bought here after failing to get past the co-op board at the San Remo (145 to 146 Central Park West).

270 Riverside Dr.: After leaving the Star Hotel, Madonna lived in a spare bedroom in an apartment at the decidedly more well-heeled building at 270 Riverside Dr.

Yeshiva of Congregation Tifereth Israel (108-44 53rd Ave., Queens): Madonna lived and rehearsed in the yeshiva of this synagogue for a period between 1979 and 1980 after returning from a disenchanting trip to Paris.

Terrace on the Park (52-11 111th St., Queens): During her time living in Queens, Madonna reportedly worked a variety of jobs at this iconic banquet hall, including serving as an elevator operator.

MADISON SQUARE GARDEN/FELT FORUM/ THE THEATER AT MADISON SQUARE GARDEN
4 Pennsylvania Pl.

Opened in 1968 as the home of the New York Knicks and New York Rangers, the current Madison Square Garden is actually the fourth in the city's history, its erection leading to the creation of the New York City Landmarks Preservation Commission after the public bristled at the demolition of much of **Pennsylvania Station** on the same site.

Madison Square Garden was just three years old when it was used for the Concert for Bangladesh, a pair of sold-out shows on August 1, 1971, that were organized and headlined by former Beatle George Harrison that served as an example of the charitable possibilities for large-scale rock concerts. Among the performers at the shows were Bob Dylan, Eric Clapton, Ringo Starr, Ravi Shankar, Billy Preston, Leon Russell, and Badfinger.

On October 20, 2001, Madison Square Garden was the location of the Concert for New York City, organized by another former Beatle, Paul McCartney, to honor the city's first responders and others in the September 11 terror attack that felled the World Trade Center. McCartney, Elton John, David Bowie, the Who, Eric Clapton, Billy Joel, and Mick Jagger and Keith Richards of the Rolling Stones were among the performers.

Though it's gotten some competition from Brooklyn's Barclays Center (620 Atlantic Ave., Brooklyn) in recent years, Madison Square Garden continues to host major rock concerts in a space that holds around 20,000 fans. Elton John, Billy Joel, Madonna, Bruce Springsteen, and U2 are among the artists who've returned to "the world's most famous arena" repeatedly.

Among the many live albums recorded at Madison Square Garden are the Rolling Stones's *Get Yer Ya Ya's Out!* from their 1969 tour and Led Zeppelin's *The Song Remains the Same*, compiled during the group's three-night July 1973 stand.

Also opened in 1968 as part of the same complex was the much smaller Felt Forum, now the Theater at Madison Square Garden. The venue has been used over the years for concerts, including shows by the Doors, Van Morrison, Neil Young & Crazy Horse, the Band, the Grateful Dead, Bob Dylan, Anthrax, Sting, and others.

ANTHRAX'S SCOTT IAN'S PRE-FAME DAY JOB
240 W. 30th St.

Prior to making it with metal band Anthrax, guitarist Scott Ian worked for his father's jewelry manufacturing business here.

NANCY SPUNGEN'S APARTMENT
323 W. 23rd St.

Nancy Spungen, former girlfriend of Sid Vicious, had an apartment here before moving into the **Hotel Chelsea**.

MOTHERS
267 W. 23rd St.

Even if it was only for a year or two in the mid-'70s, Mothers was a key venue in the city's developing punk scene with mainly gay clientele. Wayne County's manager Peter Crowley started booking groups in 1975, with an enviable run between September and December of that year of shows by the Ramones, Blondie,

Talking Heads, Television, the Heartbreakers, Mink DeVille, the Fast, Wayne County, and many others.

THE HOTEL CHELSEA
222 W. 23rd St.

Built in 1884, the Hotel Chelsea is justly famous for the many illustrious personalities associated with it, including Mark Twain, Jack Kerouac, Arthur Miller, William Burroughs, Arthur C. Clarke, Andy Warhol, Diego Rivera, Willem de Kooning, Robert Mapplethorpe, and Allen Ginsberg. For many years, a large percentage of the sprawling edifice was devoted to long-term residents, most of whom were artists, musicians, writers, photographers, filmmakers, and other creative denizens of New York's cultural community. During the '60s it was frequently the go-to destination for traveling bands who were often shunned by Manhattan's fancier hoteliers. Some of the artists who are known to have spent time here include Jim Morrison, Tom Waits, Iggy Pop, Phil Ochs, Patti Smith, the Grateful Dead, Bob Dylan, Madonna, and Leonard Cohen,

Bob Gruen

Leonard Cohen onstage at the Bottom Line

who wrote two songs about a sexual encounter here with Janis Joplin. The adjoining El Quijote bar and restaurant was a popular hangout for residents and rock & roll royalty.

In 1966 Andy Warhol and Paul Morrissey filmed *Chelsea Girls*, an experimental production chronicling the lives of some of the people who lived at the Chelsea, including Warhol superstars Nico, Brigid Berlin, Ondine, Mary Woronov, and Gerard Malanga. When released in 1967, the film did well commercially and helped to amplify the Chelsea legend and mythology.

In what is probably the Chelsea's most notorious incident, Nancy Spungen, girlfriend of former Sex Pistol Sid Vicious, was found stabbed to death in the hotel on October 12, 1978. The couple had moved in together to Room 100 on August 24 of that year. Vicious was immediately charged with the crime, but released on bail. He died of a drug overdose before the trial, leaving the case officially unresolved.

Beginning in 2011, the Chelsea changed ownership and began an extensive renovation that will most likely end its time as a Bohemian haven. Many long-term residents remain, protected by law, but one suspects the character of the Chelsea will be irrevocably changed.

GREEN DOOR/PURPLE DOOR/RED DOOR/ PLUGG CLUB ⊘
140 W. 24th St.

In 1978 filmmaker and music manager Giorgio Gomelsky moved into an industrial space in Chelsea and converted it into a private events and music space intended to give emerging artists a chance to cultivate their craft. The space featured everyone from Richard Hell to Richard Lloyd, Bad Brains to Sonic Youth to the Walkmen. The name of the venue was based upon the color of the door at the time; a legendary series of glamorous punk parties dubbed Green Door parties were put on by Jesse Malin and other founding members of D Generation in response to the flannel-draped aesthetic of the Grunge scene. Attendees at the parties reportedly included Joe Strummer, Joey Ramone, Iggy Pop, Madonna, and Debbie Harry.

"All these things would happen out of necessity," said Malin. Gomelsky "put on a lot of hardcore shows in his loft and the kids would break the toilets, but he seemed to love it. And he and I became friendly, and he had this idea that he wanted to do *West Side Story* with hardcore kids and hip-hop kids from the downtown ghetto. He was very supportive of me

at a young age. Flash forward to the late '80s and early '90s, and me and my friends hated everything that was going on in rock music. Funky, short pants, metal, the hair band thing. We couldn't stand these big clubs. New Years' Eve was coming and we wanted to have this party where we would actually be able to hang out and listen to music and get people to dance. We all rented turntables and went into a beer distributor in Brooklyn and brought in cases of beer and had our girlfriends sell the beer for two or three dollars. And we called Giorgio and said, 'Can we have your house?' He said, 'Yeah, $500!'"

The Green Door parties, which later moved into what became **Coney Island High (15 St. Marks)**, had a less salacious name than one might expect.

"The door was green," Malin said. "It had nothing to do with the porno movie or the Cramps song ("The Green Door"). We brought in the booze, we brought in the turntables, we told our friends to dress up and we handed out flyers, the old New York handshake. We went out every night, 'Come to our thing.' It was packed like crazy. And the best part was people were dancing to the Stooges, and Funkadelic, and Sly & the Family Stone, the Cramps. It went on until six in the morning, made lots of money, we trashed the place. And someone said, 'Let's do it again!'"

TRAMPS
125 E. 15th St./51 W. 21st St.

Opened by Terry Dunne in 1975 on 15th Street, and moved a little over a decade later to 21st, Tramps had a largely blues and soul vibe, with legends such as Sam & Dave, Buddy Guy, Solomon Burke, Darlene Love, and Lightnin' Hopkins all playing shows. But the venue wasn't strictly soul, with the Jon Spencer Blues Explosion, Stiff Little Fingers, Robyn Hitchcock, the Flaming Lips, and even Bob Dylan having hit the stage. On February 21, 1995, Bruce Springsteen reunited with the E Street Band for the first time since 1988 by playing a selection of old favorites and several takes of "Murder Incorporated" for a Jonathan Demme–directed music video produced to coincide with the release of the Boss' greatest hits compilation.

DANCETERIA
252 W. 37th St./30 W. 21st St./The Martha Washington Hotel (now the Redbury), 29 E. 29th St., first-floor ballroom

In a city where residents seem to constantly change addresses, it's only natural for music venues to do the same. In the case of the long-departed Danceteria, its first two locations are likely its most important.

Originally opened at 252 W. 37th St. in 1979 by Rudolf Pieper and Jim Fouratt, Danceteria's primary focus was as a dance club and video lounge, soaking up after-hours customers of

Danceteria's second location at 30 W. 21st St.

rock venues such as the **Mudd Club, Tier-3,** and **CBGB**.

The space had two floors with separate DJs, and the video lounger was designed by video artists Emily Armstrong and Pat Ivers, who programmed an eclectic mix of found footage, art, early music videos, and musical performances.

In 1982, Pieper and Fouratt were hired by John Argento to bring Danceteria to a six-floor facility on 21st Street, a space that allowed them to expand upon their original mission into a space large enough for a VIP lounge and live music. Within months Ruth Polsky was hired to replace Pieper and Fouratt to promote and book live music, making Danceteria one of the era's preeminent venues, with shows and appearances by Duran Duran, Wham!, New Order, Depeche Mode, Madonna, the B-52s, Bauhaus, Nick Cave & the Bad Seeds, Violent Femmes, Beastie Boys, Sonic Youth, Swans, Berlin, and many others. The Smiths' New York City debut took place at Danceteria on New Year's Eve 1983, with singer Morrissey refusing to wear his eyeglasses and falling off the stage.

Danceteria closed in 1986, reopening between 1990 to 1993 at the Martha Washington Hotel. It also operated as a Hamptons outpost for around a decade beginning in 1984.

BLANK TAPES STUDIO
37 W. 20th St.

Blank Tapes was a legendary independent studio founded by Bob Blank, where everyone from Afrika Bambaataa to Chaka Khan, Lydia Lunch to Larry Levan, recorded from the mid-'70s to the mid-'80s. Blank frequently worked with Arthur Russell on the composer's dance tracks. The studio closed in 1986.

LIMELIGHT
47 W. 20th St.

Opened in 1983 in a deconsecrated Episcopal church, the Limelight was unofficially dubbed the Church of Rave in honor of its reputation as a popular dance club. But the venue also hosted occasional live shows before closing in 2007, including performances by Pearl Jam, Prince, Cyndi Lauper, Gang of Four, Killing Joke, and Smashing Pumpkins. In its early '90s heyday, the Limelight drew unwanted attention from authorities when its party promoter Michael Alig was arrested for the murder and dismemberment of Angel Melendez, an alleged drug dealer who operated in the club.

41 W. 16th St.

The former Limelight

JONI MITCHELL'S HOME
41 W. 16th St.

Joni Mitchell moved into a one-bedroom apartment at 41 W. 16th St. in 1967, penning many of her songs for her album *Clouds* here, the appropriately titled "Chelsea Morning" among them.

LESTER BANGS'S HOME
542 6th Ave.

Legendary rock critic Lester Bangs lived and died in an apartment at 542 6th Ave. Bangs, who famously recounted a caustic encounter with Lou Reed in a story called "Let Us Now Praise Famous Death Dwarves," moved to New York City from Michigan after establishing himself in the pages of *Creem* magazine. Bangs also wrote for the *Village Voice*, the *NME*, *Rolling Stone*, and *Penthouse*. Bangs was found in his apartment after an accidental overdose on April 30, 1982. He had supposedly been listening to the Human League's 1981 album *Dare*.

542 6th Ave.

at Stratosphere are Television, A Perfect Circle, R.E.M., Depeche Mode, Jesse Malin, Carly Simon, Moby, and many others.

THE COOLER
416 W. 14th St.

It might be easier to list the musicians and DJs and electronic artists who didn't play the Cooler after it opened in 1993 than those who did. Located in the Meatpacking District, the Cooler condensed the melting pot ethos of New York City into a club, where avant-jazz trio Medeski, Martin, and Wood; hip-hop trio the Fugees; and electronic duo Autechre each headlining three consecutive nights made total sense. It was the site of one of the first shows by NYC-indie heroes Yeah Yeah Yeahs. The Cooler closed on June 2, 2001, and its final weekend of shows included a performance by Suicide.

WATERWORKS RECORDING
408 W. 14th St.

Since relocated to Tuscon, Arizona, Jim Waters' Waterworks Recording was a studio in the Meatpacking District that saw numerous luminaries cut tracks in its intimate space, including Sonic Youth, the Jon Spencer Blues Explosion, Gumball, Richard Hell, Dim Stars, former Velvet Underground drummer Mo Tucker, the Posies, and Jonathan Fire*Eater.

STRATOSPHERE SOUND RECORDING STUDIOS
408 W. 14th St./239 11th Ave.

Stratosphere Sound Recording Studios was founded in 1998 by James Iha of Smashing Pumpkins, Adam Schlesinger of Fountains of Wayne, and his fellow Ivy bandmate Andy Chase. The studio moved from 14th Street to 11th Avenue in 2001, where it lasted until its closure in 2012. Among the artists who worked

HIGHLINE BALLROOM
431 W. 16th St.

Open since 2007, the roughly 700-person-capacity Highline Ballroom's early highlights included shows by Lou Reed, Amy Winehouse, Art Brut, Nashville Pussy, and a rare club date by Paul McCartney on June 13 of that year in support of his *Memory Almost Full* album. The Highline Ballroom is still open, regularly hosting rock, hip-hop, avant-garde, and other shows.

THE ROXY ⊘
515 W. 18th St.

Initially opened in 1978 as a roller disco, the Roxy soon began hosting dance nights and early hip-hop pioneers such as Grandmaster Flash, Cold Crush Brothers, and Afrika Bambaataa. Other performers included Madonna, Beastie Boys, Run-DMC, New Edition, Kraftwerk, Cyndi Lauper, Whitney Houston, Beyonce, and Grace Jones. The Roxy closed in 2007.

MARQUEE
547 West 21st St.
A short-lived early '90s venue named after London's landmark club, the Marquee had a decidedly British feel. Performances by groups from across the pond included Ride, Blur, Lush, Curve, the La's, the Kitchens of Distinction, the Wonder Stuff, and Pop Will Eat Itself. But there were also plenty of American acts at the Marquee as well, with shows from the Rollins Band, fIREHOSE, Soul Asylum, Primus, and TAD.

THE PUNK DUMP ⊘
356 10th Ave.
Ged Dunn, John Holmstrom, and "Resident Punk" Legs McNeil, three friends from Connecticut, rented this space in November 1975 for $195 a month, turning it into the production headquarters for *Punk Magazine*, which they'd begin publishing the following year. A cross between a music magazine and comic book, *Punk* blended irreverent humor and

The second Punk Dump, 225 Lafayette St.

a sharp visual aesthetic to spread the word about CBGB and the downtown scene during its most celebrated era. The Punk Dump later moved to **225 Lafayette St.**, a building that was fittingly the original home of EC Comics and *Mad* magazine.

JIMI HENDRIX & ELECTRIC LADY

Though it's come to be known as the place where artists like the Clash, the Rolling Stones, Bob Dylan, David Bowie, and U2 have recorded and produced, **Electric Lady Studios (52 W. 8th St.)** will forever be associated with Jimi Hendrix, the legendary guitarist who helped design the facility to be conducive to creativity and comfort, while also giving musicians a state-of-the-art recording experience.

52 W. 8th St.

Already feeling like New York City was his home, Hendrix and manager Michael Jeffrey bought the former short-lived Generation nightclub in 1968 with an initial eye on renovating the existing space and reopening it as another live venue. Hendrix had already jammed at Generation, which in its brief existence was host to shows by Sly & the Family Stone, Chuck Berry, Big Brother & the Holding Company, and many others. But then Hendrix had jammed just about anywhere with a stage and backline in Manhattan, so what was it about Generation that caught his attention? Perhaps it was the location, as his various apartments—**321 E. 9th St., 59 W. 12th St., 61 Jane St.**, and even the **31 Bedford St.** apartment

Band of Gypsys, recorded live at the Fillmore East in 1970

of a friend where he used to like to crash—were all a short walk from Generation. Hendrix spent a lot of time in and around the Village.

Generation was only open for about a year, but the address was previously home to the country-themed **Village Barn,** opened by Meyer Horowitz in 1930 and maintained by various family members until 1967.

While Hendrix saw the venture as a new live venue and place to jam, he was convinced by

61 Jane St.

Jimi's Bedford Street crash pad

The Experience with *Alice* in Central Park

producer Eddie Kramer and Bearsville Studio manager Jim Marron, to turn it into a recording studio. With designer John Storyk, Hendrix helped shape the look and feel of the studio, which he saw as the antithesis of the antiseptic feel of other studios in which he'd recorded, with round windows and high-tech mood lightning meant to stimulate creativity. Work got underway later in the year.

But construction would prove slow and costly, with the work slowed by both bureaucracy and the discovery that a tributary of the Minetta Creek flowed underneath the building. Because of the delays, Hendrix would spend only about a month making music at Electric Lady, his final studio recording there—or anywhere—the instrumental "Slow Blues," took place just one day after he hosted a grand opening party attended by Eric Clapton, Patti Smith, Steve Winwood, Ron Wood, and many others. Hendrix boarded a flight to England the next day, where he would die less than a month later.

MORE JIMI HENDRIX

NOTEWORTHY LIVE PERFORMANCES

Fillmore East (105 2nd Ave.): The Jimi Hendrix Experience played on a double bill with Sly & the Family Stone at the Fillmore East on May 10, 1968. Hendrix would later famously return with Band of Gypsys.

Cafe Wha? (115 MacDougal St.): Hendrix's short-lived group Jimmy James and the Blue Flames had a regular gig at Cafe Wha? in 1966.

Cafe Au Go Go (152 Bleecker St.): The Jimi Hendrix Experience played three nights at Cafe Au Go Go between July 21 and 23, 1967, during their first extended stay in the city.

Village Gate (160 Bleecker St.): The trio of Jimi Hendrix, Billy Cox, and Mitch Mitchell played a benefit alongside the Grateful Dead and a poetry-reading Jim Morrison for psychedelic philosopher Timothy Leary at the Village Gate on May 4, 1970.

Madison Square Garden (4 Pennsylvania Plaza): Band of Gypsys played their final show at the Winter Festival for Peace on January 28, 1970, at the same venue where the Experience played one year earlier.

Salvation (1 Sheridan Square): The Jimi Hendrix Experience played the Salvation nightclub August 3, 5, and 7, 1967.

Steve Paul's the Scene (301 W. 46th St.) ⊘: The Jimi Hendrix Experience's New York debut took place over two nights at Steve Paul's the Scene on July 3 and 4, 1967. Also on the bill were the Seeds and the ubiquitous Tiny Tim.

Cheetah (Broadway and 53rd Street) ⊘: Hendrix played the Cheetah with Curtis Knight and the Squires in May 1966.

Wollman Rink, Central Park: The Jimi Hendrix Experience opened for the Young Rascals as part of the Rheingold Central Park Music Festival on July 5, 1967.

Hunter College (695 Park Ave.): The Jimi Hendrix Experience played two shows in the 800-person-capacity auditorium at Hunter College on March 2, 1968.

Apollo Theater (253 W. 125th St.): Jimi Hendrix won first prize in the Apollo Theater's celebrated amateur contest in February 1964.

United Block Association Benefit Concert (139th Street and Lenox Avenue): Hendrix's Gypsy, Sun & Rainbows extended their brief post-Woodstock run at this benefit, playing on a stage in the middle of the street at 139th and Lenox for the United Block Association Benefit Concert on September 5, 1969.

Downing Stadium, Randall's Island ⊘: Hendrix played the doomed New York Pop Festival at Downing Stadium on July 17, 1970.

Forest Hills Tennis Stadium (1 Tennis Place, Queens): The Jimi Hendrix Experience's brief, ill-conceived run opening for the Monkees would culminate with three nights of shows at the Forest Hills Tennis Stadium between July 14 and 16, 1967.

Singer Bowl (Flushing Meadows-Corona Park, Queens) ⊘: The Jimi Hendrix Experience headlined the Singer Bowl on August 23, 1968. Also on the bill were Big Brother & the Holding Company, the Soft Machine, and the Chambers Brothers.

NOTEWORTHY RECORDING LOCATIONS

Record Plant (321 W. 44th St.): Initial work on *Electric Ladyland*, the third studio album by the Jimi Hendrix Experience, included a great many impromptu jam sessions that took place at the recently opened Record Plant between April and May 1968.

Sound Center Studios (247 W. 46th St.) ⊘: Hendrix booked two days of sessions at Sound Center Studios on May 13 and 14, 1968, during a brief break in the Experience's US tour.

Mayfair Studios (701 7th Ave.): The Jimi Hendrix Experience recorded "Burning of the Midnight Lamp" at Mayfair Studios on July 6, 1967, more than a year before it would appear on the final album by the group, *Electric Ladyland.*

OTHER NOTEWORTHY LOCATIONS

Alice in Wonderland **Statue, Central Park:** The Jimi Hendrix Experience was photographed sitting with children on the *Alice in Wonderland* statue sometime in 1968 by Linda Eastman.

Baggie's/Baggy's (71 Grand St.): Band of Gypsys rehearsed at Baggie's in December 1969 ahead of their legendary New Year's Eve shows at the Fillmore East.

Warwick Hotel (65 W. 54th St.): In town as the support act for the Monkees at Forest Hills Tennis Stadium in Queens, the entire touring party, including the Jimi Hendrix Experience, stayed at the Warwick Hotel from July 13 to 16, 1967.

Lowe's Motor Inn (790 8th Ave.): The Jimi Hendrix Experience booked rooms at the Lowe's Motor Inn upon arrival in New York City in early July 1967.

Wellington Hotel (871 7th Ave.): The Jimi Hendrix Experience stayed at the Wellington Hotel for a week in early March 1968 while in town for an appearance at Hunter College.

Hotel Theresa (2090 Adam Clayton Powell Jr. Blvd.): A pre-Experience Jimi Hendrix stayed here in 1963. Other notable guests included musicians Ray Charles, Little Richard, Louis Armstrong, and Lena Horne.

THE PRINCE GEORGE HOTEL
14 E. 28th St.

In February 1963, 17-year-old Lesley Gore had aspirations of a career in show business. She had been working with a vocal coach and occasionally sang with her cousin Allen's band, which played weddings, Bar Mitzvahs, and sweet sixteen parties. For one such gig at the Prince George's Ballroom, she agreed to step in for the regular singer, who was ill. Unbeknownst to Lesley or her cousin, Mercury Records president Irving Green was in attendance, ostensibly to hear the band. He was unmoved by the group but impressed with Lesley, and soon after he brought her to Mercury and introduced her to producer Quincy Jones. Jones picked through more than 200 songs with Lesley before

settling on a tune to record entitled "It's My Party." Mere days later, Jones bumped into Phil Spector, who mentioned in passing he planned to record the same tune with the Crystals. With little time to waste, Jones rushed the single into production and sent several copies to influential DJs around the country.

All of this was unknown to Lesley, of course. Driving home from school less than a week after her recording date, she was stunned to hear herself on the radio belting out "It's My Party." Before her 18th birthday in May, Lesley Gore would have the number-one record in the country. She followed this success with several other hits, including the proto-feminist anthem "You Don't Own Me." Prior to her death in February 2015, Lesley had made something of a comeback, touring and performing regularly across the country.

The Prince George eventually fell on hard times. It was a crime-ridden welfare hotel for many years before being closed and left to decay in 1990. The story has a happy ending, though, as it was eventually acquired and renovated by Common Ground, an organization dedicated to serving the at-risk community by providing safe affordable housing. The Ballroom has been restored to its former glory and is once again available for rental.

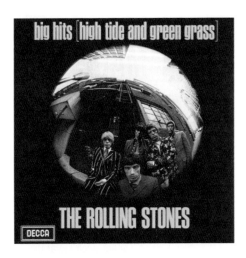

THE MODS & ROCKERS BALL
333 Park Ave. South

The Rolling Stones played two shows at the **Academy of Music (126 E.14th St.)** on October 24, 1964, kicking off their second American tour. The second show was attended by Andy Warhol, his new protégé socialite Baby Jane Holzer, and journalist Tom Wolfe, who wrote about the event in his essay "Girl of the Year." Wolfe went on to describe a party held later that evening or possibly the next at photographer Jerry Schatzberg's studio and apartment at 333 Park Ave. South in honor of Holzer's 24th birthday. In attendance were the Stones plus various assembled '60s glitterati, including Nicky Haslam, Sally Kirkland, Ahmet Ertegun (who would sign the Stones to Atlantic in seven years' time), and supermodel Jean Shrimpton, whose absent younger sister Chrissie was Mick's then-current main squeeze. Entertainment was provided by the all-female Goldie & the Gingerbreads, who would impress Ertegun enough to sign them to Atlantic. The

333 Park Ave. South

124 E. 24th St.

festivities continued until the wee hours, at which point the remaining guests, including Goldie & Co. but sans the Stones, piled into taxis and headed over to **The Brasserie (100 E. 53rd St.)**.

Two years later Schatzberg would take some now-iconic pictures of the Stones. In the late spring he would photograph them on the S.S. *Sea Panther* (79th St. **Boat Basin)** to promote the group's album *Aftermath* and by having them pose with debutante Alexandra Chace for the cover of *Town & Country* magazine. Later that year he shot them for the American cover of their new single "Have You Seen Your Mother Baby, Standing in the Shadow?" The front of the sleeve is in color through a fisheye lens—a picture also used for the UK cover of their *Big Hits (High Tide and Green Grass)* compilation. The image on the back is a black-and-white shot of the group in drag. Both pictures were taken at the same location just around the corner from Schatzberg's studio at 124 E. 24th St. According to Keith Richards, after the photoshoot, they sauntered into a local bar still in drag and failed to raise an eyebrow.

ELVIS PRESLEY AT RCA STUDIOS ⊘

151 E. 24th St.

Elvis Presley flew to New York with his manager, Colonel Tom Parker, on January 25, 1956, in anticipation of his performance on the Dorsey

Brothers Stage Show on January 28. They checked in to the **Warwick Hotel (65 W. 54th St.)** and had dinner at **The Hickory House (14 W. 52nd St.)** ⊘. After performing for the Dorsey Brothers **(CBS Studio 50, 1697 Broadway)**, Presley took a day off before joining up with his band on January 30 at RCA Studio 1 to spend seven hours recording for his new label. The following day, he and the musicians returned for another three hours. The two sessions yielded the songs "Blue Suede Shoes," "Tutti Frutti," "My Baby Left Me," "One Sided Love Affair," "So Glad You're Mine," and "I'm Gonna Sit Right Down and Cry Over You." Most of the tracks appeared on his debut RCA album that March.

Elvis returned to the studio on February 3 just prior to his second appearance on Stage Show the next day. This time he cut "Lawdy Miss Clawdy" and "Shake, Rattle, and Roll," both of which appear on the UK edition of his premier LP in 1956.

The day after Presley's appearance on the *Steve Allen Show* at the **Hudson Theater (141 W. 44th St.)** on July 1, 1956, he made his final recording date in New York at RCA, cutting "Don't Be Cruel," "Hound Dog," and "Any Way You Want Me."

GRAMERCY PARK HOTEL

2 Lexington Ave.

Built in 1925, the Gramercy Park Hotel has a long history of appealing to familiar faces. Babe Ruth was reportedly a regular in the hotel bar, and a young John F. Kennedy was a guest for several months. Humphrey Bogart married his first wife, Helen Menken, at the hotel a year after it opened; the couple divorced a year after that.

Bob Dylan, Bob Marley, the Beatles, U2, and the Clash have all stayed in the hotel.

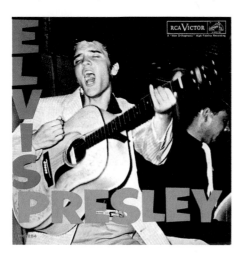

MAX'S KANSAS CITY
213 Park Ave. South

The Max's Kansas City story is an epic saga covering two distinct periods with a brief denouement. Opened by Mickey Ruskin in 1965 as a restaurant— "Steak-Lobster-Chick Peas"—and live music venue, Max's soon became a fabled hangout of artists and film stars, with Andy Warhol and his entourage frequently occupying the back room. Bands played upstairs, including the final Velvet Underground shows with Lou Reed during a nine-week residency in the summer of 1970. A recording by Warhol superstar Brigid Polk of the Velvets' performance on August 23 was released two years later as the *Live at Max's Kansas City* album.

Max's Kansas City, April 1977

Bob Gruen

Other performers at Max's during its first incarnation include Bruce Springsteen, Bob Marley & the Wailers, the New York Dolls, Wayne County, Tim Buckley, Tom Waits, and Aerosmith, who signed their deal with Columbia Records in the club.

Max's hip popularity had waned by 1974, and Ruskin closed the venue in December of that year. But in 1975 it was given a new lease on life by new owner Tommy Dean Mills. Under the direction of booker Peter Crowley, Max's Kansas City was reborn as a crucial live venue, first hosting shows by punk acts such as Blondie, the Ramones, the Patti Smith Group, the Heartbreakers, the Cramps, Sid Vicious, Devo, and others, before expanding to include hardcore bands.

Talking Heads played the second incarnation of Max's a handful of times in 1975 and '76, but their drummer Chris Frantz said it wasn't what he'd hoped it would be.

"It still had a certain cache, but nothing compared to the Warhol days, and the days that everybody from the Stooges to the Wailers would play there, and Bruce Springsteen or whoever," said Frantz. "We played there a few times, but they never paid us as well as [CBGB owner] Hilly [Kristal] did, so we just said, 'To Hell with this.'"

But Jesse Malin, who failed to impress during an audition at CBGB with an early version of his hardcore band Heart Attack, said the band was invited to play a birthday celebration for Johnny Thunders instead and he was impressed, especially with Crowley.

"The two best things Peter Crowley taught me were, 'Take this money and stick it in your underwear,' because it was all about the two-hour train ride and the half hour bus ride," said Malin, who was living at home in Queens at the time. "[He] also taught me, 'You've got to go to J&R Records, the only record store, because they've got Motörhead in the rock & roll section, not the metal section.'"

Max's closed again in November 1981, with Bad Brains and Beastie Boys playing its final night.

In Max's final act, Mills reopened the club in January 1998 at 240 W. 52nd St., but after a rights dispute with Ruskin's widow, Yvonne Sewall-Ruskin, it was closed for good.

Sewall-Ruskin later founded the Max's Kansas City Project, which serves the arts and youth communities.

IRVING PLAZA
17 Irving Place

After nearly three decades as a Polish-American community center, Irving Plaza was turned into a rock venue in 1978, hosting shows by Talking Heads and the B-52s in its early days. The club has gone through numerous owners since then, opening and closing and surviving efforts to demolish the building and erect condominiums. The Ramones played the last night of one of its closures on New Year's Eve 1988, but it reopened once again in the early '90s under the direction of promoter Ron Delsener.

Between 2007 and 2010, Irving Plaza was renamed the Fillmore New York at Irving Plaza in an attempt to draw a parallel between the former **Fillmore East (105 2nd Ave.)** and the

still thriving Fillmore in San Francisco. But without an historical connection, the rebrand didn't stick, and the venue once again reverted to being known as Irving Plaza. It's still open and hosting rock shows today, including a surprise gig by Paul McCartney in 2015 announced only that morning on Twitter.

MOUNT SINAI BETH ISRAEL HOSPITAL
10 Nathan D. Perlman Pl.

Television guitarist Richard Lloyd wound up at Beth Israel Hospital in 1978 for endocarditis, an inflammation of the inner layer of the heart often characterized by lesions, during the recording of the group's second album, *Adventure*. According to photographer David Godlis in *Please Kill Me*, Lloyd was selling pot from his hospital room, openly weighing it on a scale, much to the consternation of an elderly roommate on the other side of the curtain.

STUYVESANT HIGH SCHOOL
345 E. 15th St.

Notable alumni during the school's time on 15th Street include Walter Becker of Steely Dan, Eagle-Eye Cherry, Thelonious Monk, and Bobby Colomby, the original drummer for Blood, Sweat & Tears. Stuyvesant High moved to 345 Chambers St. in 1992. The 15th Street school is now known as the Old Stuyvesant Campus, housing three different schools: The Institute for Collaborative Education, the High School for Health Professions and Human Services, and P.S. 226.

ACADEMY OF MUSIC/PALLADIUM ⊘
126 E. 14th St.

On September 20, 1979, the Clash's Paul Simonon swung his Fender Precision Bass over his head and smashed it into the stage at the Palladium. It was a spontaneous act of frustration that, thanks to photographer Pennie Smith, has become one of the most

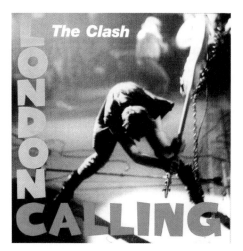

iconic images in the history of rock & roll as the cover of the group's third album, *London Calling*.

The 3,000-person-capacity theater at 126 E. 14th St. had by then already seen its share of great moments, beginning in the '60s in its prior incarnation as Academy of Music. The Rolling Stones rolled through on May 1, 1965, around a week into their first North American tour, followed by three shows on May 29 as the tour wrapped up. The Band's 1972 live album *Rock of Ages* was culled from shows as the Academy of Music between December 28 and 31, 1971. Lou Reed released two live albums recorded at the Academy of Music, starting with *Rock 'n' Roll Animal* in 1974.

By the mid-'70s, the name changed to the Palladium, with notable runs of shows by Bruce Springsteen & the E Street Band, Judas Priest, Ozzy Osbourne, Duran Duran, U2, Roxy Music, the Cramps, the Ramones, Chuck Berry, and many others. New Year's Eve 1976 saw the Palladium play host to a show headlined by the Patti Smith Group, with support from Television and John Cale.

The Grateful Dead played extended stands at the Academy of Music between March 21 and 28, 1972, and the Palladium between April 29 and May 4, 1977. Recordings from both runs have since been officially released.

The final live shows at the Palladium were a pair of sold-out gigs by post-hardcore icons Fugazi on May 2 and 3, 1997.

NEW YORK DOLLS

New York Dolls onstage at the Mercer Arts Center on December 31, 1972

If it wasn't inevitable that the **University Hotel (673 Broadway)** ⊘ would collapse, it might not have been unexpected either. Opened as the Grand Central Hotel in 1870 on the site of the first Winter Garden Theatre, the once-opulent hotel had long since lost its luster, serving a decidedly less well-heeled clientele than in its salad days. On August 9, 1973, just after 5 p.m., the hotel fell, spewing dust and rubble into the street, taking four lives and destroying not only the hotel, but also the thriving **Mercer Arts Center (240 Mercer St.)** ⊘, which for around two heady years was home to a handful of performance spaces dedicated to off-Broadway shows, dance, film, poetry, and music that would in part transform rock & roll

with early performances by two of the city's key groups: Suicide and the New York Dolls.

The New York Dolls, an aggressively flamboyant gang that sounded a bit like the Rolling Stones on a runaway subway train, may be the group most associated with the Mercer Arts Center, where they had an extensive residency in the Oscar Wilde Room on Tuesday nights in 1972. During that period, they grew popular enough that they were moved into the Mercer Arts Center's larger Sean O'Casey Theatre, with Sundays added to their steady Tuesday-night gig.

In mid-October 1972, the New York Dolls took a break from their Mercer Arts Center run for a tour of England, where they would go on

The former Endicott Hotel

to variously support Lou Reed, the Faces, Kevin Ayers, and others. But the tour was very nearly their last, when on November 2, 1972, drummer Billy Murcia died asphyxiated in a bathtub following an accidental overdose.

The Dolls returned from England, and in an effort to keep the group together, began

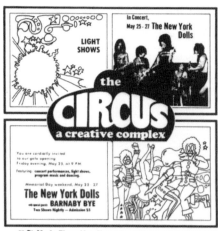

Gem Spa, 131 2nd Ave.

auditioning drummers at the **Leslie West's Charles Lane Studios (7 Charles Lane)** ⊘ , with pre-Kiss Peter Criss and pre-Voidoids and Ramones Marc Bell, a.k.a., Marky Ramone, reportedly turning up. The job went to Jerry Nolan, who debuted with the New York Dolls at the **O'Casey Theatre** ⊘ on December 19, 1972. The Dolls' Tuesday-night engagement continued through their Valentine's Day celebration on February 11, 1973, when they shared the bill with Suicide, Wayne County, the Magic Tramps, and Ruby & the Rednecks.

MORE NEW YORK DOLLS

NOTEWORTHY LIVE PERFORMANCES

Endicott Hotel (101 W. 81st St.): The band's first gig with singer David Johansen and their last with guitarist Rick Rivets happened at this welfare hotel on Christmas Eve, 1971.

Max's Kansas City (213 Park Ave. South): The Dolls played upstairs at Max's Kansas City for the first time on July 24 and 25, 1972.

Villageast (105 2nd Ave.): The New York Dolls played the Villageast Theater, formerly the Fillmore East, on December 23 and 24, 1972, with Teenage Lust and the Magic Tramps.

Club 82 (82 E. 4th St.): The Dolls played the first date of an Easter Parade tour of venues in the city on April 17, 1974.

Bottom Line (15 W. 4th St.): The Dolls' Easter Parade tour stopped at the Bottom Line for two sets on April 21, 1974, with Suzi Quatro supporting.

Beacon Theatre (2124 Broadway): With the rest of the band having split earlier in the year, the New York Dolls featuring David Johansen and Sylvain Sylvain played the Beacon Theatre on New Year's Eve, 1975.

Kenny's Castaways (211 E. 84th St.): The Dolls frequently played the original location of Kenny's Castaways through 1973, beginning with a run of shows between January 30 and February 10.

Town Hall (123 W. 43rd St.): The New York Dolls opened for Captain Beefheart & His Magic Band at Town Hall on February 24, 1973.

Academy of Music (126 E. 14th St.): The Dolls played a St. Valentine's Day Massacre at Academy of Music on February 15, 1974, with support from Elliott Murphy. Prior to the Dolls' set, the film *Lipstick Killers*, shot by Bob Gruen, was screened.

Hotel Diplomat (108 W. 43rd St.) ⊘: The Dolls played many shows at the Hotel Diplomat, including their first on February 4, 1972, an un-billed appearance at the Dana Beal Benefit Boogie, a fundraiser for the marijuana activist and founder of the *Yipster Times*.

Gaslight Au Go Go (152 Bleecker St.) ⊘: The Dolls played the Gaslight Au Go-Go, formerly the Cafe Au Go-Go until 1969, on March 23 and 24, 1973.

CBGB (315 Bowery): Though the New York Dolls never played CBGB during their original run, the reconstituted group with singer David Johansen and guitarist Sylvain Sylvain hit the venue on March 28, 2006.

The Circus (23 St. Marks Pl.): The New York Dolls played at the newly re-opened Circus between May 25 and 27, 1973, performing two sets a night.

Sea of Clouds (5 E. 16th St.): The Ramones and the Heartbreakers, a group featuring former Dolls Johnny Thunders and Jerry Nolan played a New Year's Eve show in this fifth-floor loft space on December 31, 1975.

On the Rocks (643 Broadway): The Dolls, which by then featured only Johansen and Sylvain from the classic lineup, played the opening of new rock club On the Rocks, from November 4 through 6, 1976.

Lloyd Price's Crawdaddy (1674 Broadway): The Pox, a pre–New York Dolls group started by Sylvain Sylvain and Billy Murcia, played at Lloyd Price's Crawdaddy in the late '60s.

Felt Forum (4 Pennsylvania Plaza): The New York Dolls supported Mott the Hoople at the Felt Forum on August 3, 1973, the same night the University Hotel and Mercer Arts Center collapsed.

Radio City Music Hall (1260 6th Ave.): The New York Dolls opened for Mott the Hoople at Radio City Music Hall on October 26, 1973.

Waldorf Astoria, Grand Ballroom (301 Park Ave.): The New York Dolls played a Halloween costume party in the Grand Ballroom of the Waldorf Astoria on October 31, 1973.

The Little Hippodrome (227 E. 56th St.): The Dolls made a comeback at the Little Hippodrome, a drag club and discotheque, on February 28, 1975, at the behest of their new manager, Malcolm McLaren.

Coventry (47-03 Queens Blvd., Queens): The New York Dolls began playing shows at Coventry on May 11, 1973, returning several times through late July of the same year.

Man's Country (55 Pierrepont Street, Brooklyn): An early performance by the New York Dolls took place in this western-themed bathhouse.

NOTEWORTHY RECORDING LOCATIONS

Record Plant (321 W. 44th St.): The New York Dolls recorded their eponymous debut album at the Record Plant with producer Todd Rundgren in April 1973. The album reportedly took just eight days to record, with a budget of $17,000.

Blue Rock Studio (29 Greene St.): The New York Dolls recorded demos with manager Marty Thau in June 1972 at Blue Rock Studio, tackling early takes on many songs they'd revisit later, including "Personality Crisis," "Looking for a Kiss," and "Jet Boy." These recordings surfaced on numerous releases later.

OTHER NOTEWORTHY LOCATIONS

The New York Doll Hospital (787 Lexington Ave.): Sylvain worked across the street from the famed New York Doll Hospital in the late '60s at **The Different Drummer** (792 Lexington Ave.), which offered "antique and new direction clothing."

119 Chrystie Street: Prior to settling in at the Mercer Arts Center, the Dolls used to play rent parties in the loft where Thunders, Murcia, and Sylvain lived, charging $2 a head.

161 Grand St.: After splitting with the New York Dolls, Johnny Thunders and the Heartbreakers used to rehearse in a space at 161 Grand St.

Nobodys (163 Bleecker St.): In late 1970 Johnny Thunders met Arthur Kane and Rick Rivets, at Nobodys, a bar that would continue being a frequent hangout not only for the New York Dolls, but also other rock & rollers.

Gem Spa (131 2nd Ave.): A legendary hangout for the Beats in the '50s and hippies in the '60s, the back-cover photo for the Dolls' eponymous debut was shot in front of Gem Spa.

Quintano's School for Young Professionals (156 W. 56th St.): Quintano's had a reputation for taking in talented kids who'd been kicked out of other schools, including Thunders, Sylvain, and Murcia.

Rusty Beanie's Cycle Shop (81st St. and Columbus Ave.): The fledgling band moved to Rusty Beanie's, a bicycle sales and repair shop that doubled as a $3.50-an-hour rehearsal space, in the fall of 1971.

Talent Recon (203 W. 38th St.): The New York Dolls shared a rehearsal space at Talent Recon in 1972 with Shaker, featuring future Dolls drummer Jerry Nolan

227 E. 21st St.: Johnny Thunders' last New York City residence was a studio apartment in this building.

Mount Sinai Beth Israel Hospital (10 Nathan D. Perlman Pl.): Arthur Kane wound up at Beth Israel Hospital after being stabbed in the thumb by his girlfriend, Connie Gripp, in 1973.

Newtown High School (49-01 90th St., Queens): Among Newtown's notable musical alumni were Thunders and Sylvain, both of whom were expelled.

Martin Van Buren High School (230-17 Hillside Ave., Queens): Counts among its celebrity alumni Arthur Kane.

31-11 79th St., Queens: John Genzale, Jr., better known to the world as Johnny Thunders, grew up here.

Pratt Institute (200 Willoughby Ave., Brooklyn): Dolls bass guitarist Arthur Kane dropped out of the Pratt Institute after his third year studying food science and management.

Port Richmond High School (85 St. Joseph's Ave., Staten Island): New York Dolls singer David Johansen was a member of Port Richmond High's class of 1967.

BAR 13
35 E. 13th St.

Shout! was a weekly Sunday night mod-soul dance party at Bar 13, where in the early 2000s Yeah Yeah Yeahs' frontwoman Karen O claims she found her electrifying stage persona on the dance floor.

HOTEL ALBERT
23 E. 10th St.

There was a time in the '60s when if you walked along E. 10th Street at University Place, you ran the risk of stumbling across an eventual rock legend. Renowned as a notorious dump, the Hotel Albert was still a popular destination

for musicians playing in town, and even those based in New York.

The Paul Butterfield Blues Band was formed in the Albert, and the Lovin' Spoonful spent a productive winter of 1965 in the basement rehearsal space, fine-tuning their act and writing "Do You Believe in Magic?"

Musicians such as the Byrds, Frank Zappa and the Mothers of Invention, Jim Morrison, Muddy Waters, James Taylor, and Joni Mitchell all reportedly stayed in the Hotel Albert, Tim Buckley was a resident, and a blue-eyed blues superstar jam session between Cream and Canned Heat is also rumored to have broken out in the damp, cockroach-infested basement.

BUDDY HOLLY'S HOME
11 5th Ave., Apt 4H

By 1958 Buddy Holly was ready for a change. He had left the Crickets and his manager behind. On a visit to his music publisher earlier that year in New York, he met Maria Elena Santiago,

Hotel Albert

11 5th Ave.

whom he would marry in his hometown of Lubbock, Texas. By September the couple moved into a spacious one-bedroom apartment with a balcony in the Brevoort. Holly reportedly enjoyed his brief time in the Village, often visiting nearby **Washington Square Park** and several of the clubs in the area. He also made some home recordings that were later dressed up with backing tracks known as the "Apartment Tapes." They include the tunes "Peggy Sue Got Married" and "Crying, Waiting, Hoping." Sadly, Holly's life in the city was a brief one. In January 1959 he would embark on his Winter Dance Party tour and never return. He was killed in a plane crash, along with Ritchie Valens, J. P. "The Big Bopper" Richardson, and the pilot, Roger Peterson, on February 3, "the Day the Music Died."

WASHINGTON SQUARE HOTEL
103 Waverly Place
Originally the Hotel Earle, this formerly low-budget establishment was popular with struggling musicians for many years. The Rolling Stones, John Sebastian, and many others made the Earle their home. In 1964, Bob Dylan and Joan Baez camped here, as chronicled in her song "Diamonds and Rust." John and Michelle Phillips famously wrote "California Dreamin'" during a stay in 1965.

BOTTOM LINE
15 W. 4th St.
Opened in 1974 by Allan Pepper and Stanley Snadowsky, the Bottom Line became one of the city's top live performance venues and would be instrumental in helping launch many musical careers. In June 1974, Bruce Springsteen played here only a few months after its opening, returning for a five-night stand the following year to launch *Born to Run*, which broke him as a national star and landed him on the covers of *Time* and *Newsweek* simultaneously. Other performers who played the Bottom Line include Patti Smith, Billy Joel, Lou Reed, the Police, Prince, Laura Nyro, Linda Ronstadt, Neil Young, Hall & Oates, Van Morrison, Flo & Eddie, Joan Baez, and David Johansen. Lou Reed recorded his *Live: Take No Prisoners* album here in 1978. After a lengthy rent dispute with landlord NYU, the Bottom Line closed in 2004.

THE TIN ANGEL
145 Bleecker St.
The cafe that inspired the classic song from Joni Mitchell's album *Clouds* was located here in the '60s.

BLEECKER BOB'S
149 Bleecker St./118 W. 3rd St.
Originally opened in 1967 as Village Oldies Records on Bleecker Street, Bleecker Bob's spent over 30 years at 118 W. 3rd St., former home of the Night Owl Cafe, where it served as a longtime destination for vinyl aficionados, musicians, and suburban kids looking for an edgy place to pick up a bit of street cred back home by way of a T-shirt or rare punk 45. Everyone from Led Zeppelin to David Bowie to the Clash shopped at Bleecker Bob's. Named after owner Bob Plotnik, a lovably irascible character, the shop succumbed to rising neighborhood rent, closing in the spring of 2013.

Bleecker Bob's W. 3rd St. location before it closed

THE NIGHT OWL CAFE
118 W. 3rd St.
Groups such as the Blues Magoos and the Flying Machine (featuring a teenage James Taylor) cut their teeth at the Night Owl Cafe, but none were more successful than the Lovin' Spoonful, who played a key residency at the club in early 1965. It was during that period that they fielded offers from record labels, settling on Kama Sutra. According to an interview with the group's John Sebastian in Richie Unterberger's *Turn! Turn! Turn!: The '60s Folk Rock Revolution*, the sight of a beautiful girl dancing to their set

one night inspired their debut single, "Do You Believe in Magic." Further, the closing track from the album *Do You Believe in Magic* was an instrumental called "Night Owl Blues." Rumors abound of a Lovin' Spoonful live set being recorded during that 1965 residency, but it has yet to surface more than 50 years later.

CAFE AU GO GO/GARRICK THEATRE ⊘
152 Bleecker St.
Open from February 1964 through October 1969, the Cafe Au Go Go hosted a nearly two-week residency by the Grateful Dead in June 1967 during their first visit to the city. Other acts to hit the 400-person-capacity basement venue included the Moody Blues, Van Morrison, Jefferson Airplane, Cream, Canned Heat, the Yardbirds, Lightnin' Hopkins, Joni Mitchell, Tim Buckley, and the Blues Project, who recorded their debut album, *Live at the Cafe Au Go Go*, there over four nights in late November 1965.

Frank Zappa & the Mothers of Invention played a six-month, six-nights-a-week residency in the upstairs Garrick Theatre, a small performance space, in 1967. The run was reportedly a freewheeling affair, with those buying entry for $3.50 never quite sure what they were going to get from the mercurial group. According to legend, two kids from Long Island, dubbed Leopold and Loeb by the band, hit 65 different shows during the residency.

The original building that housed the Cafe Au Go Go and Garrick Theatre was demolished in 1977.

VILLAGE HOTEL ⊘
154 Bleecker St.
Tom Miller, inspired by an acid trip, moved to New York in 1968 and stayed with his friend Richard Meyers before taking a room at the Village Hotel. Miller soon became Tom Verlaine, Meyers became Richard Hell, and they started the Neon Boys before morphing into Television.

(LE) POISSON ROUGE
158 Bleecker St.
Located since 2008 on the site of the former Village Gate, (Le) Poisson Rouge is a live music venue covering a wide range of styles, as well as occasional comedy, theater, and burlesque. Among the many artists who played intimate shows here are Living Colour, Iggy Pop & the Stooges, Kings of Leon, and Atoms for Peace, a group featuring Thom Yorke of Radiohead and Flea from Red Hot Chili Peppers.

FRANK ZAPPA'S HOME
180 Thompson St.
During a self-imposed exile from Los Angeles, Frank Zappa took up residence here in 1967 to '68. It was during this time that the Mothers of Invention had a six-day-a-week, six-month residency at the Garrick Theatre, quite literally a one-minute walk around the corner.

ZILCH
217 Thompson St.
In 1967 Davy Jones of the Monkees opened a boutique at 217 Thompson St. called Zilch, the name based on the title of a track on the group's then-current album, *Headquarters*. The shop sold hip clothes and accessories, with customers given the option of designing their own ensemble. Though the boutique didn't last, the custom metal Z-shaped door handles remain.

AFTER THE GOLD RUSH
Northwest corner of West 3rd Street and Sullivan Street
Photographer Joel Bernstein shot what would become the cover of Neil Young's 1970 album *After the Gold Rush* during a stroll through Greenwich Village earlier that year.

CAFE WHA?
115 MacDougal St.
An institution in Greenwich Village since 1959, the Cafe Wha? was opened by Manny Roth (uncle to Van Halen's David Lee Roth) as a kind of entertainment free-for-all, featuring various kinds of music, comedy, spoken word performance, and just about anything interesting or provocative that came around. Many performers took advantage of their liberal policy of allowing amateurs of all kinds to test themselves in the subterranean club before a live audience. A hat was typically passed around to collect tips for the performers. Bob Dylan famously played here soon after arriving in the city in 1961. Others who would appear in the '60s included Bill Cosby, Richard Pryor,

Woody Allen, Lord Buckley, Tiny Tim, Jimi Hendrix, and Bruce Springsteen with his high school band the Castiles. Manny Roth sold the Wha? in the late '60s, and it became a Middle Eastern club, the Feenjon, for several years. In 1987 a new owner recovered its identity as the Cafe Wha? On January 5, 2012, David Lee Roth and the other members of Van Halen played a special gig here to promote their forthcoming album *A Different Kind of Truth*.

HOUSE OF OLDIES
35 Carmine St.
Owned and operated since 1968 by Bob Abramson, House of Oldies specializes in rare and out-of-print records from the '50s to the '70s.

was inspired by advance production stills from the film *Bonnie and Clyde*, which would come out later that year. Posing in dapper cinematic gangster attire before a vintage car, the two male members of the group—Peter Yarrow and Paul Stookey—provocatively held guitar cases instead of machine guns. In some territories, the image was swapped for one of the group sitting on a park bench holding balloons.

LOU REED'S RESIDENCE
53 Christopher St.
Lou Reed lived in an apartment above the Stonewall Inn at 53 Christopher St. during the early '70s, his *Rock 'n' Roll Animal* period.

53 Christopher St.

THE DEATH OF SID VICIOUS
63 Bank St.
On February 1, 1979, former Sex Pistol Sid Vicious attended a small party held in an apartment at 63 Bank St. in his honor to celebrate his having made bail. Though he'd come out of his 55-day stint at Rikers Island clean, Vicious had heroin delivered to the party, and he overdosed. Though the attendees felt they'd successfully revived him, Vicious was reportedly found dead the next morning by his mother, Anne Beverly.

ALBUM 1700
70 Bedford St.
The cover of Peter, Paul & Mary's *Album 1700*, which was released in 1967 and featured the hit "Leaving on a Jet Plane," was shot here. The trio

63 Bank St.

TODD RUNDGREN AND BEBE BUELL'S HOME
51 Horatio St.

Todd Rundgren and Bebe Buell moved into a three-story town house at this address in the summer of 1973, paying $600 a month. Iggy Pop came to stay for a few weeks when Rundgren was on tour.

DFA RECORDS/PLANTAIN RECORDING HOUSE
225 W. 13th St./609 Washington Ave., Brooklyn

DFA Records' longtime headquarters and fabled recording studio was located at 225 W. 13th St. in a building owned by the late father of one of the label's co-founders, Tyler Brodie. That building sold for $14 million in 2017, by which point DFA had set up shop at 609 Washington Ave. in Brooklyn in a building purchased for just over $2.5 million.

CINEMABILIA
10 W. 13th St.

A few members of the literary side of the CBGB scene had day jobs in the early '70s at Cinemabilia, a film-focused bookshop where Ork Records founder Terry Ork was the manager, and Richard Hell and Tom Verlaine were still putting the Neon Boys together. The group would soon morph into Television, and their first single, "Little Johnny Jewel," was put out by Ork.

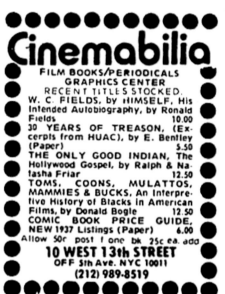

BOB DYLAN

The man who merged folk with rock. The artist who imbued rock & roll with the artistic weight of literature. The anointed "conscience of a generation." Nobel Prize winner. Bob Dylan has been many things since he first arrived in New York City in the winter of 1961.

In many ways, his is the quintessential New York musical immigrant story. Dylan's journey and creative coming-of-age is emblematic of the city's unique ability to inspire. Encouraged by his success, countless others have followed in his path.

The former Robert Allen Zimmerman grew up in Hibbing, Minnesota, a mining town where his Jewish parents owned an appliance store. He developed a deep appreciation for rock & roll, blues, R&B, and country music, but it was his discovery of Woody Guthrie while a student at the University of Minnesota that truly ignited and focused his creative energies. Guthrie's music and memoir, *Bound for Glory*, became a talisman and a kind of guidebook for the person he aspired to be. He was determined to meet Guthrie and forge his own path as a folk music performer. Dylan would embark on a journey just after Christmas of 1960 that would take him cross country to the city that would ultimately help him realize his dreams and ambitions.

By Dylan's own account, the first stop he made after alighting in the snowy city was **Cafe Wha?** **(115 MacDougal St.)**, a Greenwich Village club known for giving new performers of all kinds a chance. He had done his homework and knew that the coffeehouses of MacDougal Street were ground zero for the kind of music he wanted to make and the people he wanted to meet. He did get to play at the Wha?, often

Dylan in Rolling Thunder regalia, 1975

backing other performers on harmonica and vocals for a hamburger and whatever minuscule cut of the proceeds was offered from passing a hat around the audience. It wasn't glamorous, but it was where the 20-year-old Dylan wanted to be. Along MacDougal Street were other venues he would play and other locations he would frequent. Across the street from the Cafe Wha? was the more prestigious **Gaslight Cafe** **(116 MacDougal St.)**, a subterranean haunt that had catered to the Beats and was now an important folk music den. Dave Van Ronk, "the Mayor of MacDougal Street," who had recorded for Folkways and was often the main draw, hosted Tuesday-night Hootenannies, a kind of open mic for new talent. Van Ronk would be an important mentor to Dylan and would eventually give him a place to stay. Dylan would hone his craft at the Gaslight over many performances in 1961 and '62, some of which can be heard on the album *Live at the Gaslight 1962*, officially released in 2005. As there was often no place for performers to relax (or drink) at the liquor-less Gaslight, they typically socialized next door at the **Kettle of Fish (114 MacDougal St.),** a bar that served as both pit stop and hangout for the folk community. Down the block was the **Folklore Center (110 MacDougal St.),** owned and managed by Israel "Izzy" Young, and a nexus for all things related to folk music. Records, sheet music, books, and instruments could all be bought, borrowed, and sold here. Musicians could be contacted, and mail could be delivered, as many in the folk community, including Dylan, often had no fixed address. The Folklore Center became the best way to find out about new performers and new information related to their world, and often the surest way to find people. **The Commons (105 MacDougal St.),** later known as the Fat Black Pussycat, and also the Cafe Feenjon, was a relatively large coffeehouse that also hosted some of Dylan's earliest NYC gigs. He is said to have written "Blowin' in the Wind" here in 1962.

Another early stop was the home of the Guthrie family (159-13 85th St.) in Howard Beach, Queens. He had learned of Woody Guthrie's New York address, but probably already suspected his hero would not be found here, as he was suffering from Huntington's chorea and living at the Greystone Park Hospital in Morris Plains, New Jersey. Dylan showed up anyway, and he was turned away a couple of times before being let in to entertain the kids for a little while before departing. He eventually met and befriended Guthrie at a mutual friend's home in New Jersey and visited him several times thereafter.

Until he made enough money to get his own place, Dylan camped out on friends' floors, couches, and wherever he could find a friendly host. Dave Van Ronk and his wife Terri Thal often let him stay with them, first in their tiny apartment at 219 W. 15th St., and later in their home at 190 Waverly Pl. Terri also booked gigs for Dylan for several months.

On April 5, 1961, Dylan played for the Folk Music Society at the **NYU Loeb Student Center (566 LaGuardia Place)** ⊘ and finally got his shot on April 11 at **Gerde's Folk City (11 W. 4th St.)** ⊘, then the biggest and best folk venue in the city, opening for John Lee Hooker. Before he could take the Gerde's stage, however, he had to get his union card at the **American Federation of Musicians, Local 802 (261 W. 52nd St.)** ⊘. As Dylan was still under 21, Gerde's owner Mike Porco served as legal guardian. The gig paid $90 for each of the two weeks; it was by far the most Dylan had earned to this point. He

The White Horse Tavern

New York Public Library, where Dylan read old newspapers on microfilm

hoped the gig would lead to better things, but he was met initially with disappointment. He was shooed away by **Folkways Records (165 W. 46th St.), Vanguard Records (154 W. 14th St.),** and shown the door by *Sing Out!* (121 W. 47th St.), the most widely read folk music magazine. He played a few shows out of town, but the only immediately forthcoming New York gig outside the usual Village orbit was a show for the Kiwanis Club at the **Fifth Avenue Hotel (24 5th Ave.)** in July. Around this time Dylan got his first taste of the recording studio, playing harmonica for Harry Belafonte's *Midnight Special* album for **RCA (Webster Hall, 125 E. 11th St.),** but he reportedly did not enjoy having to do multiple takes of tracks and left disillusioned.

Washington Square Park was well established as the open-air place of congregation for folk singers and political activists. It was a place where Dylan and his colleagues in the folk community often got together to meet fellow musicians; try out songs for the students, locals, and tourists who frequented the park; and generally enjoy themselves. In those days, performing music in public required a formal permit, which the folkies ignored. The Washington Square Association, annoyed by the music, appealed to the Parks Department to rid them of these troublemakers, and the police were dispatched to clear the park. Izzy Young, on behalf of the musicians, applied for a permit and was denied. Three thousand protesters, including Dylan, came to the park on Sunday, April 9, 1961, to play in defiance of the ban. Many were beaten and arrested, but eventually the ban was overturned. Future New York City mayor Ed Koch was one of the attorneys who represented the folkies in court. The "Folk Riot" or "Beatnik Riot" is often credited for helping kick-start the counterculture movement of the 1960s.

On July 29, 1961, Dylan, along with many performers he knew from the Village, including Ramblin' Jack Elliott and Danny Kalb, appeared as part of a WRVR radio 12-hour folk music marathon at **Riverside Church (490 Riverside**

Dr.). It was there he met Suze Rotolo, who became his love and muse. Suze was well-read, artistic, and politically active. She took him to theaters and museums and educated him about contemporary politics. Their relationship inspired many of Dylan's early written tunes. He and Suze became inseparable, and Dylan often spent time at the Rotolo home on the top floor of **1 Sheridan Square**. He also sometimes crashed downstairs at the home of Miki Isaacson, who regularly opened her home to itinerant folk singers. Suze would later work the concession stand in the off-Broadway theater on the street level of the same building.

385 Broome St.

10 W. 28th St.

Another frequent campsite for Dylan was the home of Eve and Mac McKenzie (10 W. 28th St.). The couple were audience regulars at Gerde's and often hosted folk music parties at their apartment. Bob frequently slept on Eve and Mac's couch and entertained their young son

Peter. Dylan would make some fascinating home recordings here that demonstrate his continued growth as a performer and songwriter.

Harry Jackson, born Harry Aaron Shapiro Jr., was an artist with a colorful past. He grew up in Chicago and developed a fascination with cowboys and western culture helping in his mother's lunchroom at the Union Stockyards. He ran away from home as a teenager and become a cowboy himself. In World War II he joined the marines and became a combat artist. By the late '50s he was in New York specializing in western-themed painting and sculpture. He was also a folk music performer and recorded a couple of albums of cowboy music for Folkways. He formed a friendship with Dylan and gave him another place to stay in his spacious loft at 385 Broome St.

Jackson painted Dylan's portrait and was quoted in the liner notes for his second album. Jackson was also a highly vocal opponent of the planned expressway that would have obliterated Broome Street and collaborated with public advocate Jane Jacobs in protest. In 2015 a typed manuscript of a protest tune "Listen, Robert Moses" by Bob Dylan was discovered in the NYU library archives. Moses was the city's "master builder" who spearheaded much urban redevelopment and was behind plans to gut much of the Village and environs until thwarted by Jacobs and her allies. Many are skeptical of the authenticity of the document, but one never knows.

Dylan was perpetually working to improve and expand his repertoire, as well as deepening his understanding of American music. Suze's older sister Carla Rotolo worked as an assistant to Alan Lomax, son of folklorist and musicologist John Lomax, and one of the country's foremost authorities on vernacular music. Dylan became a regular at the Lomax home (121 W. 3rd St.), where he gleaned what he could from Alan and got the opportunity to hear and meet many of the regional musicians recorded in the fifth-floor apartment. Lomax was also central to the formation of the Newport Folk Festival, which would prove critical to Dylan's career.

Around this time Dylan also met Joan Baez for the first time, at Gerde's, while he accompanied Mark Spoelstra. Baez was only a few months older than Dylan but was an established folk star with a successful album and another on the way. Their relationship would blossom, but not quite yet.

56 W. 11th St.

Carolyn Hester was another folk chanteuse Dylan knew, and she asked him to play harmonica on her forthcoming third album, the first for Columbia and producer John Hammond, the legendary talent scout who had been critical to the success of many important musical

figures since the early '30s, including Billie Holiday, Ella Fitzgerald, and Benny Goodman. Hester and her husband, writer Richard Farina, were in temporary digs at the apartment of poet Ned O'Gorman (56 W. 11th St.), who was away in South America. A rehearsal was arranged, and the assembled musicians played under the watchful eye of Hammond, who took an immediate interest in Dylan. His sound, appearance, and overall demeanor fascinated Hammond, and he suggested that Dylan come up to Columbia to cut some demos.

In late September 1961, Dylan was given another two-week stint at Folk City, this time opening for the Greenbriar Boys. Robert Shelton of the *New York Times* was there and wrote a highly enthusiastic review published on September 29. Folk singers who played coffeehouses and had no record contract simply didn't get reviewed in the magisterial *Times*, so this was a major event, and a tipping point that would ultimately elevate Dylan's career from those coffeehouses to the concert halls. Interest in him increased exponentially, and it wasn't long before would-be managers and agents

began to descend upon him. The day the *Times* review ran, Dylan went into the Columbia studio to cut his tracks with Carolyn Hester.

On October 29 Dylan gave his first radio interview with Oscar Brand, host of WNYC's Folksong Festival, at their studio in the **Municipal Building (1 Centre St.).** In addition to dispensing the usual fictitious biographical hokum that was part of his early repertoire, he performed "Sally Gal" and "The Girl I Left Behind."

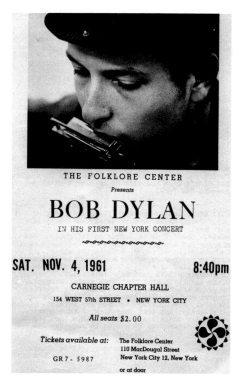

THE FOLKLORE CENTER

Presents

BOB DYLAN

IN HIS FIRST NEW YORK CONCERT

SAT. NOV. 4, 1961   **8:40pm**

CARNEGIE CHAPTER HALL

154 WEST 57th STREET • NEW YORK CITY

All seats $2.00

Tickets available at: The Folklore Center
                        110 MacDougal Street
GR 7 - 5987   New York City 12, New York

or at door

On November 4, Izzy Young booked Dylan into **Carnegie Chapter Hall (154 W. 57th St.),** a small space within the larger historic concert hall. The venue seated around 200 people, but a mere 53 tickets at $2 each were purportedly sold. Despite the meager turnout, Dylan sounded poised and confident on a widely circulated bootleg of the event as he ran through nearly two dozen tunes, including Woody Guthrie's

"This Land Is Your Land" and "Talking Merchant Marine." He finished the show with two songs of his own, "Song to Woody" and "Talkin' New York." Financially speaking, the concert can't be considered a success, but it did get him noticed outside of the Village, and would point to better things to come.

Shortly thereafter Dylan received and signed his Columbia contract, which was essentially a deal for one album and the option to record four more. Evidently there were no demos, and on November 20, Dylan went directly into **Columbia Studio A (799 7th Ave.)** ⊘ for the first of two sessions that would ultimately produce his debut album, *Bob Dylan*. Hammond would joke much later that the recording cost only $402, and bemoaned Dylan's obvious inexperience working in a studio setting. Hammond's colleagues at Columbia were even less enthusiastic about Dylan, and referred to him as "Hammond's Folly." Their reticence would delay

161 W. 4th St.

the album's release until March 1962. Like his Chapter Hall gig a couple of weeks previous, the album would feature several folk standards and but two of Dylan's own tunes, "Song to Woody" and "Talkin' New York."

With the modest advance he received from Columbia, Dylan finally moved into his own place for $60 per month on the top floor of a four-story walkup at 161 W. 4th St. When she turned 18, Suze Rotolo moved in with him. Just down the block was the **Music Inn (169 W. 4th St.)**, a shop filled to the rafters with all kinds of guitars, violins, banjos, records, and other equipment for the folk community, and next door, **Allan Block's Sandal Shop (171 W. 4th St.)**. Ostensibly a destination for footwear, Block was an accomplished fiddler and he and fellow musicians routinely played his shop informally. Dylan dropped in to both establishments regularly.

Sometime in January or February 1962, Dylan recorded a lengthy performance and interview with Cynthia Gooding for her radio program *Folksinger's Choice* at **WBAI (30 E.39th St.)**. Gooding was a folk singer herself, and the pair had a natural repartee. The show would air March 11 in anticipation of Dylan's first album's release. Over the next few years, Dylan would appear several times at the WBAI studio for hosts Billy Faier and Skip Weshner. In 1966 he actually took listeners' calls with Bob Fass, host of *Radio Unnamable*.

Still waiting for his album's release, Dylan's songwriting and political awareness developed dramatically. Suze worked with CORE (Congress of Racial Equality) and enlisted him to perform at a benefit in the Great Hall at City College (160 Convent Ave.) in February. He would premiere his first so-called protest song, "The Death of Emmett Till," about a black teenager who was lynched in Mississippi in 1955.

February also marked the premiere of *Broadside*, a new publication devoted to folk songs and the requisite socio-political issues

they represented. It was the creation of Agnes "Sis" Cunningham and her husband Gordon Friesen. Fleeing political harassment in Oklahoma due to their Communist leanings, they arrived in New York in 1941 and moved into Almanac House in the Village. Sis had been a singer and songwriter and performed for a time with the Almanac Singers, which included Woody Guthrie and Pete Seeger. Dylan and other songwriters would journey uptown to their small apartment in the **Frederick Douglass Houses (140 W. 104th St., Apt 11E)** to sing and have their material recorded so Sis could transcribe it and publish it in *Broadside*. The first issue would include the lyrics to Bob's "Talking John Birch," a satirical and comical dig at the right-wing John Birch Society. "Blowin' in the Wind" would appear on the cover of the sixth issue well before it was recorded. Suze Rotolo provided the illustration that graced his "Train a-Travelin'" on the cover of issue 23. He also performed in *Broadside*-sponsored live shows on WBAI and contributed some of his demos for record albums they produced. Because he was a Columbia artist, his recordings, which

140 W. 104th St.

included "Ramblin' Gamblin' Willie," "Talkin' Bear Mountain Massacre Blues," and "Emmett Till" appeared under the moniker Blind Boy Grunt. Dylan would continue his association with *Broadside* for the next couple of years until he generally lost interest in topical material.

By the time Dylan's debut album was released in March 1962, he was practically a different artist. In the four months since he'd completed it, he had grown substantially as a songwriter and knew that his future would be determined by creating his own material. It was just as well, since the album sold only a few thousand copies. He would begin recording his next album in April at Columbia, but he would take his time refining his songwriting craft and recorded many demos at the office of his publisher between sessions. The initial demos for Leeds were recorded at the **Leeds Music Building (322 W. 48th St.).** The remainder were recorded in a small room on the fifth floor at the offices of **M. Witmark & Sons (488 Madison Ave.).**

Unlike Dylan's first album, *The Freewheelin' Bob Dylan* required multiple sessions at Columbia Studio A and marked a dramatic creative shift as 11 of the 13 tracks are Dylan originals. The strength of those original compositions, including "Blowin' in the Wind," "A Hard Rain's A-Gonna Fall," and "Don't Think

Twice, It's All Right," would cement his position as the preeminent folk songwriter of his time. The album's cover, with its iconic Don Hunstein photo of Dylan and Suze strolling through the snow, was taken on Jones Street just around the corner from their apartment. They are walking toward West 4th Street with Bleecker Street at the end of the block behind them. Aside from the period cars, Jones Street looks very much like this today, if a bit leafier. The image was captured in February 1963, not long after Suze had returned from a six-month sojourn in Italy. Her prolonged absence inspired the Dylan tune "Boots of Spanish Leather," which would appear on his third album.

Jones Street

On April 12, 1963, Dylan would play the **Town Hall (123 W. 43rd St.),** the first of his major concert hall headlining appearances, and by all accounts, a rousing success. Significantly, it consisted almost entirely of original material. In addition to the forthcoming tunes from *Freewheelin'*, he included a handful of older tunes and some, such as "Spanish Leather," that didn't appear until his third album, as well as "Tomorrow is a Long Time," which would not get an official release until 1971. He closed with a long recited poem, "Last Thoughts on Woody Guthrie." Billboard gave him a rave review and declared him a "Folk Poet." The evening was

HAROLD LEVENTHAL presents

Bob Dylan

AT **TOWN HALL**
123 W. 43rd St.
FRI. EVE., APRIL 12th 1963 at
8:30 P.M.
Tickets 3.00, 2.75, 2.00 on sale at Town Hall Box Office &
Folklore Center, 110 MacDougal St, GR 7-5987

"BOB DYLAN is . . . the most exciting, most
potentially great new city Folksinger in recent
years. He is absolutely unique. . ."
—LITTLE SANDY REVIEW

"Among the trends is BOB DYLAN . . . this 21-
year-old ragamuffin minstrel's songs continue
to captivate this listener . . . his songs are
musically well proportioned . . ."
—NEW YORK TIMES

"He's so goddam real, it's unbelievable"
—SING OUT

"One of the most compelling blues singers
ever recorded"
—BBC RADIO TIMES

". . . the very best of the newest generations
of citybillies"
—HI/FI STEREO REVIEW

Columbia Records

recorded for a possible live album, but never officially released.

In anticipation of the release of the new album in May 1963, Dylan was scheduled to appear on the *Ed Sullivan Show,* the most highly rated TV variety show in the country and a launch pad for Elvis Presley and many others. In rehearsals on May 12 at **CBS Studio 50 (1697 Broadway)**, Dylan performed "Talkin' John Birch Paranoid Blues," but CBS executives balked and strongly suggested he play something less inflammatory. He refused, and the appearance was called off. The song was dropped from the final release of the album as well.

Dylan began an association with manager Albert Grossman at this time, though he would not sign a formal contract until August 1963.

Also in May, not long before *Freewheelin's* release, Dylan traveled to California to appear at the Monterey Folk Festival, where he would join Joan Baez on stage. The pair would begin a tempestuous personal relationship that would continue through a series of concerts over the summer, fracturing his relationship with Suze

Rotolo. As her awareness of the affair grew, she moved out of the West 4th Street apartment and moved in with her sister at **106 Ave. B,** but Dylan was a frequent visitor. He was with Baez in California when his second album was released on May 27, 1963, and would stay on the road through most of the summer, typically appearing with Baez for a few numbers. He would perform at her gig on August 17 at **Forest Hills Tennis Stadium (1 Tennis Place, Queens).** The two would perform again at Martin Luther King's March on Washington on August 28 of that year.

In June, Peter, Paul, and Mary—also managed by Grossman—released a version of "Blowin' in the Wind" that would eventually reach number 2 on the pop charts, greatly enhancing Dylan's status as a songwriter with appeal beyond the traditional folk audience.

Around this time Dylan decided to vacate the West 4th Street apartment and stayed in California with Joan Baez for a time before heading back out onto the road. Back in New York he began to stay at the home of his manager, Albert Grossman, upstate in Bearsville, near Woodstock. Joan came and stayed with him too. When the couple did come into the city, they stayed at the **Hotel Earle (103 Waverly Place)**, a somewhat sordid and disreputable place that Baez would immortalize in her 1975 song "Diamonds and Rust."

On October 26, 1963, Dylan would play **Carnegie Hall (881 7th Ave.)**, his most prestigious gig to date. He even flew his parents in for the event. Like his earlier Town Hall show, it was recorded by Columbia for a live album but only released officially in pieces many years later. He opened the show with "The Times They Are A-Changin'," which would become a popular countercultural anthem, and followed with several others that were among his most topical, including "The Ballad of Hollis Brown,"

"With God on Our Side," and "Talkin' World War III Blues."

On December 13, 1963, in the wake of the assassination of President John F. Kennedy a few weeks earlier, the Emergency Civil Liberties Committee, a liberal civil rights organization, chose to honor Dylan with the Tom Paine Award at their annual fundraising dinner at the **Americana Hotel (811 7th Ave.).** The intention was to honor someone who, like the previous recipient, Bertrand Russell, embodied the ideals of freedom and equality. Dylan was immediately uncomfortable with the whole thing. Not only did he feel unworthy, but out of place among the suit-and-tie patriarchs of the political left. It did not go well. He likely had a few glasses of red wine at the dais sitting beside James Baldwin before accepting the award and delivering a rambling, stream-of-consciousness oration that managed to offend or befuddle just about everyone present. There were confusing references to Lee Harvey Oswald, bald people, and Cuba, among other things. Shortly thereafter, he sent an almost equally inscrutable letter of apology. In any event, Dylan made it crystal clear he wasn't interested in being anointed by anyone's establishment.

The day after Christmas 1963, Dylan met poet Allen Ginsberg at the apartment of Ted Wilentz, above his store, the **Eighth Street Bookshop (32 W. 8th St.).** The event was engineered by *New York Post* reporter Al Aronowitz, who had written extensively about both men, and knew they were admirers of each other's work. Despite some initial awkwardness, the two became lifelong friends and occasional creative collaborators.

The new year would see the release of *The Times They Are A-Changin'* in January, Dylan's most overtly topical album, and a final breakup with Suze Rotolo the following month, though they would remain friendly for some time afterward. The first half of the year was spent primarily on the road, but Dylan returned to New York to record his next album, *Another Side of Bob Dylan*, in one marathon all-night session at Columbia Studio A on June 9, 1964. It contained a collection of songs that seemingly had nothing to do with politics or current events. It would also be his last album without a group of backing musicians, at least for many years. Many of the old Village crowd were confounded, but Bob was moving on.

On August 28, 1964, Dylan first met the Beatles at the **Delmonico Hotel (502 Park Ave.).** Once again, Al Aronowitz pulled a few strings and arranged for Dylan and his confidante Victor Maymudes to have an audience with the visiting Fab Four. It was also Aronowitz's idea to bring a generous supply of marijuana to help make the proceedings more convivial. First, though, the Dylan camp had to get through the throngs of screaming teenagers that surrounded the hotel. Beatles press officer Derek Taylor escorted them through, though not without incident. Maymudes was initially knocked to the ground by a police officer, but finally allowed in, which was fortunate, as he was carrying the all-important stash of pot. Introductions were made, and eventually Victor rolled the joints and got the party started. Contrary to popular myth, the Beatles may not have been entirely unfamiliar with pot, but evidently hadn't experienced weed of this quality before, and really, really, enjoyed themselves. Dylan, on the other hand, exhausted from lack of sleep, and apparently something of a lightweight, fell fast asleep after a few puffs and few glasses of wine. Maymudes and the Beatles kept themselves entertained for a few hours until Dylan roused himself. He and Victor joined the Beatles again backstage on September 20 at the **Paramount Theater (1501 Broadway)** and later at the **Riviera Idlewild Hotel (151-20 Baisley Blvd,. Queens)** before the group returned to England.

On Halloween night Dylan performed at **Philharmonic Hall (10 Lincoln Center Plaza)**, a show that was recorded by Columbia but not officially released until 2004. The set list was an interesting combination of his earlier topical material along with newer songs like "Mr Tambourine Man" and other tunes not yet recorded, such as "Gates of Eden" and "It's Alright Ma (I'm Only Bleeding)." Joan Baez joined him for three songs near the end of the performance. The two would tour again together in 1965.

Late in 1964 Dylan was in a serious relationship with Sara Lownds, a former model who was also a friend of Sally Bueler, Albert Grossman's fiancée. He and Sara attended the wedding on November 12 in Woodstock. That's Sally in red on the cover of 1965's *Bringing It All Back Home*. Not long after Dylan and Sara moved into Room 211 of the **Hotel Chelsea (222 W. 23rd St.)**, renowned for its historic collection of eclectic creative guests and residents. It was a modest one-bedroom suite with a piano and would be their New York headquarters when not on the road or in Woodstock. Sara, long estranged from her first husband, brought her three-year-old daughter, Maria. The Chelsea proved to be a creatively fertile place for Dylan, and he would write many of the most important songs of his career here, including several for his next three albums, *Bringing It All Back Home, Highway 61 Revisited,* and *Blonde on Blonde.* Not many knew of Dylan's relationship with Sara, and few knew he lived at the Chelsea. Dylan kept a low profile and, unlike many of the other residents, stayed out of trouble.

When not at home, Dylan often went downtown to his old stomping grounds at the Kettle of Fish and held court in the upstairs bar with buddy Bobby Neuwirth, who would work as his road manager and all-around lieutenant. The pair would tease and taunt all who

approached them, even old friends. Those who passed the test were permitted an audience. One such recipient was Edie Sedgwick, the troubled Warhol superstar. She and Neuwirth would have an affair, and she is thought to have inspired some of Dylan's songs, such as "Leopard Skin Pillbox Hat," and possibly "Like a Rolling Stone."

Later that year, Dylan showed up with Neuwirth at Andy Warhol's **Factory (231 E. 47th St.)**. He was filmed sullenly gazing into the camera for one of Warhol and Gerard Malanga's "Screen Tests," then abruptly grabbed a 7-foot double portrait of Elvis as recompense, strapping it to the roof of his station wagon and bringing it back to Woodstock. He would later trade it to Sally Grossman for a couch.

In January 1965 Dylan returned to Columbia Studio A to cut *Bringing It All Back Home,* the most ambitious album he'd yet made. It was the first album to combine his increasingly sophisticated songwriting with the sound of rock & roll, and upon its release in March it polarized the traditional folk audience. This is where folk rock begins, a term Dylan reportedly hated. The album contained signature tunes "Mr. Tambourine Man" and "Subterranean Homesick Blues," songs that baffled many of his old fans, but brought him legions more.

On February 17, 1965, Dylan appeared on *The Les Crane Show* at **WABC TV (7 W. 66th St.)**. Crane was ABC's more provocative late-night answer to Johnny Carson and had hosted the Rolling Stones a few months earlier. Dylan performed "It's All Over Now, Baby Blue," and "It's Alright Ma (I'm Only Bleeding)," and kibitzed with Crane and the other guests. Unfortunately no video of the show survives.

Dylan would hit the road in March and travel around the UK from late April through early June. The UK tour was captured for the D. A. Pennebaker film *Don't Look Back.*

Almost immediately upon returning to New York, Dylan was back at Columbia recording the tracks for the forthcoming album *Highway 61 Revisited*, which ventured even further into rock than its predecessor. It contained the single "Like a Rolling Stone," recorded on June 16, 1965, which at 6:13, was initially considered far too long to be released as a 45. Shaun Considine, a new-releases coordinator for Columbia was a big fan of the song and brought it to what was then the hottest discotheque in town, **Arthur (154 E. 54th St.)** ⊘, where he insisted that DJ Terry Noel play it. The crowd loved the song and had it spun repeatedly. Radio programmers were present, who then demanded copies from Columbia. Memos were written, heads rolled, and the tune was released on July 20. It would hit number 2, behind the Beatles' "Help," Dylan's most successful single to date. In 2004, *Rolling Stone* declared it the greatest song of the rock era.

On July 25, 1965, Dylan appeared at the Newport Folk Festival wielding an electric guitar backed by Mike Bloomfield and other members of the Paul Butterfield Blues Band and proceeded to blast through some of the tracks from his forthcoming album. He then abruptly left the stage. The crowd was, depending on which account you believe, stunned, aghast, horrified, or excited. Certainly, many in the crowd reacted negatively, either to Dylan, the amplified sound, or both. He would return, after much cajoling, to finish up on solo acoustic guitar. The event took on a life of its own, and by the time Dylan kicked off his American tour on August 28 at Forest Hills Tennis Stadium, the audience would be neatly divided between the younger pro-electric Dylan fans and the traditional folkies who felt betrayed. The show would have an acoustic first half, and he would then be joined by a band, which by

now included Robbie Robertson, Levon Helm, Harvey Brooks, and Al Kooper, a concert format he would employ for the remainder of the tour. The response to the first half of the show was positive and respectful, but after the short intermission, Dylan reemerged with the backing band and powered into "Tombstone Blues." He was met with boos, obscenities, and even some hurled fruit by some of the 15,000 in attendance. The next several dates of the tour followed suit. A couple of weeks later, Kooper and Brooks would drop out, to be replaced by Garth Hudson, Rick Danko, and Richard Manuel of the Hawks. The die had been cast.

Two days later on August 30, 1965, *Highway 61 Revisited* was released. It featured a now-iconic Daniel Kramer photograph on the cover showing Dylan sitting in a doorway with a Triumph motorcycle shirt and someone standing behind him. The doorway was at Dylan's manager Albert Grossman's home (4 Gramercy Park West), and the legs behind Dylan in the picture belong to Bob Neuwirth.

BOB DYLAN HIGHWAY 61 REVISITED

On September 7, the single "Positively 4th Street," a track not included on the album, was released. In it Dylan calls out his old

4 Gramercy Park West

neighborhood, rebuking the folkniks for turning on him.

Eventually, the tide began to turn, and the booing generally subsided. By his Carnegie Hall gig on October 1, 1965, Dylan was met with overwhelming applause.

Four days later, he was back at Columbia to work on his next album, *Blonde on Blonde*. Dylan would wrestle with the new songs on and off through January 1966 before relocating in February to Columbia's recording studio in Nashville and completing the album there. It would be released in May. He would not cut another track in New York until 1970.

In between gigs on November 22, 1965, Dylan married Sara in Mineola, New York, in a ceremony kept secret, even from Dylan's family. Their son, Jesse Byron Dylan, was born the following January. In February 1966, Nora Ephron revealed the marriage in the *New York Post*.

Dylan continued on the road throughout the year, eventually traveling to Hawaii,

Australia, Europe, and the UK, wrapping up in London on May 26. He would return to their new home in Woodstock for some badly needed rest and relaxation. On July 29, 1966, he had a motorcycle accident. How serious it was is unknown, but it caused Dylan to essentially drop out of the public eye, with a few brief exceptions, for eight years.

On January 20, 1968, Dylan, in his first public appearance in 18 months, appeared at Carnegie Hall as part of a tribute to Woody Guthrie, who had died 3 months prior. The assembled artists included Odetta, Pete Seeger, Judy Collins, Richie Havens, Tom Paxton, Ramblin' Jack Elliott, and Woody's son Arlo Guthrie. Will Geer and Robert Ryan read from Guthrie's writings. Dylan performed three Guthrie tunes with "The Crackers," the same group that supported him on his last tour as the Hawks. Later that year they would rename themselves the Band.

Dylan's attempt at seclusion in Woodstock proved problematic. He was frequently harassed by overzealous fans, reporters, nosey neighbors, and people who were just obnoxiously curious. Perhaps impulsively, and sight unseen, he purchased a pair of conjoined town houses at 92-94 MacDougal St., close by his formative stomping grounds, in late 1969.

If Dylan thought the familiar streets of Greenwich Village would put an end to the invasions of his privacy upstate, he was in for a rude awakening. He was greeted with protests, demonstrations, and general harassment, organized primarily by one AJ "the Scavenger" Weberman, a disaffected Dylanologist who dug through trash cans looking for clues to hidden meaning in Dylan's music. Weberman, a militant Yippie, and his loud band of cranks felt that Dylan had let them down, sold out, and turned his back on the radical political struggle of the '60s. Weberman even went so far as to make a series of harassing phone calls, some of which

124 W. Houston St.

92–94 MacDougal St.

were recorded and distributed. Even when Dylan was out of town, loud demonstrations took place outside his home, harassing his wife and children. The neighbors weren't particularly thrilled either, and eventually Dylan had had enough and confronted Weberman in the street, allegedly slamming him to the ground.

During this time Dylan maintained a rehearsal space on the ground floor of a building at **124 W. Houston St.**, a short walk from his MacDougal Street home, where he worked on new songs and stored equipment. He kept a piano here and is known to have practiced material that would appear on *Blood on the Tracks.*

Not surprisingly, the Dylans eventually packed up and moved. First, they would relocate to the East Side enclave of **Turtle Bay Gardens**, at **242 E. 49th St.**, where they rented a town house next door to Katharine Hepburn. The only trouble they had here was the mess their dog Brutus would deposit in Ms. Hepburn's shrubs.

242 E. 49th St.

Their stay at this address was not long, and later in the '70s they would pull up stakes again and settle in Point Dume, California, in an estate Dylan maintains to this day.

In 1974, Dylan took painting classes with Norman Raeben, the youngest son of Yiddish author Sholem Aleichem, author of the stories that inspired *Fiddler on the Roof.* The classes, which transpired over two months or more, were held in an 11th floor studio at Carnegie Hall and would prove to have a profound effect on Dylan, rekindling his approach to writing songs. His intense devotion to the classes and Raeben himself, however, would exacerbate an already tense relationship with his wife Sara, whom he would eventually divorce in 1977.

Dylan's temporary return to New York in the '70s is also notable as the time he was formulating and collecting various musicians and personalities for his Rolling Thunder Revue in 1975. For the first time in several years, he was seen around the Village, often dropping in to see his old friends perform at clubs such as the **Bottom Line (15 W. 4th St.)** and **The Other End (147 Bleecker St.)**, occasionally joining them on stage. It was at The Other End that he first met Patti Smith on July 26. He had hoped to recruit Patti to the Revue, and even invited her to a Rolling Thunder warm-up at the new

265 W. 139th St.

Gerde's Folk City (130 W. 3rd St.), but she ultimately turned him down. Another Other End appearance is notable: On July 3, Dylan performed impromptu a new song, "Abandoned Love," at a Ramblin' Jack Elliott show. It chronicles his then-deteriorating relationship with Sara and did not appear officially until its inclusion in the *Biograph* set 10 years later.

MORE BOB DYLAN

NOTEWORTHY LIVE PERFORMANCES

Limelight (91 7th Ave. South): Dylan played here in February and March 1961 with Fred Neil, Dave Van Ronk, Mark Spoelstra, and Ramblin' Jack Elliott.

Cafe Bizarre (106 W. 3rd St.) ⊘: Dylan came here with Mark Spoelstra in 1961 and is believed to have played a few times. Not strictly a folk club, the Bizarre offered an eclectic variety of acts.

Madison Square Garden (4 Pennsylvania Plaza): Dylan played many gigs here, the most historic being George Harrison's Concerts for Bangladesh (August 1, 1971); three shows with the Band (January 30 and 31, 1974); and the Night of the Hurricane (December 8, 1975) with the Rolling Thunder Revue, a benefit for the wrongly imprisoned boxer Rubin "Hurricane" Carter.

On October 16, 1992, a 30th anniversary tribute concert for Dylan featured guest stars including Johnny Cash, Stevie Wonder, Lou Reed, and Willie Nelson, in addition to Dylan himself.

Academy of Music (126 E.14th St.) ⊘: Dylan appeared for the encore and performed three songs at a date by the Band on December 31, 1971, as documented on the albums *Rock of Ages* and *Live at the Academy of Music 1971.* Earlier that year on February 8, he premiered his film *Eat the Document* here, a somewhat muddled documentary of his 1966 tour of the UK.

The Lone Star Cafe (61 5th Ave.) ⊘: On February 16, 1983, Dylan made a surprise appearance at a Levon Helm–Rick Danko show and performed five songs with the former Band members. He would drop in on Helm again at the same venue on May 29, 1988.

The Supper Club (240 W. 47th St.): On November 16 and 17, 1993, Dylan played four shows and recorded 41 tracks at this intimate dinner theater, known today as the Edison Ballroom, in anticipation of a live album, which has never been officially released.

Brooklyn Academy of Music (30 Lafayette Ave., Brooklyn): As part of a star-studded tribute to George Gershwin on March 11, 1987, Dylan performed the 1927 classic "Soon."

Apollo Theater (253 W. 125th St.): Dylan performed at the theater's 70th anniversary celebration concert on March 28, 2004, playing two songs with the Wynton Marsalis Quartet, "It Takes a Lot to Laugh, It Takes A Train to Cry," and "Don't Think Twice, It's All Right."

NOTEWORTHY RECORDING SESSIONS

Cue Recording Studios (117 W. 46th St.) ⊘: Dylan, on harmonica, recorded with Victoria Spivey and Big Joe Williams on October 21, 1961. The material was released in 1964 on Spivey's album *Three Kings and a Queen.*

Columbia Recording Studio A (799 7th Ave.) ⊘: In addition to the sessions detailed elsewhere, Dylan recorded the following albums (or parts of them) at this studio, which was sold to Phil Ramone and changed to A&R Studios in 1967.

- *Self Portrait* (1970)
- *New Morning* (1971)
- *Blood on the Tracks* (1974)
- *Desire* (1975)

Columbia Recording Studios B & E (49 E.52nd St.)
- *New Morning* (1970–71)

Blue Rock Studios (29 Greene St.)
- *New Morning* (1971)

Record Plant (321 W. 44th St.)
- *New Morning* (1971)

Power Station (441 W. 53rd St.):
- *Infidels* (1983)
- *Empire Burlesque* (1985)
- *Knocked Out Loaded* (1985)

Clinton Studios (653 10th Ave.) 🚫
- *Love and Theft* (2001)
- *Modern Times* (2006)

OTHER NOTEWORTHY LOCATIONS

McGowan's Off-Broadway (57 Greenwich Ave.):
A bar where Dylan often went after Gerde's gigs, since it stayed open until 4 a.m. The kindly McGowans happily supplied Dylan with food and beverages when needed.

The White Horse Tavern (567 Hudson St.): A bar with deep literary and musical associations. Dylan Thomas came here often in his last days. Bob Dylan often came to hear and socialize with The Clancy Brothers and Tommy Makem, along with the varied mix of writers, musicians, and longshoremen who spent time here.

Mills Tavern (160 Bleecker St.): Another hangout popular with writers, artists, and musicians, with a proprietor known to be generous with free food on occasion. Dylan wrote "Song to Woody" here on February 14, 1961.

Cafe Figaro (184 Bleecker St.): Frequented by Dylan and his folk colleagues, and a favorite hangout for Village creative types since the Beat days of the '50s.

Columbia Records (485 Madison Ave.):
Headquarters of CBS and Columbia Records, where John Hammond's office was located, and where Dylan signed his record contract.

Theatre de Lys (121 Christopher St.): Suze was working at the theater when Bob caught a performance of *Brecht on Brecht* in early 1962. The songs had a profound effect on him with

their intense imagery and symbolism, especially the performance of "Pirate Jenny."

Pythian Temple (135 W. 70th St.): Lou Levy of Leeds Music, Dylan's new music publisher, brought him here to show him the studio where Bill Haley & His Comets recorded "Rock Around the Clock" in 1954.

Jack Dempsey's Restaurant (1619 Broadway): Levy brought Dylan here in 1962 to celebrate their new contract and introduce him to the former world heavyweight champ, who wished him luck. The restaurant was at street level in the Brill Building, epicenter of New York's pop music business.

New York Public Library (476 5th Ave.): Dylan frequently enjoyed reading old newspapers from the 19th century on microfilm here. According to *Chronicles, Volume 1*, he was "intrigued by the language and rhetoric of the times."

Waverly Theater (323 6th Ave.): Dylan saw two of his favorite films here, *Lonely Are The Brave* and *A Face in the Crowd*. In 1978, Dylan's own *Renaldo & Clara* would play on this screen.

Village Gate (160 Bleecker St.): Dylan wrote "A Hard Rain's A-Gonna Fall" here on Chip Monck's IBM electric typewriter in 1962. Monck, the Gate's lighting engineer, had a basement apartment beneath the club. Dylan would later meet subversive comic Lenny Bruce here in 1964 and write a song for him years later for *Shot of Love*.

Albert Grossman's Office (75 E. 55th St) 🚫:
Dylan signed with manager Albert Grossman at his office here in August 1962. Grossman had previously managed Odetta and would form and also manage Peter, Paul, and Mary, as well as Janis Joplin. He and Dylan would part ways rancorously in 1970.

Videotape Center (101 W. 67th St.) ⊘: Dylan's first American television appearance was in the second program of this two-part Westinghouse television special, *Folk Songs and More Folk Songs*, hosted by John Henry Faulk. Dylan performed "Blowin' in the Wind," "The Ballad of Hollis Brown," and "Man of Constant Sorrow."

WNEW (565 5th Ave.): Dylan performed "Blowin' in the Wind" and "Only a Pawn in Their Game" for the *Songs of Freedom* television special on July 30, 1963.

Macmillan Publishers (62 5th Ave.): In 1964 Dylan was given a $10,000 advance to produce a book of his writings by editor Robert Markel, whom he visited here with Joan Baez. Written over the course of the next two years, the result was *Tarantula*, a collection of poems and prose very much in the spirit of Dylan's recordings of that time. It was eventually published in 1971, at which point multiple bootleg editions had already surfaced.

NBC (30 Rockefeller Plaza, Studio 8H): In his only appearance to date on *Saturday Night Live*, Dylan premiered three songs from his first gospel album *Slow Train Coming*, "Gotta Serve Somebody," "I Believe in You," and "When You Gonna Wake Up," on October 20, 1979.

New York Hilton (1335 6th Ave.): At a ceremony on March 15, 1982, Dylan was inducted into the Songwriter's Hall of Fame.

Late Night with David Letterman **(NBC 30 Rockefeller Plaza):** On March 22, 1984, Dylan appeared and performed on Letterman's NBC program promoting *Infidels*. He played Sonny Boy Williamson's "Don't Start Me Talkin'," as well as radically re-arranged renditions of "License to Kill" and "Jokerman."

Waldorf Astoria (301 Park Ave.): Dylan was inducted into the Rock & Roll Hall of Fame on January 20, 1988. He performed "All Along the Watchtower" surrounded by a stage full of stars that included George Harrison, Ringo Starr, Mick Jagger, Elton John, Little Richard, John Fogerty, and Bruce Springsteen.

Radio City Music Hall (1260 6th Ave.): Dylan played four shows here in October 1988. It was also the site of two other significant performances. On January 18, 1992, he taped *Late Night with David Letterman*'s 10th Anniversary show, which aired February 6. He performed "Like a Rolling Stone" backed by Letterman's band with Chrissie Hynde, Carole King, and a host of backup singers, including Mavis Staples, Nanci Griffith, and Emmylou Harris. On February 25, 1998, at the Grammy Awards, *Time Out of Mind* won for best album. At the televised ceremony, Dylan performed "Love Sick" while renegade performance artist Michael Portnoy danced crazily beside him with "Soy Bomb" painted on his chest. Dylan continued unperturbed.

Tommy Makem's Irish Pavilion (130 E. 57th St.): The party following Dylan's 30th Anniversary concert at Madison Square Garden was held here. Many of the featured performers mingled and celebrated here until the wee hours.

Sony Music Studios (460 W. 54th St.): In November 1994, Dylan filmed *MTV Unplugged* here, which he released as an album in 1995.

265 W. 139th St.: Dylan owned this McKim, Mead, and White home on Harlem's historic Striver's Row from 1986 until 2000.

Ed Sullivan Theater (1695 Broadway): On May 19, 2015, Dylan performed the Matt Dennis standard "The Night We Called It a Day" on the penultimate episode of the *Late Show with David Letterman* from his album *Shadows in the Night*. This is the same theater where 52 years earlier—almost to the day—he walked out on Ed Sullivan rather than change the song he wanted to play.

TODD RUNGDGREN'S HOME
206 E. 13th St.

Todd Rundgren lived at 206 E. 13th St. in the early '70s. Bebe Buell, in her book *Rebel Heart*, talked about the place being so sketchy you had to toss a coin at the window and he'd throw down a key. Soon after, she moved in with him. They also let David Johansen and Cyrinda Foxe stay for a couple of weeks.

NIGHTINGALE LOUNGE
213 2nd Ave.

Affectionately known as Nightingale's, the former Nightingale Lounge was once home to then-fledgling Big Apple jam bands in the late '80s and early '90s, such as Blues Traveler, Spin Doctors, and God Street Wine, with much of the scene spilling out onto the street during shows.

CLUB HOLLYWOOD
181 2nd Ave.

On October 13, 1978, desperate to make a splash to turn their fortunes around and keep publishing, the editorial staff at *Punk Magazine* held their first—and subsequently last—awards ceremony in the incongruously glamorous Club Hollywood. Though the news had broken only that morning that former Sex Pistol Sid Vicious had been arrested and charged with the murder of his girlfriend Nancy Spungen, the ceremony went on. With a live appearance by Shrapnel, scene stars such as Lou Reed, Blondie, the Ramones, Johnny Thunders, Lester Bangs, and former Sex Pistols manager Malcolm McLaren (winner of the "Con Man of the Year" award) were on hand.

FOOL FOR THE CITY
E. 11th St. and 2nd Ave.

The cover of Foghat's 1975 album *Fool for the City* features a photo of the group's drummer, Roger Earl, fishing in a manhole in the middle of the street. The album featured Foghat's biggest hit single, "Slow Ride."

WEBSTER HALL/THE RITZ
119 E.11th St.

Built in 1886 as a theater and event space, Webster Hall was largely dedicated to non–rock & roll forms of popular music for much of its first century, with the '50s bringing on performances by Woody Guthrie, Pete Seeger, and Tito Puente.

It wasn't until the space reopened as the Ritz on May 1, 1980, that rock & roll truly kicked the doors in. Through 1989, the Ritz hosted shows by U2, Beastie Boys, Aerosmith, Ramones, the Dead Boys, Fishbone, Murphy's Law, Sting, the Pretenders, and many more. The Ritz then moved into the former **Studio 54**

(**254 W. 54th St.**), continuing its rock & roll trend with shows by Guns N' Roses, Buzzcocks, Soundgarden, Public Image Ltd, Big Audio Dynamite, and others.

Webster Hall reopened in 1992 as a state-of-the-art facility with as many as five different rooms. Dance music was usually on the menu in the main hall, though numerous other acts have played the largest room in the venue, including Sonic Youth, Green Day, Faith No More, Modest Mouse, and, for the first two shows of their 2016 reunion, LCD Soundsystem.

Webster Hall closed for renovations in August 2017, with more live concerts and fewer dance nights likely in its future.

UKRAINIAN NATIONAL HOME
140 2nd Ave.

Though not a regular rock & roll venue, the Ukrainian National Home hosted occasional concerts throughout the '80s, including shows by Blues Traveler, Phish, and, on November 18, 1981, New Order, a show that was filmed and officially released by the group.

KIWI CLUB
432 E. 9th St.

The Kiwi Club was a bar where a shot and a beer were $1 and the jukebox was stocked with Janis Joplin. It had a pool table and pinball machine and was also a late-night hangout for some of the CBGB set, including Legs McNeil, Joey Ramone, Lester Bangs, and the Dead Boys, who shared an apartment upstairs. Inside the oven of the Dead Boys' place was a melted vinyl copy of Cream's *Disraeli Gears*. According to writer and former WFMU DJ James Marshall, the Kiwi Club shut down after the owner shot a patron who'd insulted Janis Joplin. The club would later become the Aztec Lounge, a punk bar.

CLUB 57
57 St. Marks Pl.

Open between 1978 and 1983, Club 57 was a nightclub, art and performance space with Dany Johnson serving as resident DJ and others, including Afrika Bambaataa, serving as guest DJs. Founded in the basement of the Holy Cross Polish National Church, the club was managed by Ann Magnuson and featured a broad range of cultural events. Musicians who either hung out or performed there included Cyndi Lauper, the B-52s, the Fleshtones, and Madonna. Club 57 also presented rock shows at the much larger **Irving Plaza (17 Irving Place)** in the late '70s.

PLEASE KILL ME
87 St. Marks Pl., Apt. 2B
Apartment 2B on St. Marks Place was the former apartment of *Punk Magazine* co-founder and longtime journalist Legs McNeil. Much of *Please Kill Me: The Uncensored Oral History of Punk*, McNeil's book with co-author Gillian McCain, was written here.

PHYSICAL GRAFFITI & "WAITING ON A FRIEND"
96-98 St. Marks Pl.
Designer Peter Corriston used these two adjoining tenements for the front and back covers of Led Zeppelin's *Physical Graffiti* in 1975. Astute fans will notice that the actual buildings stand five stories tall, not four as portrayed on the album. One of the stories was cropped out so the image would fit within the square confines of the sleeve. The Rolling Stones' 1981 video for "Waiting on a Friend" also uses this location. In the video Mick Jagger and Keith Richards meet on the stoop of 96 St. Marks, then adjourn to the nearby **St. Mark's Bar & Grill (132 1st Ave.)**, where they meet up with the rest of the band. The song would appear on *Tattoo You*, which, coincidentally, also sported a Peter Corriston–designed album cover.

SIN-É
124 St. Marks Pl./142 N. 8th St., Brooklyn/150 Attorney St.
Perhaps best known as the venue where the late Jeff Buckley recorded his intimate EP *Live at Sin-é*, this former Irish bar lasted just seven years in its original St. Marks location, where Iggy Pop might stop by for a drink. Sinead O'Connor, David Gray, Marianne Faithful, the Hothouse Flowers, the Waterboys, and many other acts played here as well. After a brief, months-long stopover in Williamsburg in 2000, Sin-é moved back into Manhattan to Attorney Street, where it remained open between 2003 and 2007.

PEACE EYE BOOK STORE
383 E.10th St. ⊘/147 Ave. A
The Fugs were a raffish synthesis of politically conscious beatnik, hippy culture that epitomized the emerging counterculture of the East Village in the mid-'60s. They made a series of albums and played shows that defied conventional expectations of what a band was supposed to do. They were troublemakers, but made trouble with a healthy dash of sly humor and anarchic wit.

Ed Sanders came to the Village from his native Missouri to attend NYU. By 1962 he had done time for protesting against nuclear submarines and was publishing his own underground literary magazine, *Fuck You/A Magazine of the Arts*. In 1964 he rented a storefront at 383 E.10th St. in what used to be a kosher butcher shop to establish the Peace Eye Book Store. It read "Strictly Kosher" in both English and Hebrew. He left it that way. He met a kindred spirit in a neighbor, Tuli Kupferberg, whose work he published. Kupferberg was several years older, but he shared similar tastes in literature and politics. He had also published his own literary magazine a few years before. The current confluence of folk music and pop/

rock inspired the duo to form their own group, the Fugs, named for the ridiculous euphemism in Norman Mailer's *The Naked and the Dead*. They would write a bizarre selection of songs and be the Fugs as a creative vehicle for poking and prodding the establishment and the US Constitution. They recruited a drummer, Ken Weaver, and members of the Holy Modal Rounders to perform at the grand opening of the Peace Eye in February 1965, which attracted William Burroughs, George Plimpton, James Michener, and a big crowd of locals. The Peace Eye became a popular destination and meeting place for the burgeoning East Village music and literary scene.

Harry Smith was a folk musicologist who befriended the Fugs and brought them to the attention of Moe Asch of Folkways Records, who would produce and release their first album, *The Village Fugs Sing Ballads of Contemporary Protest, Point of Views, and General Dissatisfaction*, since reissued as simply *The Fugs First Album*, in 1965. It contained the underground classics "Swinburne Stomp," "Nothing," "Slum Goddess," and "Boobs a Lot." They would hit the road in support of the album and play gigs with Allen Ginsberg, the Mothers of Invention, and Country Joe & the Fish. In New York they would play gigs at various venues in the Village, including **Cafe Au Go Go (152 Bleecker St.)⊘**, **Astor Place Theatre (434 Lafayette St.)**, and others before beginning a residency at the **Players Theater (115 MacDougal St.)** that lasted more than 700 performances. It was at the Players that they truly established themselves as a Village institution, attracting many fans, including Jimi Hendrix, Frank Zappa, and a host of other celebrities, including Richard Burton, Tennessee Williams, and Kim Novak, who was awarded a free T-shirt. They also had numerous run-ins with the law, from which they always managed to extricate themselves.

The Fugs would release a few more albums with varying degrees of success in the '60s, and Sanders would even make the cover of *Life Magazine* in 1967 as a leader of the "Other Culture." By 1968 The Peace Eye moved a few blocks west to 147 Ave. A, where it continued as an important cultural nexus for the neighborhood. That year it featured an exhibition of the new school of underground comix artists, including R. Crumb, Spain Rodriguez, Kim Deitch, Art Spiegelman, and others.

**FINAL U. S. A. PERFORMANCE
PRIOR TO CONCERT TOUR OF ENGLAND**

IN CONCERT

**AMERICA'S NEWEST FOLK / ROCK GROUP
THE**

FUGS

**GIVING THE WILDEST SOUNDS OF BODY–POETRY,–
PEACE–MANTRAS AND SKINFLOWERS**

TOWN HALL

113 WEST 43rd ST. - N.Y.C.

ONE PERFORMANCE ONLY · 8:30 PM

SUN. JUNE 12

TICKETS $2.50 3.00 3.50 4.00 • ON SALE AT TOWN HALL BOX OFFICE
MAIL ORDER REMITTANCE TO HENRY ABRAMSON, 165 CHRISTOPHER ST. N Y C 10014
or PHONE 929-4369
ENCLOSE STAMPED SELF-ADDRESSED ENVELOPE

In 1968 after their run at the Players Theater came to an end, the Fugs played a show with Moby Grape at the **Fillmore East (105 2nd Ave.)**, which would be captured on the album *Golden Filth*. That spring they recorded their final album of the '60s, *The Belle of Avenue A*, at **Apostolic Studios (53 E. 10th St.)**, and then called it quits. The constant harassment from the police, FBI, and post office, as well as bomb threats, had taken their toll and the group had had enough. Not long after Ed Sanders would move upstate to Woodstock.

Sanders and Kupferberg would continue to write and publish prolifically, and eventually they did reform the Fugs in 1985. They occasionally performed and recorded until Kupferberg's death in 2010. They may yet return.

BROWNIES
169 Avenue A.
For over a decade until its closure as a live music venue in 2002, Brownies was indie rock heaven, hosting early shows by the Strokes and Interpol, as well as groups like Spoon, Blonde Redhead, and the Fall. It later reopened as the **HiFi Bar,** with an expansive jukebox and very occasionally a live performance, before closing in autumn 2017.

171A
171 Avenue A
In keeping with the DIY philosophy of the blooming NYC hardcore scene, 171 Avenue A has a rich, if brief, hands-on history that began with an abandoned glass shop on the ground floor of a building that had been gutted by a fire. Jerry Williams cleared out the space, built a stage, and 171A was born anew as a live venue. After the New York City Fire Department shut the illegal venue down, it was converted into a recording studio, where the Beastie Boys recorded their debut EP, *Polly Wog Stew*. After moving up from Washington, D.C. in 1981,

Bad Brains lived and recorded at 171A, and their debut album largely consisted of studio recordings, with a handful of live tracks recorded at a show there earlier in the year. Black Flag, visiting from California, auditioned singer Henry Rollins, who was visiting from D.C., at 171A.

The basement at 171A was the original location of Dave Parsons' Rat Cage Records, one of the key hardcore labels covering the NYC scene. In 1983, Parsons moved Rat Cage to 307 E. 9th St., but it closed for good by the end of the year.

TOMPKINS SQUARE PARK BAND SHELL
Built in 1966, the Tompkins Square Park band shell was eventually knocked down during a comprehensive renovation of the historic park in the '90s. The band shell was the scene of the first ever New York City show by the Grateful Dead on June 1, 1967. In town for an 11-night stand at the Cafe Au Go Go, the Dead played a free afternoon show in the band shell, an experience, according to the *Village Voice*, preceded by a parade of around 80 hippies marching down St. Marks Place with a white carnation key to the East Village, which they presented to Ron "Pigpen" Kernan. The show rolled into the late afternoon until ended by a noise complaint.

CHRISTODORA HOUSE
143 Ave. B
Iggy Pop reportedly lived here while recording his 1999 album *Avenue B*.

LEAD BELLY'S HOME
414 E.10th St.
Huddie William Ledbetter was born in Louisiana and had been a traveling musician in the first decades of the 20th century. He ran afoul of the law on more than one occasion, however, and did a few stints in jail, including hard time for murder in Louisiana's notorious Angola State

414 E. 10th St.

Prison, where he was discovered and extensively recorded by musicologist John Lomax in 1933 and 1934. After appeals by Lomax, Ledbetter was released from prison for good behavior.

He married his wife Martha Promise and moved into an apartment at 414 E. 10th St. around 1936. He became an important figure in the burgeoning New York folk community and often played to college groups and leftist political audiences. He would host his own radio show on **WNYC (1 Centre St.)** in 1940 and became associated with Josh White, Sonny Terry, Woody Guthrie, Pete Seeger, and other important and influential folk music figures who often gathered at the apartment. It was the Ledbetters' permanent residence until his death in 1949.

Lead Belly wrote many songs that became folk standards, including "Midnight Special," "Goodnight Irene," "Cotton Fields," and "Black Betty." He was also an influential guitarist and is considered pivotal to the development of folk,

blues, and R&B. Lead Belly was inducted into the Rock & Roll Hall of Fame in 1988.

MANITOBA'S
99 Avenue B
Owned and operated by Dictators (now Dictators NYC) frontman Richard "Handsome Dick" Manitoba, Manitoba's was inspired by a childhood visit to boxing legend **Jack Dempsey's Broadway Restaurant & Bar (1619 Broadway)**, which served as something of a public hangout and clubhouse. Manitoba's is a punk version of Jack Dempsey's, with rock & roll photos on the wall.

TU CASA SOUND STUDIO
95 Ave. B
Before drummer Brian Chase entered the picture and Yeah Yeah Yeahs were complete, Karen O and Nick Zinner used to rehearse at Tu Casa Sound Studio.

PLANT BAR
217 E. 3rd St.
Now closed, Plant Bar was for a time a key hangout by groups associated with DFA Records. LCD Soundsystem frontman and DFA co-founder James Murphy and Luke Jenner of the Rapture both served as bar backs, and DJs such as Fatboy Slim, Felix da Housecat, and Adam Horovitz and Kathleen Hanna would occasionally drop in to spin. To circumvent the city's arcane cabaret law, Plant Bar reportedly had a light in the DJ booth to indicate when the cops were nearby. When the light went on, the DJ would play Radiohead, and the dancing would cease.

SIDEWALK CAFE
94 Avenue A
Opened in 1985, the Sidewalk Cafe was a key location for the early 2000's anti-folk scene, with the Moldy Peaches, Regina Spektor, Lana Del Rey, pre-Interpol Paul Banks, and many

others playing early shows here. Before forming Yeah Yeah Yeahs, Karen O performed open mic shows at the Sidewalk Cafe, returning as one half of Unitard with future Yeah Yeah Yeahs guitarist Nick Zinner. The Sidewalk Cafe is still in operation, hosting a wide range of musical performances on its busy calendar.

A7/NIAGARA
112 Ave. A

Between 1980 and 1984, A7 was the unofficial center of New York City's nascent hardcore scene, hosting shows by such visiting bands as Black Flag and then-DC-based Bad Brains, as well as giving rise to a decidedly NYC form of the music. Punk was often played lightning fast in an aggressive but generally accepting scene. Groups such as Beastie Boys, Murphy's Law, Reagan Youth, Agnostic Front, and many others played early shows here.

Joe Strummer mural adjacent to Niagara

"Down on the corner of 7th and A, all of us found each other, meaning my little crew where things began," said Jesse Malin, former Heart Attack front man who would later go on to form D Generation and break out as a solo performer. "We all came from Staten Island, New Jersey, Brooklyn. A lot from Queens, but not my neighborhood, necessarily. Some from Astoria, some from Long Island City. We found each

other on this corner without cell phones, without computers. We had to use the 'Schwartz,' as they say in Spaceballs. And we found ourselves at A7. The place didn't start until one in the morning, and it was five bucks to get in. And it wasn't listed in the *Village Voice*."

Frequently raided by police, A7 was owned by Dave Gibson, who operated his club without a liquor license and hired some of the young musicians playing shows to work on staff. The floor was tiled, the ceiling stained, and the atmosphere undeniably electric.

"(Gibson) would come out of his control room, and he'd put you on the lineup in magic marker on the door on the side street, and they'd open up at midnight," Malin recalled. "And you might play at 4 a.m. or 5 a.m., but he'd pay you. To get $150 and not have to promote the gig was great. The equipment was nailed to the stage, and we'd be in there until 6 or 7 in the morning, and many of us were definitely underage."

Years later, Malin became part-owner of Niagara, a rock & roll bar with framed gig posters on the walls and a popular Joe Strummer mural along the exterior wall along East 7th Street.

"I just wanted a little place, a Frank Sinatra fantasy," Malin said. "We took over Niagara, and we didn't expect it to do so well. You want to have a place when you're not playing music where you can talk about music, and drink, and talk to girls, and play records you like. And whenever I toured I'd always want to find that bar with the guy who's got Clash stories or they're playing Motörhead. Where do you go in each city? We tried to make it that place for bands, and we had a policy that touring bands could come through and drink free. Queens of the Stone Age and Green Day when they weren't as huge as they are now, would come in. It just became a place."

PYRAMID CLUB

101 Ave. A

In operation since 1979, the Pyramid Club opened as an East Village hangout for many of the artists, drag queens, and musicians in the area. Performers at the club over the years included Nirvana, Deee-Lite, Red Hot Chili Peppers, Swans, Book of Love, They Might Be Giants, and others. Though the scene has changed, the Pyramid Club remains, hosting regular retro-themed dance nights. In the '60s, the building was the home of the East Village In, a coffeehouse and intimate live music space during a time when Nico lived in an apartment upstairs.

ANDERSON THEATRE/CBGB SECOND AVENUE THEATER

66 2nd Ave.

A former theater at 66 2nd Ave. that twice served as a live rock venue. Reportedly opening as a Yiddish theater in the '20s, by the '60s the space was called the Anderson Theatre, which was open at least in the late '60s, and possibly into the first couple of years of the '70s. It played host to shows by the Grateful Dead, Moby Grape, Procol Harum, the Yardbirds, Big Brother & the Holding Company, B.B. King, and many others. A benefit concert for the War Resisters League was held on March 6, 1968, featuring Country Joe & the Fish, the Fugs, Bob Fass, and Paul Krassner.

The space briefly reopened as **CBGB Second Avenue Theater** on December 27, 1977, with

a show by Talking Heads, the Shirts, and Tuff Darts. The theater was CBGB-owner Hilly Kristal's doomed attempt to stretch beyond the Bowery: Following a three-night run of shows into New Year's Eve headlined by the Patti Smith Group with support from Richard Hell & the Voidoids, the Erasers, and Mars, the experiment was nearly over. Bruce Springsteen took the stage with the Patti Smith Group on the second night of their stand to share vocals on "Because the Night," a song co-written by Springsteen and Smith. The Jam played a pair of dates at the venue (still called the CBGB Second Avenue Theater on tickets) in late March 1978.

FILLMORE EAST

105 2nd Ave.

Only open between March 8, 1968, and June 27, 1971, Bill Graham's Fillmore East was the ideal rock & roll venue of the era, large enough to meet the demand of a growing audience for live music, at least until that demand forced many contemporary acts into stadiums. It was originally built as the Commodore Theater in the mid-'20s when 2nd Avenue was known as the Yiddish Theater District. After years as a cinema, it became known as the **Village Theatre** in 1967, showing its rock & roll potential with shows by the Who, the Byrds, Vanilla Fudge, Cream, the Seeds, Chuck Berry, a radio show featuring the Doors and the Blues Project, along with various folk and jazz shows.

Former entrance to the Fillmore East

Bill Graham was born in Germany, but at the age of 10 found himself in a Bronx foster home. Though he made a name for himself as a promoter and owner of the Fillmore Auditorium in San Francisco, Graham had attended **DeWitt Clinton High School (100 W. Mosholu Pkwy. S., the Bronx)** and **City College (160 Convent Ave.)** and longed to bring his success back east. He found it in the dilapidated Village Theatre, in which he quickly adapted the Fillmore's busy calendar and psychedelic lights, first with the Joshua Light Show, and later the Pig Light Show.

Many of the era's biggest groups played the Fillmore East, including the Allman Brothers Band, the Grateful Dead, Jefferson Airplane, Jimi Hendrix, Iron Butterfly, Led Zeppelin, the Byrds, the Flying Burrito Brothers, Sly & the Family Stone, the Kinks, and Crosby, Stills, Nash, and Young.

As groups such as Led Zeppelin began eyeing larger venues where they could reach more people with fewer shows, the Fillmore East's fortunes began to turn, and a final invite-only show took place on June 27, 1971. Among the performers on the last night of the Fillmore East were the Allman Brothers Band, the J. Geils Band, Albert King, the Beach Boys, Mountain, Country Joe McDonald, and Johnny Winter's White Trash. But the end of the Fillmore East wasn't the end of 105 2nd Ave. as a rock venue. In November 1972, it reopened as **Villageast**, first with Virgin: A New Rock Opera Concert by the Mission, and later with shows by Elephant's Memory, the New York Dolls, Chuck Berry, Foghat, the Steve Miller Band, and others.

In late 1974, the venue was renamed the NFE—or New Fillmore East—but after Graham raised objections it was dubbed the Village East until its closure in 1975. For most of the '80s, the site housed The Saint, a gay dance club.

Though the marquee and theater are gone, the building itself remains, housing a bank on the ground floor and apartments above. A plaque identifying the building as the former Fillmore East was dedicated by the Greenwich Village Society for Historic Preservation in October 2015.

CLUB 82/WOODY'S
82 E. 4th St.

By most contemporary accounts a run-down basement drag revue bar, Club 82 was an important venue for the transition from glam to punk, with live rock music beginning around 1972, roughly 20 years into its existence. Performers such as Wayne County & the Backstreet Boys, the New York Dolls, Television, Teenage Lust, the Brats, Suicide, the Miamis, the Stillettoes, and others would play on the stage set behind the bar. David Bowie and Lou Reed, who served as compere during a weekend showcase of NYC rock in March 1976, frequented Club 82.

Years later, Rolling Stones guitarist Ron Wood opened his ill-fated Woody's in the former Club 82 space, a live venue where such groups as the Rave-Ups, the Chills, and Eleventh Dream Day played in a room adorned with its owner's artwork and photographs. It was there in the very late-'80s and very early-'90s, and then it was gone.

TRUCK AND WAREHOUSE THEATER
79 E. 4th St.

Primarily the home of '70s off-off-Broadway productions like *Billy Noname*, *The Dirtiest Musical in Town*, and *The Faggot*, a musical by Al Carmines; the Truck and Warehouse Theater was also the site of an early gig by key punk groups Television and the Ramones in November 1974.

GREAT GILDERSLEEVES
331 Bowery

Opened in the late '70s as nearby **CBGB (315 Bowery)** continued making waves, Great Gildersleeves was a popular venue cut from similar cloth. Though it lasted less than a decade, Great Gildersleeves kept a busy schedule, filling out a calendar mostly comprised of unfamiliar faces, with early appearances by Public Image, Ltd., Elvis Costello & the Attractions, Sonic Youth, Black Flag, Beastie Boys, Husker Du, the Brats, the J. Geils Band, and others.

MARS BAR ⊘
25 E. 1st St.

For many, Mars Bar was the last remaining link to the gritty East Village of yore, a dive bar in the truest sense that opened in 1985 and outlasted CBGB, Coney Island High, and almost the rest of the neighborhood, before finally succumbing in 2011. It may have gone past its

sell-by date, because by the time word got out that you might spot one of the main instigators of the early aughts guitar explosion hunched over the bar, they'd already stopped coming. Mars Bar's specter lives on with a series of terrifying stories on its Yelp page, of which, if you have a thing about hygiene, you might want to steer clear.

STUDIO 10
10 Bleecker St.

An extension of a Yippie squat across the street, Studio 10 opened in 1979 as a short-lived rock venue, hosting shows by Bad Brains, the dBs, DOA, and other punk groups before they were evicted soon after.

SILK BUILDING
14 E. 4th St.

Built in 1912 as a silk factory, the Silk Building is a 55-unit, 12-story apartment building that runs along East 4th Street between Broadway and Lafayette. Numerous musical names have called the Silk Building home, including Cher and Britney Spears, who owned PH1109 from 2002 through 2006. Def Jam Recordings co-founder and hip-hop impresario Russell Simmons also lived in the building, selling his 3,400-square-foot penthouse PH1108 in 1996. Keith Richards also lived in the building in the '80s, taking up one floor as a residence and another as a recording studio.

OTHER MUSIC
11-13 E. 4th St.

Though they remain online, the beloved brick-and-mortar location of Other Music closed its doors in 2016 after more than two decades of giving NYU students and music lovers across the city an alternative to what was on sale first at nearby Tower Records, and then at the Virgin Megastore, both of which it outlasted. In addition to an eclectic stock, Other Music

CBGB

315 BOWERY

Though synonymous with the downtown punk scene of the mid-to-late '70s, CBGB lasted over three decades as a crucial live music venue, with new and established artists taking its shaky stage in the back of the room, using its notoriously disgusting bathroom for a variety of disgusting reasons, and following in the footsteps of the legends that came before them.

Founded in December 1973, CBGB & OMFUG—Country, Bluegrass, Blues and Other Music for Uplifting Gormandizers in its full form—was an effort by owner Hilly Kristal to give some distance between his bar of four years in the same location, Hilly's on the Bowery, and the future. Earlier in the year, the Mercer Arts Center (240 Mercer St.) had collapsed, leaving a void in venues for bands to play and people to hear new music. Mercer bands like

Ramones outside GBGB on July 18, 1975
Bob Gruen

Suicide, the Fast, and Wayne County all wound up regularly playing CBGB.

hosted occasional in-store performances, including Animal Collective, which counts former employees of the store among its members.

THE LOOKING GLASS STUDIOS

632 Broadway

The former Looking Glass Studios was located on the ninth floor of a building just to the left of what is now an Urban Outfitters. Among the artists who recorded or mixed music there are Lou Reed, Patti Smith, David Byrne, Iggy Pop,

TV on the Radio, Beck, Grace Jones, and David Bowie.

PROJECT OF LIVING ARTISTS ⊘

729 Broadway, 2nd floor

One night in 1970, Alan Vega was performing improvised electronic and looped tape in a loose artists and musicians collective at the Project of Living Artists when Martin Rev of free jazz band Reverend B joined in, playing a beat on metal tins with pencils. Soon the pair would become Suicide, returning to play the loft numerous

Though improvisational guitar band Television weren't the first to play CBGB, their willingness to smooth-talk Kristal into either believing they could play country, bluegrass, or blues, or could at least attract plenty of beer-buying friends, that he gave them a shot. In March 1975, the group played CBGB for the first time, unwittingly setting in motion the shape of things to come. Soon they were followed by the Ramones, Mink De Ville, the Dead Boys, the Heartbreakers, Talking Heads, Blondie, Richard Hell & the Voidoids, Wayne County, the Patti Smith Group, the Cramps, the Dictators, and virtually every other band associated with those leading lights. As word spread across the Atlantic, groups such as the Police, the Damned, Elvis Costello, and Gang of Four all booked shows at CBGB during North American visits.

But while the first wave of punk bands outgrew CBGB, Kristal's space bucked trends set in motion by other venues, adapting at least

enough to incorporate the growing hardcore scene into its calendar, adding matinee shows and welcoming other new groups onto its already legendary stage. Beastie Boys, Bad Brains, Agnostic Front, the Misfits, the Fleshtones, and countless others all played early shows at CBGB.

Though its cache faded into the '90s, CBGB still had plenty of life left in the years before its closure. Even between 2000 and 2006, as the venue settled into an ultimately unsuccessful bid to stay afloat in an increasingly expensive neighborhood, the music continued. CBGB closed in mid-October 2006, with Blondie and Patti Smith returning to play one last time before the end. Within two years, designer John Varvatos had opened a shop there, one that pays homage to the history of the building. And in 2013, 315 Bowery was added to the National Register of Historic Places as part of the National Bowery Historic District.

times in the early '70s. When the Project of Living Artists moved to 133 Greene St. in 1973, Suicide followed.

KMART

770 Broadway

U2 held a press conference next to the lingerie department in the Greenwich Village Kmart on February 12, 1997, to announce their PopMart World Tour. The group performed a b-side, "Holy Joe," before answering questions from reporters. The tour, which lasted from April 1997 through

March 1998, never got closer to New York City than a trio of late-spring 1997 shows at Giants Stadium in East Rutherford, New Jersey.

ASTOR PLACE SUBWAY STATION AT ASTOR PLACE AND 4TH AVENUE
turnstiles on uptown side

The photo on the cover of Billy Joel's 1976 album *Turnstiles* was taken on the uptown side of the station. The people surrounding Joel represent different songs on a collection the Piano Man considered his most "New York" record to date.

THE CONTINENTAL
25 3rd Ave.

Though the Continental no longer hosted live music, the bar was still open through August 2018, after which the building was due to be razed. During the final years of the Continental, you could grab a beer, hit the jukebox, close your eyes, and maybe hear the echoes of 15 years of shows by artists such as Green Day, D Generation, Guns N' Roses, and Iggy Pop. Joey Ramone played his last gig here on December 11, 2000.

CONEY ISLAND HIGH ⊘
15 St. Marks Pl.

Only open from 1995 to 1999, Coney Island High was a three-story venue initially co-founded by Jesse Malin of Heart Attack as a place to hold the Green Door parties after the relationship with Giorgio Gomelsky, owner of the building where the events used to be held, soured.

"I didn't know what I was doing," said Malin. "I staffed the place with friends. And I got a record deal and went on tour. I didn't know how to run a fucking club. I took my money from (music) publishing and put it into the place, and we gave everything away and everybody got in free. If I knew how to run a place maybe we'd still be open."

In its brief history, Coney Island High hosted shows by Iggy Pop, the Misfits, the Fleshtones, the Damned, Murphy's Law, Hawkwind, and Malin's glam punk outfit D Generation. Beastie Boys, as their hardcore alter-ego Quasar, played the club in 1995.

According to Malin, Coney Island High was closed due to a zoning loophole exposed while former mayor Rudy Giuliani was in office.

"St. Marks was not residential, but it was zoned residential 100 years ago," Malin said. "Our mayor was [Rudy] Giuliani, and it was a fucking war on New York and the quality of life. He came down on us for the dancing with the cabaret laws. Even though it was like a fucking mall. We fought and fought. We had to stop the dance party, tell people, 'Don't dance!' It just was a mess."

23-25 St. Marks Pl., the only part of the original structure that has not been extensively remodeled.

THE DOM/OPEN STAGE/BALLOON FARM/ ELECTRIC CIRCUS/THE CIRCUS
19-25 St. Marks Pl.

In April 1966, the Velvet Underground performed as part of Andy Warhol's Exploding Plastic Inevitable in an upstairs venue called the Open Stage at the Dom, a restaurant and nightclub opened on the former site of the Polish National Home. By the time Warhol's revue returned for a run of dates spread out from September to October of the same year, the Dom had been renamed to suit the then-contemporary trend toward the psychedelic surreal as the Balloon Farm. The name only lasted a few months before it changed to the Electric Circus, a futuristic venue that stuck around for four years, hosting shows by the Grateful Dead, the Stooges, Sly & the Family Stone, the Allman Brothers Band, and others. In 1973 The Circus opened in the same spot, with shows by, among others, the New York Dolls.

32 ST. MARKS PLACE, APT. #1

Former residence of Lady Miss Kier of house and club group Deee-Lite, this St. Marks Place apartment was also listed as the address of Deee-Lite Enterprises, Inc. on an NYSDOS domestic business corporation filing on August 10, 1990, three days after the release of the group's debut album, *World Clique*, which produced the smash hit "Groove Is in the Heart."

SOBOSSEK'S SUPPER CLUB ⊘
35 Cooper Sq.

Located just off the Bowery, Sobossek's Supper Club hosted a series of free shows by cellist, singer, and experimental composer Arthur Russell in 1976.

BLONDIE

Bob Gruen

Blondie in NYC, September 1976

Though apparently few within the downtown music scene of the mid-'70s would have imagined it possible, Blondie became one of the biggest groups on the planet by the end of the decade. For most of the world, Blondie's chart-storming ascent on the strength of worldwide #1 smash hit "Heart of Glass" and the Mike Chapman–produced album *Parallel Lines* was a sudden breath of fresh air.

As with many of the groups in their circle, Blondie are, even today, most-often associated with legendary punk club **CBGB (315 Bowery)**,

Mural by Shepard Fairey on Bleecker Street near The Bowery

a venue they played over 60 times under various guises, beginning with the band that brought Debbie Harry and Chris Stein together, the Stillettoes.

The Stillettoes ("Two Is and two ts," confirmed Stein in 2017, though he added, "I've seen it a lot of ways, and I'm never really 100 percent sure myself") were a dramatically campy girl group in the tradition of the Shangri-Las and the Supremes, featuring Harry, Elda Gentile, and Amanda Jones on vocals, with backing from, among others, Tom and James Wynbrandt, who would go on to form the Miamis. Stein turned up with Eric Emerson of the Magic Tramps at the second Stillettoes gig, on November 29, 1973. Though their romantic relationship would develop over time, the connection between Stein and Harry was immediate. **The Bobern Bar & Grill (42 W. 28th St.)** was a small saloon where, according to legend, the legs were removed from the pool table during gigs to make a stage.

"That's Debbie's recollection of it, and I'll go with that," said Stein. "It was just this little bar."

Soon the Stillettoes included Stein on guitar, Fred Smith on bass guitar, and Billy O'Connor on drums, and it was with this lineup that the group that would eventually morph into Blondie first played CBGB, opening for Television on May 5, 1974, with the pair returning to play together four more times over the next month and a half. Over a two-month period in mid-1974, the Stillettoes also played twice at **The Mushroom (22 E. 13th St.)**, opened for Wayne County & the Backstreet Boys at **Club 82 (82 E. 4th St.)**, and hit **Bacchus Rock Palace (209 W. 48th St.)** ⊘ with Eric Emerson's Star Theater.

As befitting a period of great change, the latter-day Stillettoes split, with its members making a two-gig CBGB pitstop on August 16 and 31, 1974, as Angel and the Snake. By the time they returned to the club on October 12,

1974, they were called Blondie, sometimes performing as Blondie and the Banzai Babes (sometimes showing up as "Banzai Babies" in ads) with backing vocals from Tish and Snooky Bellomo, later of the Sic Fucks and **Manic Panic (33 St. Marks Pl.)**, a boutique that grew into a cosmetics empire.

CBGB would come to play a role in other significant Blondie gigs: On April 7, 1975, Clem Burke made his debut there on drums, taking over for O'Connor, who left to resume his academic studies at the University of Pittsburgh. It would also be the last gig for Smith on bass guitar, as he reportedly told the group between sets he was leaving to join Television, who'd recently parted ways with Richard Hell. When Blondie returned to CBGB to open for the Ramones on July 4 through 6, 1975, Gary Valentine was on bass guitar.

266 Bowery

The neighborhood wasn't just where Blondie played and hung out; they also lived there, in a loft above a liquor store at **266 Bowery** in a building where the hall reeked from a mixture of cat and human urine.

"Me, Debbie, Gary, and various other people lived there," recalled Stein. "A lot of crazy parties went on there with everybody from the scene. And we rehearsed there. That was when the whole CBGB's scene was up and flourishing, so it was a central location, that and Arturo (Vega)'s loft, you know?"

The group thought the building might be haunted, and though it had no heat at night and an only semi-functional bathroom, the location combined with the reasonable rent of $350 a month was too good to pass up. Artist and fashion designer Stephen Sprouse lived in a unit above the Blondie loft for a time; later, he'd help shape their iconic style.

Two other residences played a role in the early days of Blondie, beginning with **18 1st Ave.,** an apartment where Stein lived after returning to the **School of Visual Arts (209 E. 23rd St.)** following a year spent in San Francisco.

"It was near a funeral home and a bathhouse," Stein said. "I think the funeral home is still there."

Eric Emerson of the Magic Tramps, for whom Chris had arranged to play the School of Visual Arts Christmas party, moved in with him for a while, with the pair causing mayhem in a building largely populated by non-freaks. Later, Tommy Ramone sublet the place from Stein, with Dee Dee living there as well.

Stein moved in with Harry at 105 Thompson St., her first place in the city after moving from New Jersey following an experience that would later inspire one of Blondie's singles, "One Way or Another."

"That was when she was getting stalked by her boyfriend and left New Jersey," Stein said.

Before they all decamped to 266 Bowery, Valentine lived with Stein and Harry on Thompson Street, reporting back to his

18 1st Ave.

105 Thompson St.

Chris Stein's childhood homes at 1144 (left) and 1043 (right) E. 13th St., Brooklyn

probation officer in Bayonne, New Jersey, every week following his arrest for statutory rape at the age of 18 after getting his 16-year-old girlfriend pregnant. The charges were eventually dropped.

Seemingly always on the move, Stein and Harry would eventually leave the Bowery for a place on 17th Street, before they moved uptown altogether. Valentine moved on as well, leaving Blondie in 1977, and eventually being replaced by Nigel Harrison on bass guitar. Harrison, along with Harry, Stein, Burke, keyboardist Jimmy Destri (who joined soon after Valentine in 1975), and guitarist Frank Infante, were Blondie from late-1977 until the group split in 1982.

MORE BLONDIE

NOTEWORTHY LIVE PERFORMANCES

Whyte's Pub (80 Wall St.): Blondie would perform at Whyte's Pub a handful of times between 1974 and 1975. Harry and Anya Phillips, eventual Mudd Club co-founder and manager of James Chance & the Contortions, also worked at Whyte's as bikini bartenders.

"It was weird," Stein said. "This guy once gave Debbie a tip on the daily double, but we didn't have any fucking money so we put like $10 down and got $100. If I'd had $1,000 I'd have been able to clean up."

Continental Baths (2109 Broadway): Original drummer Billy O'Connor claimed Blondie played a show at Continental Baths, a gay bathhouse in the basement of the Ansonia Hotel, sometime in the fall of 1974.

The Mushroom (22 E. 13th St.): The Stillettoes played the Mushroom on May 11, 1974; Blondie's early resume lists the venue as well, though the date they played is unknown.

Bacchus Rock Palace (209 W. 48th St.) ⊘: The Stillettoes and Eric Emerson's Star Theater each played two sets at Bacchus Rock Palace on July 1, 1974.

The Gymnasium (474 E. 71st St.): Chris Stein played with a loose group that opened for the Velvet Underground during their run of shows at the Gymnasium in 1967.

Monty Python's (12th St. and 3rd Ave.): Blondie played Monty Python's numerous times in the mid-1970s, with the most significant show taking place on November 8, 1975, reportedly the debut of keyboardist Jimmy Destri.

Performance Studios (23 E. 20th St.): Blondie first opened for the Ramones at Performance Studios on December 7, 1974.

Village Gate (160 Bleecker St.): Blondie played three straight nights at the Village Gate from July 1 through 3, 1977. These were the final Blondie gigs with Gary Valentine on bass guitar.

Quando Gym (9 2nd Ave.) ⊘: Blondie shared the bill with the Dictators, Mink De Ville, and Demons at New York Rock, a mini-festival held at Quando Gym on October 23, 1976.

Broadway Charly's (813 Broadway): Though the dates are unknown, Blondie listed Broadway Charly's as a venue they played in an early press kit.

Club 82 (82 E. 4th St.): Though the dates are unclear, Blondie's early resume cites Club 82 among the venues they played.

Mothers (267 W. 23rd St.): Blondie played Mothers several times in 1975, opening three nights for the Fast in September and returning the following month for a three-night stint supporting the Ramones.

Max's Kansas City (213 Park Ave. South): Like many groups in the downtown scene, Blondie played Max's Kansas City numerous times. Debbie Harry had previously waited tables there for around seven or eight months in 1969 before leaving for a job as a Bunny at the **Playboy Club (5 E. 59th St.).**

The Palladium (126 E. 14th St.) ⊘: Blondie first played the Palladium on March 18, 1977, when the group traveled with Iggy Pop on the former Stooge's tour in support of *The Idiot*. David Bowie played keyboards and sang backing vocals in Pop's backing band.

30 Rockefeller Plaza: Blondie performed "Dreaming" and "The Hardest Part" from Studio 8H on the opening episode of the fifth season of *Saturday Night Live* on October 13, 1979.

S.I.R. Studios (310 W. 52nd St.) ⊘: Blondie recorded the bulk of the *Eat to the Beat* video album at the former S.I.R. Studios facility on 52nd Street over three days in October 1979.
The New York Hilton Midtown (1335 Avenue of the Americas): On August 27, 1977, Blondie played the National Music and Sound Show, a music industry convention, at the Hilton Midtown.
Wollman Rink (Central Park): Blondie played at Wollman Rink as part of the Dr. Pepper Central Park Music Festival on July 9, 1979, with Rockpile supporting.
Brandy's II (1584 York Ave.): Blondie and the Banzai Babes opened for the Miamis at Brandy's II on January 31 and February 1, 1975, returning later in the month to support "the funkiest sound in town," Harlem Drive.
George Seuffert Bandshell (Forest Park Dr., Queens): In a show presented by the New York Free Music Committee, Blondie played what was then called the Forest Park Bandshell on August 1, 1975.

NOTEWORTHY RECORDING LOCATIONS

Plaza Sound Studios (55 W. 50th St., 7th floor): Blondie recorded their eponymous debut for Private Stock Records with producer Richard Gottehrer at Plaza Sound Studios in December 1976, returning the following summer to record its follow-up, *Plastic Letters*.
Record Plant (321 W. 44th St.): Blondie entered the Record Plant in the summer of 1978 to record their third album, *Parallel Lines*, with producer Mike Chapman.
Power Station (441 W. 53rd St.): Blondie recorded some of their 1979 album *Eat to the Beat* with producer Mike Chapman at the Power

Station. Electric Lady Studios (52 W. 8th St.) was also used.
Hit Factory (421 W. 54th St.): For their final album before a lengthy split, Blondie recorded *The Hunter* with producer Mike Chapman at the Hit Factory in the fall of 1981 and during the first few months of 1982.
Mercy Sound Recording Studios (602 E. 14th St.): Released in 2014, *Ghosts of Download* was recorded at both Mercy Sound Recording Studios and Skyline Studios in Oakland, California.
Chung King Recording Studios (170 Varick St.): Blondie recorded some of their 1999 reunion album *No Exit* at Chung King's Varick Street facility.
Magic Shop (49 Crosby St.): One of the last albums recorded in the now-shuttered Magic Shop was Blondie's *Pollinator*, released in 2017. The Magic Shop moved to 68 Jay St. in Brooklyn in 2015, and is now MARS NYC, the Magicshop Archive and Restoration Studios.

OTHER NOTEWORTHY LOCATIONS

David's Pot Belly Stove (94 Christopher St.): In his book *New York Rocker,* former Blondie bass guitarist Gary Valentine recalled that in the early days, if the group scraped enough money together after a good gig, they'd celebrate here with cheeseburgers, fries, and milk shakes.
300 Mercer St.: The photograph for the cover of Blondie's 1980 album *Autoamerican* was shot on the roof of 300 Mercer. The image was turned into a painting by Martin Hoffman.
Music Building (584 8th Ave.): Blondie rehearsed at the Music Building sometime after it opened in 1979.
Quintano's School for Young Professionals (156 W. 56th St.): Chris Stein originally attended

Midwood High School (2839 Bedford Ave., Brooklyn) before moving to Quintano's School for Young Professionals.

"The idea was that it was a school for professional kids, but only a handful of the kids who went there were actually working in showbiz," Stein said. "The rest of us were just miscreants."

200 W. 58th St.: During the height of Blondie's popularity, Harry and Stein moved considerably farther uptown than the scene they'd been such a crucial part of in the '70s.

1144 E. 13th St./1043 E. 13th St., Brooklyn: Chris Stein grew up in Brooklyn, and before his family moved to an apartment on Ocean Avenue they lived at 1144 E. 13th St., then 1043 E. 13th St.

PS 199 (1100 Elm Ave., Brooklyn): Stein attended elementary school at PS 199, where he first found fame as a performer dressed as a leaf in the school play.

"I was a crepe paper leaf," Stein said. "My mom made me that thing."

Andries Hudde Junior High School (2500 Nostrand Ave., Brooklyn): Named after a prominent 17th-century land owner, Andries Hudde Junior High School was where Chris Stein attended middle school in the mid-'60s.

"The urban legend was that (Hudde) was hung for stealing horses," Stein said. "Whether this is true or not, I don't know. All the kids in school were always going on about that. Somebody is probably still saying that."

Maimonides Medical Center (4802 10th Ave., Brooklyn): Before joining Blondie, keyboardist Jimmy Destri worked as an emergency room orderly at Maimonides.

PARADISE GARAGE
84 King St.

The heart of the late '70s and early '80s house and garage dance scenes in NYC, Paradise Garage took its name from its location, a former parking garage. Its most celebrated DJ, Larry Levan, remains both an icon and inspiration to turntablists around the world. Known primarily as an iconic LGBT–friendly dance club, Paradise Garage also hosted live music during its decade in operation, including performances by Diana Ross, Madonna, Richard Hell & the Voidoids, Teenage Jesus & the Jerks, James Chance & the Contortions, the Stimulators, Cyndi Lauper, ESG, Whitney Houston, Grace Jones, New Order, and many more.

The building has recently been altered, removing the distinctive curved portion of the façade.

HERALD & EMBER RECORDS
469 West Broadway

Herald Records, under the ownership of Al Silver, would initially operate from a tiny basement office here on West Broadway and issue some of the most memorable R&B singles of the '50s and early '60s, including Faye Adams's "Shake a Hand," which topped the R&B charts for 10 weeks in the fall of 1953. Herald and its sister label Ember would issue several ensuing hits, including the Five Satins' "In the Still of the Night," the Silhouettes' "Get a Job," and "Stay" by Maurice Williams & the Zodiacs. Silver even pressed records early on, until he was incapable of meeting demand. Herald and Ember would move uptown to 236 W. 55th St. in 1955, but eventually close in 1964.

OK HARRIS
465 W. Broadway

Primarily an art and photography gallery open between 1969 and 2014, OK Harris was in its earliest days the site of primal shows by electronic punk pioneers Suicide.

JON BON JOVI'S HOME
158 Mercer St.
New Jersey rocker Jon Bon Jovi bought the six-bedroom, 7,837-square-foot penthouse at 158 Mercer for $24 million in 2007. He sold the unit for $34 million in 2015.

GREENE ST. RECORDING
112 Greene St.
Until its closure in 2001, Greene St. Recording was a key studio in early hip-hop, with Run-DMC's "It's Like That" and Kurtis Blow's "The Breaks" among the records mixed and recorded there. Other artists who recorded at Greene St. include Public Enemy, Sonic Youth, New Order, Mos Def & Talib Kweli, De La Soul, A Tribe Called Quest, Ice Cube, the Jungle Brothers, and many others.

DAVID BOWIE'S HOME
285 Lafayette St.
David Bowie and his wife Iman moved into this unassuming building in 1999, after having

lived in the **Essex House (160 Central Park South)** for the previous seven years. The 1886 building was just being converted from lofts to apartments in what had once been an industrial neighborhood. His last two albums, *The Next Day* and *Blackstar*, were recorded at the **Magic Shop (49 Crosby St.)** only a short walk away. When Bowie died on January 10, 2016, the sidewalk in front of his apartment building became a temporary memorial, as thousands came to pay their respects.

MAGIC SHOP
49 Crosby St.
Open between 1988 and 2016, the Magic Shop was located behind a slate-gray door in a nondescript building, the ideal setting for high-profile musicians to come and work away from the watchful eyes of the paparazzi. The studio was featured on an episode of Dave Grohl's HBO series *Sonic Highways*, and over the years it hosted recording and mixing sessions by artists Lou Reed, Sonic Youth, Soul Asylum, and many others. The late David Bowie lived nearby, managing to record his last two albums—*The Next Day* and *Blackstar*—in total secrecy.

THE KITCHEN
59 Wooster St.
Originally opened in the Mercer Arts Center in 1971 as a presentation space for visual artists, the Kitchen's most fertile period for music was during its time on Wooster Street between 1973 and 1986. Largely dedicated to experimental composition and performance, with Talking Heads playing the space in 1976, and avant-garde performers such as Laurie Anderson, Brian Eno, Glenn Branca, and Steve Reich participating in Aluminum Nights in 1981, a 10th anniversary celebration over two days, which also included film and dance. The Kitchen is now located at 512 W. 19th St.

Bowie memorial at 285 Lafayette St.

BAGGIE'S/BAGGY'S
71 Grand St.

Baggie's is a former professional rehearsal studio where Peter Frampton, Santana, and Jimi Hendrix all played. When he was still in high school, Marc Bell, a.k.a., Marky Ramone, used to jam here with friends (Velvert Turner and Scott Fine). Hendrix rehearsed here with the Band of Gypsys in December 1969 ahead of their legendary performances (NYE) at the Fillmore East. In 2002, Dagger Records released an album called *The Baggy's Rehearsal Sessions*, tracks from which had been widely circulated as bootlegs.

THE MUDD CLUB
77 White St.

Described by Michael Musto in the *Village Voice* as "an amazing antidote to the uptown glitz of Studio 54 in the '70s," the Mudd Club's legend has far surpassed its five years of operation.

77 White St.

Opened in 1978 by Steve Mass, Diego Cortez, and Anya Phillips, the club was named for Samuel Mudd, the physician who treated John Wilkes Booth following the assassination of President Abraham Lincoln. It quickly became a hotspot for underground artists and musicians.

With No Wave and such punk groups as Sonic Youth, DNA, the Cramps, and James Chance & the Contortions playing there on a regular basis, the club trafficked in experimental music and the jarring dance floor–filling sounds of post-punk. The Mudd Club lives on in song, earning lyrical mentions from Talking Heads ("Life During Wartime"), Ramones ("The Return of Jackie and Judy"), and Frank Zappa ("Mudd Club").

The Mudd Club wasn't just a live music space, it featured an art gallery curated by Keith Haring, and its stage was used for literary readings, such as performances by Beat legends Allen Ginsberg and William Burroughs.

In 1979, *People* magazine took notice, claiming "For sheer kinkiness, there has been nothing like it since the cabaret scene in 1920s Berlin."

Though it remained open until 1983, some of the Mudd Club's original crowd felt it had already lost its cool cache by then; a plaque placed in 2007 by arts organization Creative Time lists the club's run as lasting only from 1978 through 1981, though it's unclear whether that was a sly editorial comment or merely an error.

SHIMMY DISC
247 W. Broadway

This West Broadway location was the former headquarters of Shimmy Disc, an indie label founded by musician and record producer Mark Kramer. The label released albums by Kramer's own group Bongwater, as well as Galaxie 500, Daniel Johnston, Ween, Boredoms, and Gwar.

TIER 3

225 W. Broadway

Though it lasted a little over a year and a half before closing in December 1980, Tier 3 (a.k.a., TR3), was a live music and arts space that featured shows by the Stimulators, Bush Tetras, A Certain Ratio, the Pop Group, the Slits, the Raincoats, DNA, and what was reportedly the NYC debut of British ska band Madness. Though Sonic Youth played the venue after it reopened as Stillwende, Lee Ranaldo remembered visiting Tier 3 as both a musician and music fan.

WETLANDS PRESERVE

161 Hudson St.

A combined jam-friendly live music venue and center for environmental and social activism, Wetlands Preserve was a living testament to the Woodstock ideal while it was open between the late '80s and 2001, when it closed due to rising rent. Though known as a jam haven—Blues Traveler's front man John Popper once dubbed the club "Sweatglands"—Wetlands has a diverse history, including performances by hip-hop pioneers the Cold Crush Brothers, grunge superstars Pearl Jam, and the first New York City show by BritPop icons Oasis.

The Wetlands Activism Collective is still in operation fighting for environmental causes.

DON HILL'S

511 Greenwich St.

This former club and hangout hosted intimate live performances by Iggy Pop & the Stooges,

the Killers, LCD Soundsystem, Courtney Love, the Horrors, and many others. It was also the home of many popular dance parties, like SqueezeBox, Tiswas, and MisShapes, which moved there after outgrowing their space at 21 7th Ave. S. Don Hill's was named after its founder, the late Don Hill, who previously ran the **Cat Club (76 E. 13th St.)**, which was primarily devoted to metal in the '80s and '90s, but also featured performers from other genres. David Bowie announced his Glass Spider tour with a press conference and four-song set at the Cat Club in March 1987.

PUNK & NO WAVE ON WARREN ST. #1

81 Warren St.

81 Warren St. was a squat and rehearsal space for groups like the Cramps, Teenage Jesus & the Jerks, Richard Hell & the Voidoids, James Chance & the Contortions, and Lester Bangs' first band, with Robert Quine and Jody Harris, who lived in the building.

PUNK & NO WAVE ON WARREN ST. #2

83 Warren St.

Dubbed the "Home For Teenage Dirt," 83 Warren St. around 1977 was a residence for musicians Lydia Lunch, Bradly Field, and Miriam Linna; members of the group Mars; and writer and former WFMU DJ James Marshall.

SONIC YOUTH

For more than 25 years, Sonic Youth were a singular manifestation of the crossroads of the music of downtown Manhattan, a heady mix of aggressiveness and avant-garde, willing and able to stretch their squall into the cosmos.

Though they'd crossed paths before, Sonic Youth really came together when Lee Ranaldo played Noise Fest at **White Columns (325 Spring St.)**, a nine-day music and art event in mid-June 1981 organized by Thurston Moore.

325 Spring St.

"Noise Fest is a reaction to false claims made by the majority of rock/disco club owners and the overground music press," read the press release. "The fact is there are more young, new, experimental rock musicians than ever before."

Ranaldo played guitar with avant-garde composer Glenn Branca on one night and built looped sound collages as part of a duo called Avoidance Behavior with David Linton on another.

"An early version of Sonic Youth played there with Thurston and Kim, and this guy Dave Keay on drums, and a woman named Anne DeMarinis on keyboards," said Ranaldo in 2017. "At some point during that week we began getting friendlier with each other, me

Bob Gruen

Sonic Youth in 1994

and Kim [Gordon] and me and Thurston, and at one point she said, 'You and Thurston should try playing together.' And basically that lineup of Sonic Youth kind of fizzled out, and we met in the gallery space the next week and started banging stuff around, and that pretty much started it. Those were the first Sonic Youth rehearsals, in White Columns."

Ranaldo and Moore had already met, when the former was with the Fluks and the latter the Coachmen. If they didn't sound alike, they were certainly approaching music from a similar headspace.

"When we started playing around New York, we were just looking for like-minded bands," said Ranaldo. "We saw the Coachmen play in this weird little club in Chelsea. They were a similar age, they were trying to do something similar. We started to see each other here and there, and eventually we played a show together at **CBGB (315 Bowery)**, right before both of those bands kind of fizzled out and kind of led to Sonic Youth happening later."

Sonic Youth's history, from their early days until their dissolution was announced in 2011, saw them move comfortably between art galleries and music halls, cunning and commerce, unflinchingly experimental and disarmingly traditional.

On June 17, 1988, the group played at the **Knitting Factory (47 E. Houston St.)**, jamming on tracks that would become their breakthrough album, *Daydream Nation*. They returned to the venue nearly five years later, well after signing with major label Geffen Records, and played skeleton versions of songs that would make up *Experimental Jet Set, Trash and No Star* on an evening dubbed the Esctatic Peace Caravan of Stars, which also included performances from Gordon's Free Kitten, Mosquito, Alan Licht, and a solo set from Ranaldo. It was clear Sonic Youth felt relaxed enough at the Knitting Factory to unwind and let their natural experimental

nature flow in front of a crowded room. But they also felt that way elsewhere, too.

"There were always places where we felt comfortable doing that very thing, experimenting a little bit and trying things out," Ranaldo said. "The Knitting Factory was one of those places. I think we knew the atmosphere was no bullshit and wasn't about anything but the music, really. People were there for the music and it was kind of a musician-centric place. People tended to take you with a certain seriousness there in terms of what you were doing, and yet you could try almost anything you felt you wanted to try there. And we always had new material we wanted to try out somewhere. But we played **Avery Fisher Hall (10 Lincoln Center Plaza, now David Geffen Hall)** in the late '90s, and we were trying out *A Thousand Leaves* material there, an almost fully instrumental concert that night. Whether it was a small venue or a place as big as Avery Fisher, we were trying stuff out."

Brooklyn Academy of Music

Sometimes Sonic Youth would launch these journeys in the unlikeliest of places, such as the **South Street Seaport Atrium (Pier 17)**, where they played a mostly improvisational set on June 13, 1999, alongside a reunion of the New York Art Quartet. In keeping with semi-nautical settings, the group had previously played an almost entirely instrumental set under the Manhattan side of the **Brooklyn Bridge** on June 5, 1997, as part of Music in the Anchorage, curated by Creative Time.

Earlier, Sonic Youth stretched their creativity at **Artists Space (55 Walker)** on December 5, 1986, with a set of improvisational ambient music for a performance of artist Mike Kelley's "Plato's Cave, Rothko's Chapel, Lincoln's Profile"; and they played three instrumentals at former nightclub the **Cooler (416 W. 14th St.)** on March 1, 1997, billed as Male Slut. They even turned up at the **Park Avenue Armory**

84 Eldridge St.

McCarren Park Pool

(643 Park Ave.) for a Marc Jacobs runway show; and in the former **Hiro Ballroom at the Maritime Hotel (371 W. 16th St.)** for a benefit concert event for the Anthology Film Archives, performing in front of the Jonas Mekas film *Walden* on May 19, 2010, with other performers on the night including Lou Reed, Moby, and the Virgins.

MORE SONIC YOUTH

NOTEWORTHY LIVE PERFORMANCES

Stillwende (225 W. Broadway): In one of their first shows with Lee Ranaldo, Sonic Youth played Stillwende in July 1981, a venue of which Ranaldo was already a fan from its previous incarnation, Tier 3.

"When I moved to New York and started living downtown in TriBeCa, that was the nearest club and maybe the hippest club at the time," Ranaldo said. "It was short-lived, but really effective in terms of being a place where a lot of good experimental stuff happened."

Plugg Club (140 W. 24th St.) ⊘: The Plugg Club was a short-lived venue in the loft of former owner of London's Crawdaddy Club, Giorgio Gomelsky. Sonic Youth played the Plugg Club on October 8 and 15 in 1983, and they also rehearsed there.

Sin Club (272 E. 3rd): Sonic Youth played the Sin Club numerous times during its brief existence, including July 22 and September 10, 1983.

"It was just a dingy New York bar in a way," said Ranaldo. "It was conducive to playing at the time because they were letting us."

Folk City (130 W. 3rd St.): Sonic Youth played Folk City several times in the first half of the '80s, perhaps none more memorable than on June 12, 1985, shortly after Steve Shelley became their drummer.

"We did a very, very experimental show there, one of our early legendary shows just after Steve joined," Ranaldo said. "We had Steve playing drums, and we also had Bob Bert playing drums, and we had a couple of other people jumping in on guitar. We had guitars and amps scattered all around the room, and we had all these different screens hung and

Richard Kern was projecting film on all these different screens. At one point Bob Bert starts bashing on drums at the back of the room, and everybody turned around like, 'What the fuck's going on over here?'"

Just Above Midtown/Downtown (178 Franklin St.): Ranaldo's first gig with Sonic Youth reportedly took place at Just Above Midtown/Downtown art gallery sometime in July 1981.

Pyramid Club (101 Ave. A): Bob Bert's last show as the drummer for Sonic Youth took place at Pyramid on June 12, 1985. Steve Shelley, who would take over as drummer shortly thereafter, was reportedly in the crowd.

Great Gildersleeves (331 Bowery): As a warm-up for Noise Fest at White Columns later in the month, Sonic Youth played Great Gildersleeves on June 3, 1981. Ranaldo, who was soon to join Sonic Youth, was part of Glenn Branca's group at Great Gildersleeves on the same bill.

CBGB (315 Bowery): Sonic Youth played CBGB numerous times, including an April 11, 1983, memorial for Patrick Mack on a sizable bill that included hardcore Beastie Boys, Swans, and Murphy's Law. Sonic Youth's last show at CBGB on June 13, 2006, was bass guitarist Mark Ibold's first with the group.

A's (330 Broome St.): The Coachmen, Moore's pre–Sonic Youth band with J. D. King, played at A's on New Year's Eve in 1979, alongside Alan Vega (billed as Alan Suicide), Harry Toledo, and Liquid Idiot.

515 Broadway: The Coachmen played with Harry Toledo at artist Jenny Holzer's loft at 515 Broadway on December 8, 1979.

Anspacher Theater (425 Lafayette St.): Sonic Youth played the Anspacher Theater on January 11, 1982, as part of Poets at the Public. They

were called Sonic Youth Band in a preview listing of the event in the *New York Times*.

Botany Talk House (803 6th Ave.): The Coachmen, Moore's pre–Sonic Youth band, played Botany Talk House numerous times in the late '70s. This is where Ranaldo first met Moore.

Danceteria (30 W. 21st St.): Sonic Youth played Danceteria a few times, including sharing the bill with Swans on June 30, 1984.

Charas New Assembly Hall (350 E. 10th St.): Sonic Youth played an August 1983 benefit for the Vancouver Five, an anti-capitalist group who'd been arrested for bombing three locations of a chain of porn shops accused of selling snuff films.

Peppermint Lounge (100 5th Ave.): Sonic Youth and Necros played the Peppermint Lounge on February 15, 1985, with the group returning once more that July.

Cat Club (76 E. 13th St.): On October 22, 1987, Sonic Youth played the Cat Club with Pussy Galore.

The Ritz/Webster Hall (125 E. 11th St.): Sonic Youth first played 125 E. 11th St. when it was still called the Ritz on October 28, 1988, as part of their *Daydream Nation* tour. They last played Webster Hall as part of their *Rather Ripped* tour on February 16, 2007.

Irving Plaza (17 Irving Pl.): Sonic Youth first played Irving Plaza with fIREHOSE and Frightwig on November 22, 1986.

Roseland Ballroom (239 W. 52nd St.)⊘: Sonic Youth closed out their Pretty Fucking Dirty tour at Roseland on October 24, 1992, with support from the Jon Spencer Blues Explosion and Boredoms.

Academy (234 W. 43rd St.): Sonic Youth first played the Academy with the Breeders and St. Johnny on June 21 and 22, 1993.

Terminal 5 (610 W. 56th St.): Sonic Youth played Terminal 5 with Dinosaur Jr. and Cold Cave on November 21, 2009.

Central Park SummerStage: On July 4, 1992, Sonic Youth played a free show at Central Park SummerStage alongside Sun Ra & His Intergalactic Arkestra. They returned to play a pair of shows in late July 2003 supporting Wilco.

Bowery Ballroom (6 Delancey St.): Sonic Youth debuted material from their *SYR4* release at the Bowery Ballroom on April 1, 1999, also playing music by Yoko Ono, John Cage Takehisa Kosugi, and other experimental composers.

Apple SoHo (103 Prince St.): Sonic Youth performed a "secret" gig of songs from their final album, *The Eternal*, at the Apple Store in SoHo on June 9, 2009.

Anthology Film Archives (32 2nd Ave.): Sonic Youth performed an improvised score for a Stan Brakhage benefit at the Anthology Film Archives on April 12, 2003.

Spirit (530 W. 27th St.): Sonic Youth joined Blondie and the Strokes for Be Well: the Ramones Beat on Cancer, a benefit for the Cedars-Sinai Cancer Research Center and the Lymphoma Research Foundation organized by Johnny Ramone. The event took place on October 8, 2004, just weeks after Ramone's death.

Hammerstein Ballroom (311 W. 34th St.): Sonic Youth first played the Hammerstein Ballroom on February 27, 1999, with support from the David S. Ware Quartet.

Wollman Auditorium, Ferris Booth Hall, Columbia University (116th St. and Broadway) ⊘: Sonic Youth and Royal Trux played a students-only gig in Columbia University's Wollman Auditorium on Friday, September 11, 1992.

Beacon Theatre (2124 Broadway): Sonic Youth played an AIDS benefit hosted by filmmaker John Waters at the Beacon Theatre on December 2, 1994.

United Palace (4140 Broadway): Sonic Youth played the United Palace on July 3, 2009, with the Entrance Band supporting.

Subway (63rd Dr./Rego Park subway station, Queens): Sonic Youth played the short-lived Subway with Das Damen on June 8, 1985. The club was located on a lower level of the 63rd Drive subway station in Rego Park, Queens.

La Ojeva Negra (3438 38th St., Queens): Sonic Youth performed at the former La Ojeva Negra on April 10, 2005.

Trans-Pecos (915 Wyckoff Ave., Queens): Since Sonic Youth's split, Lee Ranaldo has played solo acoustic shows at Trans-Pecos, a venue and community resource center in Queens.

St. Ann's Warehouse (45 Water St., Brooklyn): Sonic Youth—minus Ranaldo—played a benefit for poet and Fugs co-founder Tuli Kupferberg at St. Ann's Warehouse on January 22, 2010.

Northsix (66 N. 6th St., Brooklyn): Sonic Youth played DIY-indie club Northsix on April 12, 2005. By the time they returned to the venue on November 24 and 25, 2009, it had been renamed as Music Hall of Williamsburg.

Union Pool (484 Union Ave.): Lee Ranaldo has played numerous shows at this venue located in a former pool supply shop.

McCarren Park Pool (776 Lorimer St., Brooklyn): Sonic Youth played McCarren Park Pool three times, including the final show on August 30, 2008, before renovations to turn it back into a public swimming area began.

Brooklyn Academy of Music (30 Lafayette Ave., Brooklyn): Sonic Youth played the Brooklyn Academy of Music during the four-night celebration of choreographer Merce Cunningham's 90th birthday that took place from April 16 through 19, 2009.

Prospect Park Bandshell (141 Prospect Park West, Brooklyn): Sonic Youth's final show in New York City took place at the Prospect Park Bandshell on July 31, 2010.

NOTEWORTHY RECORDING LOCATIONS

Echo Canyon (47 Murray St., 4th floor): Sonic Youth began renting a space at 47 Murray St. in the mid-'90s. They were there for over a decade, rehearsing and recording albums *A Thousand Leaves* (1998), *NYC Ghosts & Flowers* (2000), *Murray Street* (2002), and *Sonic Nurse* (2004) there.

"We took our earnings from *Lollapalooza* (1995) and bought a professional desk and tape recorder and we needed a space to put it," Ranaldo said. "It really became this kind of clubhouse for us, the fourth floor at 47 Murray St. for a long, long time."

Radio City Music Hall Studios (55 W. 50th St., 7th floor): Sonic Youth's eponymous debut EP was recorded at Radio City Music Hall Studios between December 1981 and January 1982.

Fun City (340 E. 22nd St.): Sonic Youth's first full album, *Confusion is Sex*, was recorded in the basement studio of co-producer Wharton Tiers during late 1982 and early 1983. The band dubbed the studio Wharton's Palace of Confusion.

"We may have called it Wharton's Palace of Confusion on some record because we didn't like the idea of calling it Fun City," said Ranaldo. "Back then we didn't smile in pictures."

Greene St. Recording (112 Greene St.): Sonic Youth recorded *Daydream Nation* (1988) and some of *Goo* (1990) at Greene St. Recording.

Sorcerer Sound Recording Studios (19 Mercer St.): Sonic Youth recorded some of their 1990 album *Goo*, their first for Geffen Records, at Sorcerer Sound.

Waterworks Recording (408 W. 14th St.): In November 1989, Sonic Youth entered Waterworks, a studio run by Jim Waters in the Meatpacking District, to record demos for *Goo*, their first album for Geffen Records.

Sear Sound Recording (235 W. 46th St.): Sonic Youth recorded *Sister* at Sear Sound in the spring of 1987 when it was still on West 46th Street. It relocated three years later to 353 W. 48th St., where the group worked on albums *Dirty* (1992), *Experimental Jet Set, Trash and No Star* (1994), and *Rather Ripped* (2006).

BC Studio (232 3rd St., Brooklyn): Sonic Youth recorded *Bad Moon Rising* (1985) and *EVOL* (1986) at Martin Bisi's BC Studio, located in an old can factory in Brooklyn. Moore dubbed it "Before Christ Studio" on *Bad Moon Rising*.

"It was a very unorthodox studio," said Ranaldo. "The control room was in the middle of the playing room without walls around it. We worked there because it was conducive. He was up for experimenting with us."

OTHER NOTEWORTHY LOCATIONS

Mike Gira's Bunker on 6th and B (northeast corner, likely 93 Ave. B): "It was like a crazy bunker where we rehearsed for a while in I would say, '83, '84, '85, somewhere in there," said Ranaldo. "I know we were working on the song "Death Valley '69" in there with Lydia [Lunch]."

262 Mott St.: Prior to moving into Echo Canyon (47 Murray St.), Sonic Youth's longtime rehearsal space was three floors below street level at 262 Mott St., on the same floor (and possibly in the same room) that the Beastie Boys set up shop and recorded their 1998 album *Hello Nasty*.

"On Mott St. we'd bought our own 8-track machine and an inexpensive mixing desk and a couple of cheap out-port pieces that Wharton [Tiers] advised us on," said Ranaldo. "We did the demos for *Washing Machine* there."

Washing Machine debuted in 1995.

178 Duane St.: Lee Ranaldo lived in an apartment at 178 Duane St. for all of the '80s.

84 Eldridge St.: Kim Gordon and Thurston Moore lived at 84 Eldridge St. in the '80s.

LOWER EAST SIDE

KNITTING FACTORY

47 E. Houston St./74 Leonard St./361 Metropolitan Ave., Brooklyn

Founded in 1987 by Michael Dorf and Louis Spitzer, the Knitting Factory was opened in a disused Avon Products office on East Houston Street as an art gallery and performance space with an eye on the avant-garde. A record label also grew out of the nascent club.

Early performances at the Knitting Factory during its time here include Sonic Youth, Yo La Tengo, They Might Be Giants, Sun Ra, the Lounge Lizards, and the Go-Betweens.

The increased popularity of the Knitting Factory precipitated a move to a larger 400-person-capacity space on Leonard Street,

where it remained for the next fifteen years. Luna, Bush Tetras, the Wedding Present, Cornershop, Lou Reed, Elliott Smith, Silver Apples, and many others played shows here.

In an effort to follow the trail of young concertgoers, the Knitting Factory moved to Metropolitan Avenue in Brooklyn in 2009, opening a 300-person-capacity venue in the former Luna Lounge, a bar that had followed a similar path a few years earlier. Japandroids, the Lemonheads, Beach Slang, and other indie groups have appeared in the Brooklyn Knitting Factory, which has a front bar space that often features live alternative comedy shows.

The Knitting Factory expanded its operations into now-shuttered locations in Los Angeles, California, and Reno, Nevada, as well as still-successful venues in Spokane, Washington, and Boise, Idaho.

WILLIAM BURROUGHS BUNKER

222 Bowery

William Burroughs lived here from 1974 through 1981 in a windowless three-room chamber that was once the locker room in an old YMCA building. It was cheap and allowed him to fire his pistols without bothering anyone. Burroughs' bunker was within walking distance of CBGB and other downtown clubs he frequented, as well as near several heroin dealers in the neighborhood. It also became a hangout for the chosen few he allowed to enter, such as Patti Smith, Lou Reed, Mick Jagger, Andy Warhol, and Frank Zappa. In 1981, Burroughs moved to Lawrence, Kansas, but his friend John Giorno took over the space and kept it preserved.

BOWERY BALLROOM
6 Delancey St.

Completed just prior to the stock market crash in 1929, the Bowery Ballroom lay dormant until the mid-'40s when it was taken over by a retail store. Various other businesses cycled in and out of the space until it was converted into a live music venue in 1998. With a capacity of 575 people, it remains a popular destination for touring musicians, hosting shows over the years by the White Stripes, Queens of the Stone Age, Nine Inch Nails, Lorde, R.E.M., and many others.

Bowery Ballroom

ARLENE'S GROCERY
95 Stanton St.

Opened on the site of a former grocery store, Arlene's Grocery is a bar and 150-person-capacity live music venue that hosted early shows by the Strokes, Arcade Fire, Jeff Buckley, and Lana Del Rey.

LUNA LOUNGE
171 Ludlow St./361 Metropolitan Ave., Brooklyn

Opened in 1995 on Ludlow Street, Luna Lounge was a bar and live music venue and home to the weekly Eating It alternative comedy night. Music at Luna Lounge was free, with groups like the Strokes, Interpol, the National, and Nada Surf all playing there early in their careers. Elliott Smith was also a frequent patron on Ludlow Street.

Luna Lounge closed on Ludlow after a developer bought the building in 2005 with the intention of knocking it down to build a larger structure in its place. Luna Lounge reopened on Metropolitan Avenue in Brooklyn in 2007, with shows by the Black Angels, the Meat Puppets, Melvins, and others. Luna Lounge closed for good in 2008, their Brooklyn space now occupied by the Knitting Factory.

MAX FISH
178 Ludlow St./120 Orchard St.

Originally opened in 1989 at 178 Ludlow, dive bar Max Fish has since relocated to 120 Orchard St., where if it hasn't retained its indie rock star clientele, it still boasts reasonably priced drinks, charmingly worn seating, and eclectic artwork. Jaleel Bunton of TV on the Radio used to work there. In Lizzy Goodman's *Meet Me in the Bathroom*, Matt Berninger of the National claimed the group used to walk from their 61st Street apartment to hang out at Max Fish when

they first arrived in New York City because they were too afraid to take the subway.

MERCURY LOUNGE
217 E. Houston St.
Opened in 1993 on the site of a former tombstone dealership, Mercury Lounge is a 250-person-capacity venue beyond a long bar, hosting independent music shows as well as special gigs by everyone from Katy Perry to Ed Sheeran to Coldplay's Chris Martin, who played a benefit for Manhattan homeless shelter the Bowery Mission in 2015. Ryan Gentles quit his job booking gigs at Mercury Lounge to become the manager of the Strokes.

ABC NO RIO
156 Rivington St.
Since 1989 art gallery and community center ABC No Rio has hosted hardcore and punk matinees on Saturday afternoons, picking up the slack in the scene a month after CBGB discontinued their matinee series. The bands are independent and must not promote racism, sexism, homophobia, or other prejudices. As of 2017, ABC No Rio's home is being demolished and rebuilt, but the matinee series is continuing in a variety of other spaces until it can return to 156 Rivington.

LADY GAGA'S HOME
176 Stanton St., Apt. #4A
Lady Gaga (a.k.a., Stefani Germanotta) lived in an apartment at 176 Stanton St. for three years as she was making her way through the NYC nightclub scene as a performer, reportedly writing many of the songs that would make up her 2008 debut album, *The Fame*, there. According to a 2010 *New York Magazine* profile, her apartment featured a futon for a sofa and a Yoko Ono record hung on the wall over her bed.

176 Stanton St.

THE STROKES

Cody Smyth

The Strokes in front of the Music Building, spring 2001

Though there's nothing to suggest they asked for it, the Strokes were shouldered with the honor or burden of saving rock & roll in the early aughts, a hype almost within moments of their debut EP for *Rough Trade* being released that might have felled a group of lesser mettle. New York City hadn't exactly been fallow ground since the heyday of CBGB, it's just that until the Strokes, the rest of the world wasn't paying all that much attention.

Comprised of five handsome guys with an eye for downtown thrift-store style and a way around a guitar riff, the Strokes were seen as something of an antidote to rap metal and the dying embers of the '90s alt rock explosion. Their debut album, *Is This It*, only hit #33 on the Billboard 200, but its impact went much deeper.

Lycee Francais de New York

THE STROKES

The Strokes recorded *Is This It* in the spring of 2001 at **Transporterraum (154 E. 2nd St.),** a studio in the East Village, where a year earlier they'd cut the demos that became their debut EP *The Modern Age*. They once again worked with producer and studio head Gordon Raphael, who helped define the group's early sound. The studio and control room at Transporterraum were bathed in purple, red, and blue, looking like a mix of an opulent sheikh's tent and a toddler's birthday cake. According to the Transporterraum website, the colors, reflective glitter, lava lamps, and Christmas lights were meant to inspire creativity in the way a sterile recording studio could not.

The songs had been fine-tuned on stage at venues such as **Arlene's Grocery (95 Stanton St.), Luna Lounge (171 Ludlow St.), Under Acme** (9 Great Jones St.), **Baby Jupiter (170 Orchard St.), Orange Bear (47 Murray St.),** and **Don Hill's (511 Greenwich St.),** and the group hoped the energy of their live shows would come through on the album.

The recording of *Is This It* was collaborative, with Raphael often taking his cues from the band in the moment, mixing on the fly to quickly give them a sense of what a song might sound like to fans, qualities that reportedly

The former Transporterraum

helped convince a skeptical label intermediary checking in mid-recording that they were on the right track. Upon release, critics praised *Is This It* for somehow managing to simultaneously be of its moment and classic, a feat achieved in a studio where Raphael had fears of being evicted during the recording.

86 E. 10th St.

MORE OF THE STROKES

NOTEWORTHY LIVE PERFORMANCES

Spiral (244 E. Houston): Not long after the Strokes added the final piece of their puzzle in guitarist Albert Hammond Jr., they played their first show at Spiral on September 14, 1999.

Mercury Lounge (217 E. Houston): With their local popularity building, the Strokes played a brief residency at the Mercury Lounge in December 2000. Ryan Gentles, who worked as a booker for Mercury Lounge, eventually quit his job to become the group's manager.

Madison Square Garden (4 Pennsylvania Ave.): The Strokes played the Theater at Madison Square Garden on October 30, 2003, returning on April 1, 2011, to a sold-out show in the significantly larger Madison Square Garden proper.

Radio City Music Hall (1260 Avenue of the Americas): The Strokes played Radio City Music Hall on August 15, 2002, with support from the White Stripes, whose frontman Jack White joined the group for a blistering guitar solo on "New York City Cops."

Randall's Island: On August 14, 2004, the Strokes performed at Little Steven's Underground Garage Festival, taking the stage just prior to a headline set by the reunited Stooges. The group returned to Randall's Island for the Governors Ball, where they headlined the first of three days of the festival on June 3, 2016.

NOTEWORTHY RECORDING LOCATIONS

TMF Studios (36 E. 12th St., 2nd floor): The Strokes rekindled their relationship with producer Gordon Raphael to record their sophomore album, 2003's *Room on Fire*, at TMF Studios.

Avatar Studios (441 W. 53rd St.): The Strokes entered Avatar Studios in early 2010 to record their fourth album, *Angles*.

Music Building (585 8th Ave.): The Strokes came together in room 203 of the Music Building, especially after guitarist Albert Hammond Jr. joined after a rehearsal in the late '90s. They continued using it as their home base even after their initial swell of popularity in the early 2000s.

OTHER NOTEWORTHY LOCATIONS

Dwight School (291 Central Park West): Guitarist Nick Valensi, singer Julian Casablancas, and drummer Fabrizio Moretti met while attending this exclusive college preparatory school on the Upper West Side.

Lycée Français de New York (505 E. 75th St.): Julian Casablancas and bass guitarist Nikolai Fraiture met as elementary school students at this school, which follows a French curriculum of study.

2A (25 Ave. A): The Strokes regularly hung out at 2A in their early days, a corner bar with a rock & roll aesthetic and plentiful windows ideal for people-watching.

352 Bowery: In anticipation of their headlining set at Governors Ball, the Strokes opened the No Room NYC popup shop and gallery at 352 Bowery between May 30 and June 5, 2016.

The Rutherford Building (305 2nd Ave.): Julian Casablancas and Albert Hammond Jr. shared an apartment here in the early aughts.

Wiz Kid Management (86 East 10th St., #1): The band's managerial headquarters during their dizzying early days and right up through mid-2015 was the elevated storefront offices of Wiz Kid Management. It has since relocated to 263 Bowery following a merger with C3 Presents.

 BROOKLYN

SADOWSKY GUITARS
20 Jay St. #5C, Brooklyn

Master Luthier Roger Sadowsky has operated this shop since 1979, with his guitars used by Lou Reed, John Fogerty, Paul Simon, Prince, Walter Becker, and others.

NORMAN MAILER'S HOME
142 Columbia Heights, Brooklyn

After seeing the Ramones for the first time at CBGB in late 1979, writer Norman Mailer befriended *Punk Magazine* writer Legs McNeil, who was a frequent guest at Mailer's epic, nautically themed Brooklyn residence, with sprawling gangways and rope ladders, and a complex Lego cityscape on the first floor. McNeil was managing Shrapnel, a punk band with a combat aesthetic, and Mailer used to book them for parties at his house. On one such occasion in the spring of 1980, Mailer and McNeil wrestled on the floor before guests such as Shelly Winters, Kurt Vonnegut, former light heavyweight fighter José Torres, and Woody Allen.

"Woody Allen hid in the bathroom all night," McNeil remembered, "And people keep knocking on the door because they had to pee or do coke or whatever, but Woody wouldn't open the door. Finally, he opened the door a little and peeked out, and [Ramones artistic director] Arturo Vega opened the bathroom door all the way and said to Woody, 'Boy, you really are shy, aren't you?' Then Arturo closed the bathroom door on him, in disgust."

BROOKLYN PARAMOUNT THEATER
1 University Plaza, Brooklyn

The '50s have often been described as a kind of golden age in Brooklyn history. The end of World War II precipitated the Boomer generation, and the borough was filled with cultural diversity, young families, and lots of teenagers. As rock & roll entered the nation's consciousness, there was no greater impresario than DJ Alan Freed. His rock & roll shows at Christmas and Easter from 1955 through 1960 made the Brooklyn Paramount the most exciting place on earth. Kids camped out overnight and waited on lines around the block for the privilege of bearing witness to some of the most incredible lineups in music history. Freed's shows regularly featured national stars such as Fats Domino,

The former Paramount

Chuck Berry, Jerry Lee Lewis, Little Richard, Ray Charles, Buddy Holly, and the Everly Brothers. Regional groups like the Harptones; the Cadillacs; the Chantels; and the Teenagers, featuring Frankie Lymon, also performed there.

Freed positioned himself, of course, as the biggest star, the High Lama of Rock & Roll. But when his star faded due to the infamous payola scandal, TV host Clay Cole became his interim successor. The shows remained hugely popular, but the building was sold to Long Island University in 1962, had its theater regalia removed, and was converted for use as a gymnasium and auditorium. It still plays that role today.

BROOKLYN FOX THEATRE

20 Flatbush Ave., Brooklyn

When Alan Freed was forced to abandon his popular live shows in 1959, WINS DJ Murray "The K" Kaufman eventually took over. The shows continued at the Paramount until 1961, moved to the Academy of Music in Manhattan, and finally to the Brooklyn Fox from 1962 to 1967. For $2.50, Brooklyn teens could see more than a dozen top acts at the popular shows, which easily packed the 4,000-seat theater at Christmas, Easter, and Labor Day. A small sampling of some of the performers who played the Fox during the '60s includes the Shirelles, the Four Seasons, the Ronettes, Jackie Wilson, Dionne Warwick, the Coasters, Stevie Wonder, Little Anthony & the Imperials, Jan & Dean, the Miracles, Jay & the Americans, Marvin Gaye, the Supremes, Martha & the Vandellas, Dusty Springfield, the Shangri-Las, the Righteous Brothers, the Marvelettes, and the Temptations.

HAVE GUITAR WILL TRAVEL

368 Livingston St., Brooklyn

Guitar legend Bo Diddley shot the cover photo for his third album, 1960's *Have Guitar Will Travel*, on Livingston Street in Brooklyn.

JAY-Z'S HOME

560 State St., #10C, Brooklyn

Hip-hop giant Jay-Z lived in a two-bedroom duplex at 560 State St. in the late '90s after his career as an MC began to take off.

O'CONNOR'S BAR

39 5th Ave., Brooklyn

The late singer-songwriter Elliott Smith lived in Brooklyn in the late '90s, singing about the F train and spending time in a booth at

O'Connor's Bar, drinking, writing songs, and playing cribbage. Smith died in 2003, but his beloved O'Connor's persevered as a dive bar until 2011, when it was renovated and reopened as McMahon's Public House.

HOYT-SCHERMERHORN STREETS SUBWAY STATION
Brooklyn

Accessible by the A, C, and G subway lines, Hoyt-Schermerhorn opened in 1936 to serve the Fulton Street line's local and express trains. It's perhaps most famous as the location of Michael Jackson's video for his 1987 single "Bad." The video, directed by Martin Scorsese and released in both single-length and sprawling 18-minute versions, featured Wesley Snipes as the antagonist and a tightly choreographed dance battle on the wide level connecting the platforms. "Weird Al" Yankovic shot his parody video, "Fat," in the same station.

Jackson was already familiar with Hoyt-Schermerhorn, having shot a scene from 1978 film *The Wiz* there. The platforms and stairs were designed to look like the Yellow Brick Road for the movie.

BC STUDIO
232 3rd St., Brooklyn

Founded by Martin Bisi with Bill Laswell in the former American Can Company factory near the Gowanus Canal, BC Studio has been at the center of numerous key recordings over the years, perhaps non more groundbreaking than Herbie Hancock's genre-busting 1983 single "Rockit," which introduced scratching and other turntablist techniques to a wide audience. Other artists who've recorded at BC Studio include Sonic Youth, Swans, the Dresden Dolls, Violent Femmes, and Brian Eno, whom Bisi credited with funding the opening of the studio in 1979.

BROOKLYN BOWL
61 Wythe Ave., Brooklyn

Opened in Williamsburg in 2009, Brooklyn Bowl is a bowling alley, bar, restaurant, and 600-person-capacity live music venue. Mac DeMarco, Yeah Yeah Yeahs, Elvis Costello & the Roots, Living Colour, Animal Collective, and many other artists have played live while bowlers knocked down pins nearby. Roots drummer and bandleader Questlove hosts a popular weekly Thursday-night residency at Brooklyn Bowl called Bowl Train, sometimes incorporating a specific theme dedicated to an artist or genre in his DJ sets.

ROUGH TRADE NYC
64 N. 9th St., Brooklyn

US outpost of the longtime London indie record shop and label, Rough Trade NYC sells mostly new vinyl and CDs, with a modest used selection of the former. They also stock books, have a small coffee kiosk, a multipurpose

Music Hall of Williamsburg

have played the 550-person-capacity space, including Bon Iver, Franz Ferdinand, Grizzly Bear, Blur, Yeah Yeah Yeahs, Iggy Pop & the Stooges, and Sleater-Kinney.

HEADGEAR RECORDING
234 Wythe Ave., Brooklyn
Headgear Recording was a key indie recording studio where Yeah Yeah Yeahs cut their first album and David Bowie recorded guest vocals on "Province" with TV on the Radio. It later became a J Crew, which members of TV on the Radio have lamented both on stage and in print interviews.

digital lounge, gallery space, and an intimate dedicated live room with shows almost daily. Among the artists who've played special shows at Rough Trade NYC's 250-person-capacity venue are Television, the Feelies, Wilco, Gorillaz, and former Oasis singer Liam Gallagher.

MUSIC HALL OF WILLIAMSBURG/NORTHSIX
66 N. 6th St., Brooklyn
Originally open between 2001 and 2007 as independent music venue Northsix, Music Hall of Williamsburg has been one of the changing neighborhood's most enduring live music venues. During its time as Northsix, the venue was seen as the location of the opening scene of the 2003 film *School of Rock,* as well as hosting shows by the National; My Morning Jacket; Animal Collective; and in 2003, what would be the last three Elliott Smith shows in NYC.

Northsix was acquired by Bowery Presents in 2007, reopening after a remodel that year and staying in operation ever since. Many artists

NICK ZINNER'S HOME ⊘
249 Metropolitan Ave., Brooklyn
Yeah Yeah Yeahs founder and guitarist Nick Zinner lived with a Brooklyn-appropriate amount of roommates at 249 Metropolitan before the group made it.

WARSAW
261 Driggs Ave., Brooklyn
Located inside the Polish National Home, Warsaw first began hosting rock shows in 2001. It remains a thriving live music venue with a cavernous main hall, a bar that serves Polish beer, and a small concession stand where the slogan "Where pierogies meet punk" regularly comes to life. Recent shows at the Warsaw

include Primal Scream, the Damned, Teenage Fanclub, Warpaint, and Weezer.

BROOKLYN STEEL
319 Frost St., Brooklyn
Brooklyn Steel is a 1,900-person-capacity hall with an industrial vibe, opening in April 2017 with a five-night residency by LCD Soundsystem and featuring shows by the Decemberists, Father John Misty, Slowdive, Ride, and others in just their first few months of operation. LCD Soundsystem returned in December 2017 for a 10-night run of shows.

DOC POMUS' HOME ⊘
75 Manhattan Ave., Brooklyn
Jerome Felder grew up here in Williamsburg, the son of Jewish immigrants. As a child he contracted polio and walked with crutches for most of his life. As a teenager he developed an intense love of the blues and created the moniker Doc Pomus when he sang in the Village and at **Club Baby Grand (319 W. 125th St.)** in Harlem. He eventually recorded over a dozen singles, including "My Good Pott" for Savoy and "Blues Without Booze" for Apollo, with little success. His friend and fellow Brooklynite Otis Blackwell introduced him to Herb Abramson at Atlantic Records, where he had the opportunity to write songs for others, most notably "Lonely Avenue" for Ray Charles in 1956. Pomus had trouble writing for the lucrative teenage market, however, and eventually partnered with Mort

Shuman, a college student who was dating his cousin. The pair would ultimately have great success teaming up for several classic hits of the late '50s and early '60s, including "Save the Last Dance For Me" and "This Magic Moment" for the Drifters, "A Teenager in Love" for Dion & the Belmonts, and several hits for Elvis Presley, such as "Little Sister" and "Surrender." In his later years, Pomus lived in Manhattan in an 11th-floor apartment at 253 W. 72nd St., where he continued to write songs with multiple collaborators, including Doctor John and Willy DeVille.

MARCY HOUSES
648 Park Ave., Brooklyn
In the mid-20th century, a series of six-story buildings called the Marcy Houses were built as part of the New York City Housing Authority's projects. Jay-Z (524 Marcy Ave., Apt. 5C) and Memphis Bleek are among its famous former residents.

BIGGIE SMALLS

226 St. James Place, Brooklyn

Biggie Smalls grew up as Christopher Wallace
in a modest apartment with his mother, Voletta
Wallace, at 226 St. James Pl.

Orient Temple

**Corner of Quincy Street and Bedford Avenue.,
Brooklyn**
Mural of Biggie Smalls, "King of NY," on the side
of a deli. It was painted by muralists Naoufal
"Rocko" Alaoui and Scott "Zimer" Zimmerman.
**Christopher "Biggie" Wallace Courts (Crispus
Attucks Playground, 1030 Fulton St., Brooklyn**
The renovated basketball courts at Crispus
Attucks Playground were renamed to honor the
memory of Christopher Wallace, a.k.a. "Biggie
Smalls," in August 2017.

226 St. James Place

Orient Temple (197 St. James Pl., Brooklyn)

Christopher Wallace was given the unofficial
title of the Mayor of St. James Place because of
his vocal prowess at Soul Power parties at the
Orient Temple.

Met Food (991 Fulton St., Brooklyn)

Christopher Wallace, a.k.a. the Notorious B.I.G.
and Biggie Smalls, bagged groceries at this
Met Food for spare change as a young boy. The
grocery store is still there, but it's a Key Food
now.

STINGER CLUB
241 Grand St., Brooklyn

In 2005, TV on the Radio played a residency in this former club that was bathed in red light. According to the group's lead singer Tunde Adebimpe in Lizzy Goodman's *Meet Me in the Bathroom,* the bar had a sign that read "Get naked, you get a free shot. Oral sex, you get three free shots. Fuck on the bar, you get an open tab."

It was during the residency the group was approached by Jaleel Bunton, who said they needed him; he was initially their drummer but has since moved over to bass guitar during live shows.

BOYS HIGH SCHOOL
832 Marcy Ave., Brooklyn

In 1955 a group of students at Boys High School, including Anthony Gourdine, formed a vocal harmony group called the Duponts. They released one single on the tiny Winley label with little success. They released another, "Prove

It Tonight" on another label in 1957, but that didn't sell either. In 1957, Gourdine left and joined another local group, the Chesters. They would release one single with that name before hooking up with End Records and becoming Little Anthony & the Imperials. Their first single, "Tears on My Pillow," was a huge hit in 1958. They followed it with "Shimmy Shimmy Ko Ko Bop," another big hit, in 1960. Anthony would attempt a solo career but return to the group by 1963. They moved a reconstituted Imperials, which consisted of Gourdine, Ernest Wright, Clarence Collins, and Sammy Strain, to the new DCP label and recorded a string of highly successful singles well into the '60s, including "Goin' Out of My Head" and "Hurt So Bad." They would have several more hits and appear on the *Ed Sullivan Show* twice, in 1965 and 1970. After a hiatus in the '80s, the group reunited and continue to tour to this day. They were inducted into the Rock & Roll Hall of Fame in 2009.

Boys High School

BIRDEL'S RECORD STORE
535 Nostrand Ave., Brooklyn

Opened in 1944, Birdel's Record Store was a longtime staple of the Bed-Stuy community, frequented by music fans and performers alike. Birdel's, which was owned by Joe Long from 1967 until its closure in 2011, was a favorite destination of a young Christopher Wallace, who later became hip-hip legend the Notorious B.I.G. Birdel's was a relatively small shop with tens of thousands of vinyl albums and singles and a handful of CDs, focusing primarily on soul, oldies, and gospel.

The stretch of Nostrand Avenue in front of the former shop was officially renamed Birdel's Records Way, with a sign at the intersection of Nostrand Avenue and Fulton Street.

CLUB BABY GRAND BROOKLYN
1274 Fulton St., Brooklyn
The Brooklyn branch of the established Harlem nightclub featured many top black performers of the '50s, including several jazz and R&B luminaries. Comedian Redd Foxx was also a regular here long before his ascent to stardom in TV's *Sanford and Son.*

ESSENCE
1662 Atlantic Ave., Brooklyn
An unassuming and comfortable neighborhood bar that serves southern American fare and live music, Essence is perhaps best known as

the venue where Daptone Records co-founder Gabriel Roth first spotted soul singer Charles Bradley performing his James Brown revue as Black Velvet. Daptone signed Bradley under his own name, leading to a series of critically and commercially successful records.

THE HALSEY HOUSE
615 Halsey St., Brooklyn
Known colloquially as "The Halsey House," this once-dilapidated house with a leaky roof was home to Dave Longstreth of Dirty Projectors and Ezra Koenig of Vampire Weekend in the mid-2000s. Dirty Projectors' 2007 album,

615 Halsey St.

Charles Bradley performing in 2012

Rise Above, a reinterpretation of Black Flag's *Damaged,* was recorded and produced by Grizzly Bear's Chris Taylor at the Halsey House.

HARRY NILSSON'S HOME
762 Jefferson Ave., Brooklyn
Singer-songwriter Harry Nilsson lived in a small, six-room apartment on the top floor of this three-story building for the first ten years of his life, he and his mother sharing the apartment with his half-sister, maternal grandparents, two uncles, an aunt, and a cousin. Nilsson's commercial peak occurred in the late '60's and early '70's with hits like "Everybody's Talkin','" "Without You," and "Coconut," as well as his animated musical children's fable *The Point!,* which included the tune "Me and My Arrow" in 1971.

DAPTONE'S HOUSE OF SOUL
115 Troutman St., Brooklyn
Founded by Gabriel Roth and Neal Sugarman, Daptone Records routinely delivers on its promise of producing the New Sound of Old Soul from the House of Soul, a former row house that was converted into a recording studio and label headquarters. From the late Sharon Jones & the Dap-Kings to Charles Bradley & His Extraordinaires to Antibalas and beyond, Daptone has used its analog studio to create some of the most heralded soul music in the past few decades. Keep an eye on the label's various social media accounts, as they sometimes hold stoop sales where you can find great deals on records and merchandise.

ERASMUS HALL HIGH SCHOOL
899-925 Flatbush Ave., Brooklyn
Marc Bell, later to become Marky Ramone, went to Brooklyn's Erasmus Hall High School. The school, founded in the late-18th century as Erasmus Hall Academy, was closed by the city in 1994 due to underperforming academic scores. It reopened as Erasmus Hall Educational Campus, where it houses five separate schools. In addition to Marc Bell, other notable alum

Daptone's House of Soul

Erasmus Hall High School

include legendary Paradise Garage DJ Larry Levan; singer-songwriter Neil Diamond (who left in 1956 and graduated from Abraham Lincoln High, also in Brooklyn); singer-actress Barbra Streisand; William "Kedar" Massenburg, former president of Motown Records; songwriter and producer Jeff Barry; Dave Getz, drummer in Big Brother and the Holding Company; Joseph Barbera, cartoonist and co-founder of Hanna-Barbera; mystery novelist Mickey Spillane; and Moe Howard, de facto leader of the Three Stooges, who dropped out of the school in 1915 after just two months.

KINGS THEATRE
1027 Flatbush Ave., Brooklyn
Opened in 1929, the Loew's Kings Theatre, as it was originally known, initially struck a balance between showing movies and showcasing vaudeville acts, with a stage show, orchestra, and pipe organ used for both. With vaudeville's rapid decline over the next few years, the Kings Theatre operated primarily as a cinema from the early '30s until its closure in 1977.

Following years of neglect and ruin, the building underwent an extensive renovation, reopening on February 3, 2015, with much of its opulence restored. Diana Ross performed during a gala event at the grand reopening. Nick Cave & the Bad Seeds, Ronnie Spector, Father John Misty, Dion, the Beach Boys, TV on the Radio, Ringo Starr and his All-Starr Band, and Wilco are just some of the performers who've played the Kings Theatre since its rededication.

L'AMOUR ⃠
1546 62nd St., Brooklyn
Dubbed "The Rock Capital of Brooklyn," L'Amour originally opened in 1978 as a disco before shifting to live, loud guitars three years later. Run by Mike and George Parente until its closure in 2004, L'Amour hosted shows by Metallica, Slayer, Suicidal Tendencies, Guns N' Roses, Anthrax, Faith No More, and a great many others. During the venue's mid-'80s heyday, the brothers opened **L'Amour East (77-00 Queens Blvd., Queens)** and **L'Amour Far East,** the latter on Long Island. L'Amour reopened briefly **(2354 Arthur Kill Rd., Staten Island)** in 2009.

NEW UTRECHT HIGH SCHOOL
1601 80th St., Brooklyn
Built in 1915, New Utrecht High School counts among its musical alumni record-mogul David Geffen, producer Tony Visconti, Vanilla Fudge drummer Carmine Appice, late-era Journey singer Steve Augeri, and the late Robert Merrill, known to longtime fans of the New York Yankees for his operatic renditions of "The Star-Spangled Banner."

JAMES MADISON HIGH SCHOOL
3787 Bedford Ave., Brooklyn
Carole King, then Carol Klein, graduated from James Madison High School in 1958. Other notable alumni include radio personality Bruce "Cousin Brucie" Morrow, actor Martin Landau,

James Madison High School

founding publisher of *Mad* magazine William Gaines, comedians Chris Rock and Andrew Dice Clay, and politicians Bernie Sanders and Chuck Schumer.

ZIG ZAG RECORDS
2301 Avenue U, Brooklyn
For around 35 years, Zig Zag Records was a mainstay vinyl stop for classic rock and heavy metal fans, hosting in-store performances by Metallica, Motörhead, Twisted Sister, Iron Maiden, and many others in the genre. Zig Zag closed its doors in December 2011.

ABRAHAM LINCOLN HIGH SCHOOL
2800 Ocean Pkwy., Brooklyn
Notable musical alumni include Neil Diamond, Neil Sedaka, Hank Medress (the Tokens), Buddy Rich, and Mort Shuman, who worked with Doc Pomus as a songwriting team in the Brill Building. Playwright Arthur Miller and actors

Abraham Lincoln High School

John Forsyth, Lou Gossett Jr., and Harvey Keitel also went to high school there.

POPEYE'S SPINACH FACTORY
2301 Emmons Ave., Sheepshead Bay, Brooklyn
In early 1974, the Dictators were a raucous struggling bar band, playing gigs in the outer boroughs and occasionally opening for the likes of the Stooges and Blue Öyster Cult. Richard Blum, their somewhat slovenly roadie, was remarkable primarily for his enormous Jewfro hair and general weirdness.

On March 29, the band played a gig at Popeye's Spinach Factory, a grimy bar in what was then a working fishing neighborhood in Sheepshead Bay. The Dictators played a typical set, but at the end invited Blum to join them onstage, where he blasted through an insane rendition of "Wild Thing." No one knew it at the time, but Richard Blum was to be reborn as "Handsome Dick" Manitoba, and the Dictators' path was laid clear. Blum continued to make guest appearances with the band, and in May at one such gig in the Bronx, producer Sandy Pearlman and manager Murray Krugman offered the group a contract, but only if Blum were included. They recorded their first album *The Dictators Go Girl Crazy* a few months later, and Blum/Manitoba became a bigger part of their stage act. When the album eventually came out, it promptly bombed, and the group was dropped. The band gutted it out for a few more months, but eventually called it quits.

New York's nascent Punk scene, though, loved *Girl Crazy* and embraced the Dictators' attitude. After a few fights and personnel changes, the band reformed in early 1976. In March of that year, Blum taunted the cross-dressing Wayne County at CBGB and an on-stage brawl ensued. Numerous hospital visits and lawsuits later, the Dictators, considered too obnoxious (!), found themselves banned from most venues until championed by *Punk*

Magazine. Ultimately accepted back into the fold, the band made more albums and played many more gigs, including a triumphant show at CBGB later that year.

Today, the former Richard Blum can typically be found managing his bar, Manitoba's, on Avenue B in the East Village. He occasionally takes the stage to flex his still-capable rock muscles too. No trace remains of Popeye's. That stretch of Emmons Avenue has become a nice residential neighborhood, with condominiums sitting on the former Popeye's site. An Applebee's sits next door. There is a small commemorative plaque at the site placed by fans.

WOODY GUTHRIE'S HOME ⊘
3520 Mermaid Ave., Brooklyn

Woody Guthrie lived in Apt. 1R at 3520 Mermaid Ave. in Coney Island from November 1943 through September 1950. Arlo, Joadie, and Nora were born while Woody and his second wife Marjorie Mazia lived here. Many years later the address provided the inspiration, and title, for a series of albums recorded by Billy Bragg and Wilco, who wrote music to previously unused lyrics written by Guthrie that were given to Bragg by Guthrie's daughter, Nora. The partnership yielded two albums, plus a third volume of outtakes included in the 2012 release, *Mermaid Avenue: The Complete Sessions.*

TALKING HEADS

Bob Gruen

Talking Heads in 1978

In his book *Talking Heads' Fear of Music*, author Jonathan Lethem describes the band as "the definitive New York rock band. Manhattan band if you want to give the outer boroughs to the Ramones." But while Talking Heads were indeed entrenched in the downtown CBGBs scene, with an intellectual and artful approach to music that seemed to have sprung from a whispered conversation in a Chelsea art gallery and a distinctly musical melting pot aesthetic, the group's most fertile period was actually centered in a third-floor industrial loft at **9-01 44th Dr.** in Long Island City, Queens.

The loft was where Talking Heads' married rhythm section, bassist Tina Weymouth and drummer Chris Frantz, lived since around the summer of 1976, but it also served as the band's nerve center, where they could rehearse in relative isolation.

"Tina's brother Yann was in a loft there," said Frantz in 2017. "That's where we first

9-01 44th Dr., Long Island City

stayed when we moved to New York. We liked it out there. We liked the building very much. It was cool. There was a guy named Bill Barrell. Bill had the loft adjoining Tina's brother's on the same floor. . . . He was a protege of the artist named Red Grooms, so he did sculptures of buildings and things. He would use this big freight elevator which opened right onto the street, and we thought, 'Wow, this would be so perfect for our equipment.' So when his loft became available, we jumped on it. Tina's brother called and said, 'Barrell's moving back to Australia.' So we took the place."

It was from the roof of the building, with its spectacular vistas of Manhattan across the East River, that Talking Heads experienced the New York City blackout on July 13, 1977.

"It was a very clear view," Frantz said. "We were having a little barbecue up there while we were recording our first album. We were up on the roof and the sun was going down and we

195 Chrystie St.

noticed, 'Wow, the lights went out in Harlem.' And then, Boom, the lights went out on the Upper East Side, and then Midtown, and then shortly after that, Downtown, and then finally Wall Street. But the lights stayed on in Queens. It was wild."

Footage of the group rehearsing in the loft was seen in a 1979 episode of *The South Bank Show*, an arts program produced for British television network ITV. Interview segments for the show were also shot in the loft in the same year Talking Heads recorded *Fear of Music* with Brian Eno. After initial demo recording in a professional studio left them feeling dissatisfied, the band decamped to the familiarity and creative comfort of the Long Island City loft. With a mobile recording truck supplied by the Record Plant parked on the street below, the group worked with producer Brian Eno on the basic tracks that would become their third album. Those sessions were recorded on April 22 and May 6, 1979, with writing and rehearsing also taking place around this time.

"It came on two separate Sundays," said Frantz of the mobile recording truck. "That was the only time it was quiet enough. Otherwise it was street noise, traffic and everything. Two separate Sundays we recorded basic tracks, and then we did overdubs at **Atlantic Studios" (1841 Broadway).**

Talking Heads used Weymouth and Frantz's loft until they began rehearsals with an expanded nine-member version of the group following the release of *Remain in Light* in 1980. And even then they didn't travel too far, using the large rehearsal room at **Britannia Row (21-29 45th Rd., Queens),** Pink Floyd's brief foray into the equipment rental business.

"It was an old film studio that Charlie Chaplin and people like that had made movies in," said Frantz. "It was super historic."

While much of the Talking Heads story takes place within a few square blocks in Long

Island City, the group is undeniably linked to Manhattan, where they played live, and at least for the first couple of years, lived and worked.

Weymouth, Frantz, and David Byrne met as art students at the Rhode Island School of Design, where the latter pair formed the Artistics, laying the foundational groundwork for what would later become Talking Heads. By the mid-'70s, they were all living together in a loft on the ninth floor of **195 Chrystie St.**, in a neighborhood the members of the group have at varying times described in less than savory terms.

"It was not in the least bit gentrified or anything like that," said Frantz. "It was a very interesting neighborhood. There were the five-dollar hookers on that street, and a lot of cab drivers would come down there at the end of their shift and visit."

Frantz said the trio discovered the loft on a bit of less-than-traditional advice from Yann Weymouth.

"He said, 'Oh, look in the industrial section. You'll find the rates are much cheaper,'" Frantz recalled. "So I did, and I found this place . . . And Tina, David, and I lived there. We moved in in the fall of 1974, November."

The loft, across the street from a narrow stretch of Sara D. Roosevelt Park, was a short walk from **CBGB (315 Bowery)**, where Talking Heads had their public debut in June 1975 and went on to play over 70 times between then and October 10, 1977. Frantz said he was first hooked on the location of the Chrystie Street address because of its close proximity to the venue, where they'd already begun hanging out. Once inside the loft, he was sold.

"I thought, 'Perfect.' I went and looked at it and it had this great view of the Empire State Building, Union Square, and you could see way uptown," he said.

"I remember buying a water heater, which never got hooked up," Frantz said of his fleeting

interest in DIY home renovation. "There were two sinks in the place and no walls, just big open space. I had every intention of like, you know, making it into a really nice loft, but then I realized, 'I don't know how to do any of this stuff.' Plumbing? Forget about it. And carpentry also. So we just made the best of it."

Making the best of it, as far as taking showers was concerned, involved the largesse of less-plumbing-deficient friends.

"We would have these very nice towels and we would go to visit our neighbors and say, 'Hey, mind if I take a shower?'" Frantz laughed. "Surprisingly they never said no. We would do things like bring them a nice fresh bar of soap every once in a while."

Byrne, Weymouth, and Frantz didn't just live together in the early days, they also frequently commuted together to jobs in Midtown Manhattan. Frantz recalled that Byrne ran a stat machine, likely at **Waring & LaRosa Ad Agency (555 Madison Ave.)**, a firm that counted among its clientele Prince Matchabelli perfume. Weymouth sold stationery and shoes at upscale women's shop **Henri Bendel (10 W. 57th St.)**, and Frantz worked at **D/R Design Research (53 E. 57th St.)**, an eclectic home furnishings store stocked with products by such celebrated designers as Marcel Breuer, Hans Wegner, Joe Colombo, and Alvar Aalto.

"I was in shipping and packing, and I would unload things off of trucks," Frantz said. "And when they got sold I would load them back on."

After spending their days in relatively glamorous businesses in a relatively well-heeled part of town, Byrne, Weymouth, and Frantz would then return to their decidedly less-opulent digs on Chrystie Street.

"We would work our day jobs and then we would come home and we would make dinners like spaghetti with cottage cheese, and then some tomato sauce on top of that," Frantz said. "We were very spartan. Tina had a hotplate that

421 W. Broadway

The former Kitchen, 484 Broome St.

we would cook on that she brought from college days."

But while the ninth-floor loft on Chrystie Street may not have been lavishly appointed, it did provide the former art students an ideal setting to become a band. It was in their communal home where Weymouth learned bass guitar and where the trio began the long journey to become Talking Heads, a process that sometimes involved playing for pals.

"We didn't have a proper PA system or anything like that, but we would have these impromptu concerts for our friends," Frantz

said. "It was basically, 'Come on over, have a few glasses of cheap wine, and watch our rehearsal.'"

After giving up their Long Island City loft, Frantz and Weymouth moved back into Manhattan into a loft at **421 W. Broadway** to be closer to their bandmates.

"David and Jerry [Harrison] were both living in SoHo at the time, and I thought, 'Let's get a loft by them so we're in the same neighborhood,'" Frantz said. Byrne was on Greene Street, while Harrison was on Prince Street.

MORE TALKING HEADS

NOTEWORTHY LIVE PERFORMANCES

Bottom Line (15 W. 4th St.): Talking Heads first played the Bottom Line on June 23, 1977, supporting Bryan Ferry, the suave singer of Roxy Music, less than a week after the marriage of Frantz and Weymouth in Kentucky. The group returned to headline the Bottom Line on October 27 of the same year.

Lower Manhattan Ocean Club (121 Chambers St.): Opened by Max's Kansas City–founder Mickey Ruskin, Talking Heads first played the Lower Manhattan Ocean Club as a trio in August 1976, returning as a quartet with new member Jerry Harrison on February 9, 1977.

"The Ocean Club was a nice change," Frantz said. "They had decent food and it had a real cool vibe."

Mudd Club (77 White St.): Though they immortalized the Mudd Club in the lyrics of their 1979 single "Life During Wartime," Talking Heads only played the TriBeCa club once, on August 13, 1979, where they were filmed for an appearance on *The South Bank Show.*

The Kitchen (59 Wooster St.): On March 13, 1976, Talking Heads performed at the Kitchen, an art and performance space originally started at the Mercer Arts Center before its move to SoHo in 1973.

Irving Plaza (17 Irving Pl.): Talking Heads kicked off a two-month North American tour with an early September 1979 show here.

Entermedia Theater (189 2nd Ave.): Talking Heads played the Entermedia Theatre on August 10, 1978, with the performance filmed as a promo video by Sire Records' parent company Warner Bros. Records.

Max's Kansas City (213 Park Ave. South): Talking Heads played Max's Kansas City a handful of times between December 17, 1975, and November 19, 1976.

"We played there a few times," said Frantz. "But they never paid us as well as [CBGB owner] Hilly [Kristal] did, so we just said, 'To Hell with this.'"

Village Gate (160 Bleecker St.): Talking Heads played a four-night stand at the venerable Village Gate from July 5 through 8, 1977.

CBGB Second Avenue Theater (66 2nd Ave.): Talking Heads played the inaugural show at CBGB Second Avenue Theater on December 27, 1977.

The Ritz (119 E. 11th St.): Until their 2002 induction into the Rock & Roll Hall of Fame, the last time Byrne, Harrison, Weymouth, and Frantz would play live together was during a Tom Tom Club show at the Ritz on July 17, 1989.

Mothers (267 W. 23rd St.): After playing exclusively at CBGB, Talking Heads first ventured away from the Bowery for three shows at Mothers between November 28 and 30, 1975.

Waldorf Astoria (301 Park Ave.): Talking Heads were inducted into the Rock & Roll Hall of Fame during a ceremony held at the Waldorf Astoria Hotel in March 2002. It was their first time playing together in 18 years, and it remains their final performance.

Beacon Theatre (2124 Broadway): Talking Heads played a New Year's Eve show at the Beacon Theatre on December 31, 1978.

Wollman Rink (Central Park): Talking Heads played the Dr. Pepper Music Festival on August 16, 1979, returning to the festival a little over a year later as an expanded nine-piece live group.

"Wollman Rink was really nice," said Chris Frantz. "A beautiful spot. The audiences loved

it. And it was five dollars to see two really great bands. Five bucks. Can't beat that."

Forest Hills Tennis Stadium (1 Tennis Pl., Queens): Talking Heads's final full gig in New York City took place at the Forest Hills Tennis Stadium on August 21, 1983, as part of their *Stop Making Sense* tour.

NOTEWORTHY RECORDING LOCATIONS

Sundragon Studios (9 W. 20th St.): Talking Heads recorded their debut album, *Talking Heads: 77*, at Sundragon.

Former location of Sundragon Studios

Blank Tapes (37 W. 20th St.): Talking Heads began work here in 1982 on the album that would become their commercial breakthrough, *Speaking in Tongues.*

"It was very reasonable, and the people were nice to us there," said Frantz. "We were into the studios that were reasonable and functional. We weren't impressed by whether they had a lot of potted palms or anything."

Sigma Sound Studios (1697 Broadway): Talking Heads recorded or mixed here numerous times, including work on *Little Creatures* (1985) and *True Stories* (1986), and their final album, *Naked* (1988).

Atlantic Studios (1841 Broadway): After recording basic tracks at Frantz and Weymouth's Long Island City loft, Talking Heads completed some work on *Fear of Music*, including vocals, at Atlantic Studios.

CBS 30th Street Studio (207 E. 30th St.) ⊘: Talking Heads recorded demos at the CBS 30th Street Studio in 1975, including early takes on "Psycho Killer," "Warning Sign," and "Thank You for Sending Me an Angel."

OTHER NOTEWORTHY LOCATIONS

Pier 61 (W. 21st St. and 11th Ave.): In 1983 Talking Heads spent six weeks rehearsing for their *Stop Making Sense* tour on Pier 61, which later became the ice rink at the Chelsea Piers entertainment complex.

52 Bond St.: Artist Jamie Dalglish lived in a loft where David Byrne stayed when he first came to New York City.

Murray Hill Cinema (160 E. 34th St.) ⊘: David Byrne was an usher at the Murray Hill Cinema in 1974, earning minimum wage but reportedly delighting in seeing Mel Brooks' *Young Frankenstein* numerous times.

The Public Theater (425 Lafayette St.): In January 1985, Byrne put on a performance piece, *The Tourist Way of Knowledge*, at the Public Theater as a benefit for avant-garde theater company Mabou Mines.

QUEENS

QUEENSBRIDGE HOUSES
105 & 106 41st Ave., Queens
The sprawling Queensbridge Houses public housing complex was once the home of hip-hop artists such as Nas, MC Shan, Mobb Deep, Roxanne Shante, and Marley Marl.

The former Britannia Row

BRITANNIA ROW
21-29 45th Rd., Queens
Named after their London studio and headquarters, Britannia Row was Pink Floyd's brief foray into the rehearsal and equipment rental business. Run by Mike Sinclair between 1979 and 1981, the Long Island City facility featured a large rehearsal room used by UB40, the B-52s, Adam Ant, the Stranglers, and Talking Heads, who prepared for their *Remain in Light* tour in 1980 after expanding their live group to nine members.

"While I was there, and to my knowledge before I was there, Pink Floyd did not rehearse at their sound studio," said Sinclair in 2017. "It was primarily a business venture they set up after the *Animals* tour to rent their sound system in America. The next tour, *The Wall*, they purchased a new system for themselves."

According to Sinclair, currently the VP and owner of Audio Incorporated, Britannia Row's sound equipment was used during the Clash's legendary 1981 residency at **Bond International Casino (1530 Broadway)**, along with a run of shows by the Stranglers at **Irving Plaza (17 Irving Place)** around the same time.

COVENTRY ⊘
47-03 Queens Blvd., Queens
Growing out of the former Popcorn Pub in early 1973, Coventry was a 700-person-capacity live venue that, for a few brief years, played host to some of the city's key rock & roll groups of the era: the Dictators, New York Dolls, Wayne County & the Backstreet Boys, the Brats, and the Harlots of 42nd Street. Kiss played their first-ever show at Coventry on January 30, 1973. Coventry closed in the mid-'70s, with a brief revival in 1978. **Coventry II (1550 1st Ave.)**, the venue's Manhattan satellite, opened in 1974, closing within months.

LES PAUL'S HOME
40-15 81st St., Queens
Les Paul, in addition to being a virtuoso guitarist, was a musician who altered the landscape of American popular music. He developed the solid-body electric guitar for Gibson—who still sells a popular model bearing

40-15 81st St.

his name—and a variety of other technical innovations, including multitrack recording. In his home at 40-15 81st St. in Queens in 1951, he created a home studio and recorded the hit "How High the Moon" with his wife Mary Ford on vocals. A few early takes were thwarted by a fire engine and a neighbor's toilet flush. In all, it took them about an hour to lay down the multiple vocal and instrumental tracks that distinguish the lush distinctive recording that hit number 1 and that the Library of Congress added to the National Registry in 2002. Paul and Ford would have 16 top ten hits in the '50s and would become major radio and television stars. The couple divorced in 1964, but after a period of semi-retirement, Paul returned to the stage and performed regularly into his 90s.

NEWTOWN HIGH SCHOOL
49-01 90th St., Queens
Opened in 1897, Newtown High School adopted the motto "We tower above the rest," inspired by the school's most visible architectural

feature. Among the school's notable musical alumni are Kiss bassist Gene Simmons and Johnny Thunders and Sylvain Sylvain of the New York Dolls, both of whom were reportedly expelled. Other famous Newtown alumni include comedian Don Rickles, cosmetics magnate Estée Lauder, and actor Carroll O'Connor, most renowned for having played curmudgeonly bigot Archie Bunker on *All in the Family.*

FOREST HILLS TENNIS STADIUM
1 Tennis Place, Queens
The Forest Hills Tennis Stadium was first used as a concert venue in the '60s and early '70s when such artists as the Beatles, the Monkees, Sly & the Family Stone, the Four Tops, Marvin Gaye, the Lovin' Spoonful, the Supremes, the Band, Bob Dylan, and the Doors all played an annual summer music festival. The stadium fell into disrepair after its closure in 1978, but it was revived as a live music venue in 2013, with artists such as Tom Petty & the Heartbreakers, Mumford & Sons, the National, and Van Morrison linking the past to the present.

Forest Hills Tennis Stadium

SINGER BOWL ⊘
Flushing Meadows-Corona Park, Queens
Built by the Singer Sewing Machine Company for the 1964 World's Fair, the Singer Bowl was remodeled and refurbished over the years for use as a tennis stadium before it was leveled in 2016. In the late '60s, the Singer Bowl served

as the site of rock concerts by the Doors, the Who, the Jimi Hendrix Experience, Vanilla Fudge, Steppenwolf, the Rascals, the Moody Blues, and others.

NEW YORK STATE PAVILION
111th St., Queens
Designed by architects Philip Johnson and Lev Zetlin for the 1964 World's Fair, The New York State Pavilion has fallen into disrepair over the years. But in the late '60s it was used as a concert space as part of the Singer Bowl Festival, with appearances by Three Dog Night, Led Zeppelin, the Grateful Dead, Joe Cocker, Chuck Berry, Fleetwood Mac, the MC5, and the Stooges. The Pavilion has been seen in numerous movies and TV shows, and also appeared in the video for "Don't Let's Start" by They Might Be Giants.

New York State Pavilion

SHEA STADIUM ⊘
123-01 Roosevelt Ave., Queens
Opened in April 1964 as the new home of the New York Mets baseball team, Shea Stadium hosted the Beatles in 1965 and 1966. While they were the stadium's most famous musical performances, there were plenty of other celebrated concerts at Shea after the Fab Four showed what was possible in front of such a large crowd.

The Summer Festival for Peace took place at Shea on August 6, 1970, featuring

performances by Janis Joplin, Paul Simon, Miles Davis, Creedence Clearwater Revival, Steppenwolf, and many others. Grand Funk Railroad sold out Shea in 1971, and the Who played the ballpark with support from the Clash in 1982. The Rolling Stones played six nights at Shea in October 1989 sandwiched around a jaunt to Los Angeles. Other performers at Shea included the Police, Bruce Springsteen & the E Street Band, and Elton John.

Billy Joel performed the last two concerts at Shea on July 16 and 18, 2008, with special guest appearances by Paul McCartney, Roger Daltrey, Don Henley, John Mellencamp, Steven Tyler, and others. Shea was shuttered at the end of the 2008 Major League Baseball season when the Mets moved into nearby Citi Field.

CITI FIELD
120-01 Roosevelt Ave., Queens
Soon after the New York Mets baseball club moved into their new digs, Citi Field began hosting live gigs, starting with a trio of dates by Paul McCartney on July 17, 19, and 21, 2009. The Dave Matthews Band, Foo Fighters, Beyoncé, and Lady Gaga have all performed at Citi Field since. The stadium was also home to the Classic East, two dates of shows headlined by the Eagles and Fleetwood Mac in July 2017. The Citi Field parking lot is the home of the annual Meadows Music & Arts Festival, held over three days in September, with past headliners including Jay-Z, Kanye West, Gorillaz, Red Hot Chili Peppers, and Chance the Rapper.

ST. JOHN'S EPISCOPAL CHURCH
149-49 Sanford Ave., Queens
According to Scott Ian's autobiography, *I'm the Man*, the first Anthrax show took place in the basement of St. John's Episcopal Church. The fledgling group sold $3 tickets to friends, and around 30 people turned up.

PS 169
18-25 212th St., Queens
Scott Ian of Anthrax attended elementary school at PS 169, playing stickball at the school and trying to emulate smaller major leaguers like Freddie Patek of the Kansas City Royals.

MOONSHINE RECORDS
212-91 26th Avenue, Queens
As a kid, Anthrax's Scott Ian used to shop for music at Moonshine Records in the Bay Terrace Shopping Center. He bought tickets from Ticketron to see Kiss at Madison Square Garden on December 14, 1977, at this shop. In his book, *I'm the Man*, Ian said he lined up with other fans, some of whom had been camping out all night. His ticket was $6.50, and he wound up in the back of the floor seats behind the soundboard. He claims to still have his tour program and T-shirt, though the latter is apparently a bit snug.

BAYSIDE HIGH SCHOOL
32-24 Corporal Kennedy St., Queens
Among the famous alumni of Bayside High are Anthrax's Scott Ian; rapper Action Bronson; astronaut Ellen Baker; and Jordan Belfort, a former investment banker whose memoir, *The Wolf of Wall Street,* was turned into a film directed by Martin Scorsese.

QUEENS COLLEGE
65-30 Kissena Blvd., Queens
Notable musical alumni of Queens College include Paul Simon; Ellie Greenwich; Carole King; disgraced boy band manager Lou Perlman; Marvin Hamlisch; and Robert Moog, inventor of the Moog synthesizer. Other notable alumni include comedians Jerry Seinfeld, Carol Leifer, Ray Romano, and porn legend Ron Jeremy.

Among the musical artists to play shows at Queens College were the Kinks, who performed there on March 27, 1971.

THE MUSIC BOX
177-19 Union Turnpike, Queens
Opened in 1970 by Keith West of the Brats, the Music Box was a record shop that became a central hangout for the nascent Queens glitter scene. Founding Anthrax guitarist Scott Ian was a customer of the Music Box in his youth.

RUSSELL AND JOSEPH SIMMONS CHILDHOOD HOME
205-16 109th Ave., Queens
Russell Simmons, chairman and CEO of Rush Communications and co-founder of Def Jam Recordings, and his brother Joseph, better

Queens College

known as the Rev. Run of iconic hip-hop group Run-DMC, grew up in this two-story Dutch Colonial house.

JAM MASTER JAY CHILDHOOD HOME
109-74 203rd St., Queens
Jason Mizell, who grew up to become renowned DJ Jam Master Jay of Run-DMC, grew up in the house at 109-74 203rd St. in Queens.

The intersection of Hollis Avenue and 205th Street has been officially renamed Run-DMC JMJ Way, and a memorial mural to the late Jam Master Jay near the corner just off Hollis Avenue painted by local artists shortly after his murder in 2002 has been maintained ever since.

LL COOL J CHILDHOOD HOME
185-02 Ilion Ave., Queens
Following his parents' divorce, James Todd Smith was raised by his grandmother, Ellen Griffith, in a brick house at 185-02 Ilion Ave. A fan of hip-hop from an early age, Smith adopted the stage name LL Cool J—"Ladies Love Cool James"—as a teenager and began creating demo tapes in the basement of his grandmother's home, and before long he'd signed to Def Jam Recordings, becoming one of the label's first breakout solo stars.

RUN-DMC JMJ WAY & HOLLIS PLAYGROUND
Hollis Ave. and 205th St., Queens
Named after the New Hampshire birthplace of 19th-century-developer Frederick W. Denton, the Queens neighborhood known as Hollis is almost synonymous with legendary hip-hop group Run-DMC, who even called their 1987 yuletide single "Christmas in Hollis." It was at Hollis Playground where neighborhood hip-hop groups like the Fat Boys used to congregate, and it was also where Run-DMC held their first-ever public performance.

24/7 STUDIO
9010 Merrick Blvd., Queens
Jason Mizell, better known as Jam Master Jay, the DJ for trailblazing hip-hop group-Run-DMC, was shot and killed in this recording studio on October 30, 2002.

The former 24/7 Studio

Called Quest. Legend says that it was on this corner that Phife met Q-Tip.

MUSIC BUILDING
92-32 Union Hall St., Queens
Like its Manhattan sibling, the Music Building in Queens was intended to be used by bands strictly as rehearsal and sometime recording spaces, but some ducked the rules and lived there too. More an outpost for hip-hop and metal acts than the Manhattan location, the Queens building's leading figures included Anthrax and Metallica, who lived in their rehearsal space when they arrived from San Francisco in 1983. The building was still active when it was gutted by a fire in the mid-'90s.

MALIK "PHIFE DAWG" TAYLOR WAY
Intersection of Linden Blvd. and 192 St., Queens
This intersection was renamed by the city in November 2016 in honor of the late Malik "Phife Dawg" Taylor, an MC from hip-hop-outfit A Tribe

JAMES BROWN'S HOME
175-19 Linden Blvd., Queens
The Godfather of Soul owned this home in the stylish Addisleigh Park neighborhood in the '60s and early '70s. Each Christmas he lived there,

Brown reportedly had a black Santa Claus on his lawn.

WYNONIE HARRIS HOME
114-11 178th St., Queens
The picturesque neighborhood of Addisleigh Park is justly famous for its illustrious assortment of residents from the world of jazz, including Billie Holiday, Count Basie, and Ella Fitzgerald, but it was also home to its share of notable R&B musicians, and few were as flamboyantly famous in the late '40s and early '50s as Wynonie "Mr Blues" Harris. An Omaha native, Harris had a string of R&B hits beginning just after World War II that included a cover of Roy Brown's "Good Rockin' Tonight" in 1948 (later a hit for Elvis Presley), "All She Wants to Do is Rock," and "Lollipop Mama." He was known to cruise Harlem in his Cadillac convertible waving to adoring fans and generally acting like a big shot. He was also notorious for the wild parties at his 178th Street home, which typically included neighborhood

friends Earl Bostic and Arthur Prysock, plus a regular bevy of willing young women.

Sadly, the good times didn't last. A performer who had built a primarily black adult audience could never quite cross over to the white teenagers of the '50s who now embraced the music he had helped to pioneer. His star would dim, and his career and life would begin a precipitous decline. He changed labels several times and made many fine recordings but could not find a breakout hit that would place him with the other rock & roll luminaries of his time. In 1956 he moved to more modest accommodations at 120-34 200th St. He could no longer headline the big clubs, and he earned extra bread running a bar in Bed-Stuy, Brooklyn, Wynonie's Club 884 (884 Fulton St.), not far from some of the important black venues of the time, Club Baby Grand (1274 Fulton St.), and Cafe Verona (1330 Fulton St.) ⊘. His health would decline as well, and by the end of the '50s he had relocated to Los Angeles, where he died at age 53 in 1969.

Creedmore Psychiatric Hospital

to Creedmoor, where he reportedly received a series of electroshock sessions. Reed wrote about the experiences in "Kill your Sons," a song on his 1974 album *Sally Can't Dance*. In an interview for *Please Kill Me,* Reed claimed he'd been given the treatments as a means of quelling homosexual urges, but Weiner said their parents were not homophobic.

The former Andrew Jackson High School, today known as the Campus Magnet High School

ANDREW JACKSON HIGH SCHOOL
207-01 116th Ave., Queens
Notable alumni include hip-hop stars Jam-Master Jay, LL Cool J, and 50 Cent. The '60s girl group the Shangri-Las were formed at the high school from two sets of sisters, Mary and Betty Weiss, and identical twins Marge and Mary Ann Ganser. The Shangri-Las' tough urban girl image was best exemplified through hit singles "Leader of the Pack" and "Out in the Street."

CREEDMOOR PSYCHIATRIC HOSPITAL
79-25 Winchester Blvd., Queens
Woody Guthrie was admitted to Creedmoor in June 1966 in the latter stages of his battle with Huntington's disease, a brain disorder. Guthrie died in the hospital on October 3, 1967, at the age of 55.

After being pulled by his parents from New York University during his freshman year, with his sister, Merrill Weiner, later saying it was due to what their parents called a "nervous breakdown," Lou Reed was eventually admitted

QUEENSBOROUGH COMMUNITY COLLEGE
222-05 56th Ave., Queens
Cheryl James and Sandra Denton were studying nursing at Queensboro Community College when they met. The two would go on to form hip-hop outfit Salt-N-Pepa, who after a brief run of singles that met with modest success on the R&B chart had their first big taste of crossover success with "Push It" in 1987.

CYNDI LAUPER

Cyndi Lauper grew up in New York City, wearing her roots on her sleeve, in her music, and in her accent and attitude. A singer, songwriter, and LGBTQ activist, Lauper struggled through life and rarely felt as if she belonged. She found fame around the time she embraced her uniqueness, even naming her debut album *She's So Unusual.*

Lauper spent some of her childhood in a semi-detached house at 95-11 104th St. in Queens, where she lived with her sister and mother. She first attended the High School of Fashion Industries (225 W. 24th St.), writing in her autobiography that she was riveted by fellow straphangers on the A train she'd board at 104th Street/Liberty Avenue. After flunking out of Fashion Industries, Lauper enrolled in a school much closer to home at Richmond Hill High School (89-30 114th St., Queens), a 15-minute walk down a familiar street rather than a long subway trip full of adventure. Lauper would eventually be expelled from

Richmond Hill High, though after being asked back as a celebrity alum in 1988, she agreed only with the stipulation that her expulsion was nullified and she be given an honorary degree. To her surprise, the school said yes.

Lauper's early fame on the strength of the "Girls Just Want to Have Fun" single and *She's So Unusual* album, both released in 1983, saw her embrace New York City. The album cover featured images shot by Annie Leibovitz in Coney Island, Brooklyn, including the cover image in front of the Roberto Clemente Wax Museum building on Henderson Walk, a structure that has since been torn down. The back cover of the album shows the Parachute Jump on the Boardwalk and the bottoms of Lauper's shoes, painted in the style of Vincent Van Gogh's "The Starry Night." The single sleeve of "Girls Just Want to Have Fun" showed four images of Lauper taken along the Boardwalk. The vivid video for "Girls Just Want to Have Fun" moved the action to Manhattan, with exterior shots filmed along Gay Street, a short, curved street between Christopher Street and Waverly Place.

9 5-11 104th St.

RAMONES

Bob Gruen

Ramones onstage at CBGB, April 1979

"The Ramones all originate from Forest Hills and kids who grew up there either became musicians, degenerates, or dentists. The Ramones are a little of each. Their sound is not unlike a fast drill on a rear molar." —TOMMY RAMONE, FROM A 1975 PRESS RELEASE ABOUT THE RAMONES

The Ramones weren't actually brothers, and they didn't always seem to like one another. But there are few artists more ingrained in the whole of the familial New York City experience, which carried them aggressively lurching from the leafy semi-suburbs to the gritty city streets of the Bowery just across the East River.

The four original members of the Ramones met in Forest Hills, Queens, where Johnny (John Cummings) and Joey (Jeffrey Hyman) were born

Forest Hills High School

and raised, and where Dee Dee (Douglas Colvin) and Tommy (Tamás Erdelyi) mostly grew up. All four Ramones went to **Forest Hills High School (67-01 110th St., Queens)**, which by then included among its notable rock & roll alumni Paul Simon, Art Garfunkel, Burt Bacharach, Leslie West, and Gary Kurfirst, record label executive, music promoter, and eventual manager of several New York groups, including the Ramones. (In October 2016, a stretch of 67th Avenue and 110th Street in front of Forest Hills High School was renamed Ramones Way in the group's honor.)

Joey's childhood home, the Bel-Air

Much of the Ramones story in Forest Hills is clustered in a grid a few blocks from Forest Hills High School, including Birchwood Towers. Years later, Joey claimed "Beat on the Brat" was inspired by watching unsupervised children running through a common courtyard. Joey lived with his mother, Charlotte Lesher, and brother, Mickey Leigh, in **Apt. 22F of the Bel Air (66-36**

The ramp

Johnny's childhood home

Yellowstone Blvd.) when the brothers were teenagers. Birchwood was also home to Johnny's family at some point.

Johnny's family also lived at 66-07 99th St., across the street from **Thorneycroft Apartments (66th Rd. at 99th St.).** Among the young Ramones' hangout spots was an open lot on the Thorneycroft property, and a ramp at 66th Avenue at 99th Street that led from the sidewalk up to the roof of a parking garage. The ramp was where the pre-Ramones and their friends reportedly idly spent time engaging in the sort of delinquent behavior that would inform the lyrics of many of their early songs. In a 2016 interview with the *New York Times*, Leigh recalled an incident in the early '70s when Johnny slapped a kid to make his point that it wasn't possible to defend oneself with karate, then slapped the kid's dad when he stepped in. In 2016, the ramp was dedicated to the Ramones with a mural.

Dee Dee (66-25 103rd St.) and Tommy (65-35 Yellowstone Blvd.) also lived nearby in their lean teen years. At the start of the Ramones, Tommy was using his family's home as the headquarters for Loudmouth Productions.

Because they came off like a gang of street kids with their leather jackets, torn jeans, sneakers, T-shirts, and perpetual scowls, the Ramones' image appeared less an image than an ideal, a direct link to the Dead End Kids. They grew up in Queens, but it wasn't until they

hit Manhattan that the Ramones became the Ramones, grinding out show after blistering show at lightning speed. And, as their debut gig proved, that wasn't going to happen overnight.

On March 30, 1974, the Ramones opened the doors to their rehearsal space at **Performance Studios (23. E. 20th St.),** a facility built by their friend and then-manager Erdelyi and the group's future tour manager Monte Melnick. The Ramones had been practicing at Performance Studios since that January, with Joey on drums, a friend named Richard Stern on bass, and Johnny and Dee Dee playing guitar and sharing lead vocal duties. Stern was out well before the debut, with Dee Dee taking over bass duties. Dee Dee stopped singing altogether because he couldn't sing and play simultaneously, so Joey began sharing vocals from behind the drum kit. The group's debut was its only show as a trio, and it was a mess.

Tommy's childhood home

The former Performance Studios

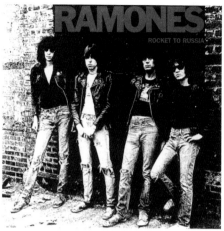

The show was a mess, sure, but an important mess. For a start, it showed at least some of what the Ramones would become was already there: They played seven short explosive songs, some of which would be reworked over the next two years before appearing on their debut album, *Ramones.* Five of the songs played at Performance Studios had "wanna" in the title, four of them preceded by "don't," with the fifth familiar to longtime fans, "Now I Wanna Sniff Some Glue." There was another "don't" song ("I Don't Like Nobody That Don't Like Me")

and, uncharacteristically, one simply called "Succubus."

By the time the group played their first public show at **CBGB (315 Bowery)** on August 16, 1974, Joey was the lanky lead singer of the Ramones, and following a string of auditions with incompatible drummers, they'd discovered the solution right under their noses when Tommy sat behind the kit. They were still sloppy, but they were headed in the right direction, a runaway, amphetamine-fueled locomotive.

Though they rehearsed and sometimes gigged at Performance Studios, the importance of CBGB in the early story of the Ramones cannot be overstated. Between their debut in August 1974 and November 17, the group played the club 25 times. The following year, they surpassed that number. And even after they began touring in '76 and '77, most of their hometown gigs happened at CBGB. Their final performance at CBGB took place nearly five years to the day after their first, when the group played a benefit to raise money to buy bulletproof vests for NYPD officers.

MORE RAMONES

NOTEWORTHY LIVE PERFORMANCES

Sea of Clouds (5 E. 16th St.): The Ramones and the Heartbreakers played a New Year's Eve show in this fifth-floor loft space on December 31, 1975, with the $7.50 cover including a champagne toast.

Mothers (267 W. 23rd St.): With support from Blondie, the Ramones played Mothers for three nights in early October 1975, returning again for a similar stand two months later.

Max's Kansas City (213 Park Ave. South): The Ramones first played Max's Kansas City as part of the club's 1976 New York Rock Festival, a 12-day event that included numerous key groups of the CBGB's scene.

Hurrah (36 W. 62nd St.): The Ramones played three consecutive nights at Hurrah in August 1978, in part as an audition for film director Allan Arkush, who was looking to cast them in *Rock 'n' Roll High School.*

Coventry (47-03 Queens Blvd., Queens): The Ramones played an early gig at the glam-rock capital of Queens, Coventry, on May 30, 1975.

NOTEWORTHY RECORDING LOCATIONS

Plaza Sound Studios (55 W. 50th St., 7th floor): With a budget of $6,400, the Ramones spent a week in February 1976 recording their debut album in this studio on the seventh floor of the same building that houses Radio City Music Hall.

Sundragon Studios (9 W. 20th St., 9th floor): For their second album, *Leave Home,* the Ramones set up shop at Sundragon Studios in October 1976.

Mediasound Studios (311 W. 57th St.): The Ramones recorded their third album, *Rocket to Russia,* at Mediasound Studios, located in the former location of the Manhattan Baptist Church. They would return to record *Road to Ruin* and *Too Tough to Die.*

OTHER NOTEWORTHY LOCATIONS

Joey Ramone Place (E. 2nd. St. at Bowery, NW corner): The city officially named this corner Joey Ramone Place on November 30, 2003.

6 E. 2nd St.: On February 3, 1975, the Ramones videotaped a live performance in their artistic director and confidante Arturo Vega's loft as a label showcase. Joey and Dee Dee lived here sporadically.

Albert's Garden (16 E. 2nd St.): The brick wall in this small serenity garden maintained by area residents is the setting of the cover of the Ramones' 1976 debut album as shot by Roberta Bayley.

Extra Place: Manager Danny Fields shot the cover of the group's third album, *Rocket to Russia,* in the small side street behind CBGB's Extra Place.

The St. Mark (115 E. 9th St.): Joey Ramone lived in an apartment on the 10th floor of the St. Mark from around the time of the release of the Ramones' *End of the Century* in 1980 until he passed away at the age of 49 in 2001.

85 E. 10th St.: Johnny Ramone lived in an apartment here for around a decade in the '80s and '90s.

Cafe Wha? (115 MacDougal St.): Before either of them adopted the last name Ramone, John Cummings first met Marc Bell at Cafe Wha? in the early '70s, when the future Ramones drummer was playing with Dust.

The Camera Mart (456 W. 55th St.): On September 3, 1977, the Ramones were filmed enthusiastically lip-syncing a handful of songs on a soundstage at the Camera Mart, a Manhattan video sales, rental, and service company.

The George Washington Hotel (23 Lexington Ave.): Dee Dee Ramone used to live in the George Washington, writing in his book *Poison Heart: Surviving the Ramones* about sneaking into his old room on Christmas Day 1991.

The Hotel Chelsea (222 W. 23rd St.): Count Dee Dee Ramone among the many famous faces who've lived in the Chelsea.

Village Plaza (79 Washington Place): During the early days of the Ramones, Dee Dee lived in the Village Plaza, a derelict hotel that, according to a 1972 article in the *New York Times,* was populated by criminals.

29 John St.: Marky Ramone lived in a converted loft on the ninth floor at 29 John St. during his first stint with the Ramones.

Daily Planet (251 W. 30th St.): Marky played with the band at this rehearsal studio when he rejoined the Ramones after Richie Ramone's departure in 1987. A decade earlier he'd auditioned for Richard Hell and the Voidoids in the same location.

World Trade Center ⊘: After high school, Johnny worked as a pipe-fitter, including a stint on the under-construction World Trade Center.

1633 Broadway: Johnny worked construction at 1633 Broadway in the late '60s at the same time Dee Dee was working in the mail room of the same building.

Waldorf Astoria (301 Park Ave.): The Ramones were inducted into the Rock & Roll Hall of Fame during a ceremony at the Waldorf Astoria on March 18, 2002. Johnny, Dee Dee, Tommy, and Marky attended the ceremony, where they were inducted by Pearl Jam's Eddie Vedder.

Inscope Arch, Central Park: The photo for the cover of the Ramones 1976 single "I Wanna Be Your Boyfriend" was shot here.

Playmates Arch, Central Park: Showing a continued fondness for arches in Central Park, the Ramones shot the cover of their 1984 album *Too Tough to Die* inside the Playmates Arch.

Metropolitan Opera House (30 Lincoln Center Plaza): The Ramones were given an MTV Lifetime Achievement Award at the Metropolitan Opera House on September 6, 2001, during the MTV Music Video Awards.

53rd & 3rd streets: An intersection made famous through "53rd & 3rd," a song written by Dee Dee featured on the group's eponymous debut album in 1976. The song is about a

hustler turning tricks and killing a john with a razor.

57th St. Subway Station: Back when the B was a 6th Avenue express train, it used to stop at the 57th Street subway station, which is now serviced by the F. The group used a B train here as the setting of the cover of their 1983 album *Subterranean Jungle*.

The Roosevelt Hotel (45 E. 45th St.): Marky's then-girlfriend Marion used to work the front desk, giving him the key to her complimentary room for naps.

Manny's Music (156 W. 48th St.): Prior to starting the Ramones, Johnny and Dee Dee visited Manny's Music, with the former buying a Mosrite guitar and the latter a Danelectro bass.

Cornell Burn Center (525 E. 68th St.): Joey Ramone was admitted to the Cornell Burn Center after he was scalded by boiling water at the Capitol Theater in Passaic, New Jersey, on November 19, 1977.

St. Vincent's Hospital (170 W. 12th St.): Johnny Ramone was taken to St. Vincent's Hospital after his skull was fractured in a fight outside his apartment building.

Spirit (530 W. 27th St.): Blondie, Sonic Youth, and the Strokes were among the performers at a Johnny Ramone–organized benefit for Cedars Sinai Cancer Research Center and the Lymphoma Cancer Research Foundation on October 8, 2004.

Rusk Institute of Rehabilitation Medicine (400 E. 34th St.): Joey was admitted here after breaking his hip following a fall on a patch of ice on New Year's Eve 2000.

Art Garden (98-87 Queens Blvd., Queens): Joey's mother, Charlotte Lesher, owned the Art Garden, where the nascent Ramones used to rehearse in the basement.

21-07 157th St., Queens: Dee Dee lived in a basement apartment here for around a decade.

147-16 230 Pl., Queens: Linda Ramone, nee Daniele, grew up here. Originally Joey's girlfriend, Linda later dated and eventually married Johnny.

Rockaway Beach, Queens: Dee Dee wrote a paean to Rockaway Beach in the style of surf songs by the Beach Boys; the song appeared on the Ramones' third album, *Rocket to Russia*.

Erasmus Hall High School (899-925 Flatbush Ave., Brooklyn): Marky Ramone, then Marc Bell, went to Erasmus Hall High School, which was closed in 1994 due to underperforming academic scores.

640 Ditmas Ave., Brooklyn: Marky's family moved in with his grandparents at 640 Ditmas Ave. in Brooklyn when he was five, moving into a different apartment in the same building seven years later.

Parkside Plaza at the southeast entrance of Prospect Park (Ocean and Parkside Avenues): Marky used to hang out here as a teenager when other young people would jam; pot, LSD, beer, and red wine circulated freely.

SIMON & GARFUNKEL

(Lewton Cole/Alamy)

Simon & Garfunkel at their Central Park reunion concert in 1981

They would emerge as one of the most influential and best-selling recording artists of the '60s, but Simon & Garfunkel's road to

Paul's childhood home

Artie's childhood home

PS 164

Parsons Junior High School

167 W. 48th St.

Before there was Simon & Garfunkel, there was simply Paul Frederic Simon and Arthur Ira Garfunkel of Kew Gardens Hills, in the borough of Queens. Paul's family had moved from Newark in 1944 and moved around the neighborhood for a few years, ultimately settling at 137-62 70th Rd. Artie grew up not far away at 136-58 72nd Ave. Although they attended the same elementary school (**PS 164—138-01 77th Ave.**), they did not actually meet until the graduation play, *Alice in Wonderland.* Paul was cast as the White Rabbit and Artie the Cheshire Cat. They would cement their friendship the following year at **Parsons Junior High School (158-40 76th Rd.**), where they enjoyed similar tastes in music and enjoyed playing together. By the time they were students at **Forest Hills High School (67-01 110th St.**), they were actually writing songs together in emulation of their idols, the Everly Brothers, and were playing sock hops and parties around the neighborhood. Paul's father Louis played the bass and fronted his own dance band as "Lee Sims," and was able to help them copyright their work and show it to publishers in the city. The pop music industry was ruled by the galaxy of music publishers and labels headquartered in **The Brill Building (1619 Broadway)** and other office towers in midtown Manhattan, and the boys would typically go door-to-door plying their latest tunes hoping for stardom. Eventually they learned they'd need to record demos, so they went to **Sanders Recording Studios (167 W. 48th St.)** to cut their latest and greatest, "Hey Schoolgirl," along with the intended B-Side, "Dancin' Wild." Sid Prosen, owner of the otherwise minuscule Big Records, overheard the boys' performance and offered them a contract on the spot. As they were underage, the contract was ultimately signed by their fathers, Louis Simon and Jacob Garfunkel. Both tunes were re-recorded with musicians, including Louis Simon on bass, at **Bell Sound Studios (237 W. 54th St.)** ⊘ in October 1957.

success began in Queens and would take many interesting twists and turns along the way.

What were they to call this duo? After some thought they settled on Tom & Jerry, after the cartoon characters. Paul was Jerry Landis, using his girlfriend's name, and Artie was Tom Graph, lampooning his facility with mathematics. With some help from Alan Freed and some likely Prosen payola, "Hey Schoolgirl" made it to number 49 and sold over 100,000 copies. They even appeared on *American Bandstand*, then in its premiere season. The boys were thrilled and became stars—at least in Kew Gardens. Follow-up singles, unfortunately, went nowhere, and Tom & Jerry appeared done for. Paul and his dad, however, incorporated a side deal into the contract, giving Paul the opportunity to give it a go as a solo act, horrifying the Garfunkels. Artie felt betrayed and the two would fall out for some time afterward. Paul would record under a variety of names, including True Taylor, Tico & the Triumphs, as well as Jerry Landis, with very little success. Eventually the Garfunkels and the Simons had to sue to recover royalties, which amounted to about a grand each. Paul bought himself a red Chevrolet Impala, which promptly caught fire and burned.

Despite his disappointment, Artie also cut at least two singles as Artie Garr. Years later, these tracks would make their way onto albums designed to cash in on the success of Simon & Garfunkel, much to their irritation.

Paul and Artie would go their separate ways for now; Paul to **Queens College (65-30 Kissena Blvd.)**, and Artie to **Columbia University (1130 Amsterdam Ave.)**. Paul continued his multi-pronged attempts to make it musically, writing songs and occasionally recording them with little fanfare. One of his classmates at Queens was Carol Klein, who shared a similar interest in making music. She had also released a few singles a few years back that disappeared into the pop music ether. They called themselves the Cousins and made some demos together, with Paul on bass and guitar and Carol on piano.

They recorded each other's songs, and songs by other writers, but never collaborated. Not long after, Carol changed her professional name to Carole King and had great success as both a songwriter and eventually a recording artist. Paul continued to develop his songwriting skills, often spending hours writing and recording demos on his own at the **Variety Arts Studios (225 W. 46th St.)** ⊘.

A few years later when Paul and Artie reconnected, they found they'd both developed an interest in folk music. They both thought rock & roll had become stale and lifeless and preferred the social and political consciousness that folk had to offer. Both were going away for the summer but agreed to reunite when they were back in town. They were both headed to graduate school; Paul to **Brooklyn Law School (375 Pearl St.)** and Artie to **Teachers College at Columbia University (525 W. 120th St.).** In addition to law school, Paul was also working

The former Brooklyn Law School

for $150 a week as a song-plugger for **Edward B. Marks Music Publishers (136 W. 52nd St.)**, selling potential tunes to record companies. He was prohibited from selling his own songs, but he continued to work on his own material, which was beginning to take on a contemporary folk music feel.

In 1963 the duo began performing in the Village as Kane and Garr, working the various folk clubs such as the **Cafe Wha?** **(115 MacDougal St.)**, **The Gaslight Cafe (116 MacDougal St.)**, and eventually **Gerde's Folk City (11 W. 4th St.)** ⊘, which all offered amateur nights during the week. They also spent weekends busking for change in **Washington Square Park**. The Village folkies weren't sure what to make of the neatly groomed collegiate pair, and little happened for them. One afternoon Paul found himself in the office of Tom Wilson, a producer at **Columbia Records (485 Madison Ave.)**. Wilson produced Bob Dylan and was

preparing another group, the Pilgrims, an African-American alternative to Peter, Paul, and Mary. Simon sensed an opportunity and pitched a couple of songs he'd written recently, "He Was My Brother" and "The Sound of Silence." Wilson was intrigued and eventually Paul brought Artie up to the office to perform the songs with him. Wilson liked what he heard and in early 1964 Paul and Artie were signed to Columbia.

Paul promptly dropped out of law school, but Artie continued at Columbia, eventually earning his masters in Mathematics Education. He would continue toward his PhD well into their run of success.

What was this new folk duo to be called? Kane and Garr? Boring. Not Simon & Garfunkel, certainly. Much too Jewish. Simon & Garfield was suggested, and Artie grudgingly agreed to go along with it. Columbia executive Norman Adler strenuously disagreed. This was 1964, after all, and Simon & Garfunkel it was.

In March, recording sessions commenced at **Columbia Studio B (49 E.52nd St.)**. Compared to their later work, *Wednesday Morning, 3 A.M.* is fairly simple affair, just the two of them with acoustic instrumentation. Simon's early originals are combined with traditional folk tunes and a cover of Dylan's "The Times They Are A-Changin.'"

Teacher's College, Columbia University

The album cover is a color photograph of Paul and Artie in the subway at **5th Avenue and 53rd Street.** Reportedly the image had to be touched up to mask some obscene graffiti on the wall behind them.

After completion, Paul was off to England for a few months to play gigs and rejoin some friends he'd met the previous year. Artie would spend the summer hitchhiking around France.

When *Wednesday Morning, 3 A.M.* was released in October 1964, it barely sold at all. For a record-buying public in the thrall of the British Invasion, it seemed oddly out of step, even for a folk album. Paul would return to England. He was having some success as a solo artist in London, and was in love with a girl he had met there, Kathy Chitty. She would inspire some of his best-known songs in the months to come. Artie would continue at Columbia University. In April of '65, at the behest of Wilson, they went into the studio to try a couple of tunes with a backing band, but those were shelved. Simon & Garfunkel, it seemed, was done.

Things went well for Paul in London. He even cut a solo album, *The Paul Simon Song Book*, which was initially released only in the UK. Meanwhile, despite the complete commercial failure of the debut Simon & Garfunkel album, college radio stations in a few parts of the country were receiving requests for "The Sound of Silence," spurring sales of the album. Back in New York, Tom Wilson was working with Bob Dylan recording *Highway 61 Revisited* at **Columbia Studio A (799 7th Ave.).** When Dylan left for the day, he asked some of the musicians to stick around for a little while and help him record a new electrified backing track to "The Sound of Silence." Perhaps there was still a chance for this song, at least. The new version was released as a single on September 13 and very rapidly became a huge hit. Paul returned to New York, and Columbia demanded new material as soon as possible.

The first thing Paul and Artie did was hire a manager, Mort Lewis, who had successfully managed Dave Brubeck and the Brothers Four. They spent many hours at **Lewis's apartment (345 E. 56th St.)** and at a neighboring deli, **The Hole in the Wall (1055 1st Ave.)** together. Lewis promised them they'd make $10,000 a week, which they did almost immediately.

Tom Wilson had left Columbia for MGM, so Paul and Artie were flown to Los Angeles to quickly put together a new album with producer Bob Johnston. The single "Homeward Bound," written while Paul was in England, was released in January 1966. The new album, *The Sounds of Silence*, would recycle some of the songs included on Paul's British album, newly recorded. This album would prove to be a major success, and Simon & Garfunkel were on their way. The following albums, which included *Parsley, Sage, Rosemary, and Thyme*, and a soundtrack to the Mike Nichols film *The Graduate* were extremely successful and increased their profile both in the US and internationally.

Bookends was recorded in multiple sessions over the course of 1966 through 1968 and utilized both **Columbia Studio A (799 7th Ave.)** ⊘ and **Columbia Studio B (49 E.52nd St.).** One of the stipulations of their contract was that Columbia would pick up the cost for recording and studio time, since originally, at least, they were merely two folk singers with a guitar. Paul and Artie took full advantage of this and spent as much time as they desired perfecting the songs and getting the performances they wanted. The experimental Moog synthesizer was brought to the studio to enhance "Save the Life of My Child," one of its very first uses in a commercial recording. In addition to the eventual classics "America," and "Old Friends," the album featured an expanded version of "Mrs. Robinson," which originally appeared in *The Graduate*. When released with the album in

Artie's pad at 40 E. 68th St.

released in January 1970, it became their most successful release to date, and it would be one of the most successful albums of all time. It would also be the duo's last studio album, as Artie told Paul he would be leaving that summer to join Mike Nichols once again to co-star in *Carnal Knowledge*. They would play out their current tour, which would end right where their careers began, in Queens at **Forest Hills Tennis Stadium (1 Tennis Pl.)**. The pair would reunite many times in the ensuing years, and both would have successful solo careers.

St. Bartholomew's Church

April 1968, it would hit number one and become their most successful single to date.

For his next film, Mike Nichols would adapt Joseph Heller's *Catch-22*, and he asked both Paul and Artie to appear in it. Paul's role was eventually written out, so he stayed behind in New York while Artie traveled to Mexico for the film. It would be only a couple of months, and he would have time to finish off some songs and work on backing tracks. Due to prolonged delays in production, Artie's absence stretched into five months. Paul, deeply frustrated, was inspired to pen the tune "The Only Living Boy in New York," revealing his mixed feelings for missing his friend and partner. Artie's absence and Paul's perfectionism caused the album to take much longer to produce than expected, so Simon & Garfunkel had to hit the concert circuit before its release. Their shows would feature many of the as-yet unreleased material contained within it, including the title track "Bridge Over Troubled Water," which Artie performed as a solo. When the album was

St. Paul's Chapel, Columbia

Simon's former home at 7 E. 94th St.

Paul's first post-breakup solo album, 1972's *Paul Simon,* spawned the hits "Mother and Child Reunion" and "Me and Julio Down by the Schoolyard," demonstrating that he had lost nothing in the way of creativity. It was merely the first of many hugely successful and award-winning albums he would produce in the ensuing years. Artie spent some time teaching mathematics at a school in Connecticut before releasing his first album, *Angel Clare*, in 1973. Simon & Garfunkel would reunite in the studio for the single "My Little Town" in 1975, which appeared on both Simon's *Still Crazy After All These Years* and Garfunkel's *Breakaway.*

MORE SIMON & GARFUNKEL

NOTEWORTHY LIVE PERFORMANCES

McMillin Theatre, Columbia University (2960 Broadway): Artie was still enrolled as a graduate student when the duo performed here on May 1, 1966, on the heels of *The Sounds of Silence*. Today the Miller Theater.

Forest Hills Tennis Stadium (1 Tennis Pl., Queens): As part of the annual Forest Hills Music Festival, Simon & Garfunkel played in their veritable back yard with the Mamas and the Papas on August 6, 1966. They played the venue again in 1967, 1968, and 1970.

Philharmonic Hall (10 Lincoln Center Plaza): Shortly after the release of their second album, the duo played this venerable concert hall on January 22, 1967. The show was eventually released in 2002 as *Live From New York, 1967*.

Carnegie Hall (881 7th Ave.): Simon & Garfunkel played the first of four shows over the next two years at Carnegie Hall on January 27, 1968.

Madison Square Garden (4 Pennsylvania Plaza): The duo's first reunion took place on June 14, 1972, at a packed fundraiser for presidential candidate George McGovern. The event also featured a reunion of Peter, Paul, and Mary.

The Great Lawn, Central Park: In a much-heralded free concert, Simon & Garfunkel played before 500,000 fans on September 19, 1981, in an event that spawned both a live album and a film. They would follow with a world tour that would include **Shea Stadium (126-01 Roosevelt Ave., Queens)** on August 6, 1983.

Paramount Theater (1501 Broadway): As part of Paul Simon's Event of a Lifetime tour, he performed a lengthy residence at the Paramount throughout October 1993 that included sets with Garfunkel, as well as the Mighty Clouds of Joy and Ladysmith Black Mambazo.

OTHER NOTEWORTHY RECORDING SESSIONS

St. Paul's Chapel, Columbia University (1160 Amsterdam Ave.): During the early sessions for *Bridge Over Troubled Water* in 1969, Paul and Artie recorded the La-La-La's for "The Boxer" here.

OTHER NOTEWORTHY LOCATIONS

190 Waverly Place: Residence of Barry Kornfeld, a friend of Paul's and his partner in the publishing firm of Eclectic Music, which used this address. Some of the rehearsals for *Wednesday Morning, 3 A.M.* took place here as well.

NBC Midwood TV Studio (1268 E.14th St., Brooklyn): Simon & Garfunkel performed live on January 3, 1968, on *Kraft Music Hall*, playing "A Poem on the Underground Wall," "For Emily Whenever I May Find Her," "Overs," "Anji," "Patterns," "The Sound of Silence," and "The 59th Street Bridge Song."

The 59th St. Bridge: Subject of the song "The 59th Street Bridge Song (Feelin' Groovy)" from *Parsley, Sage, Rosemary, and Thyme*. Officially known as the Ed Koch Queensboro Bridge, the cantilever structure opened in 1909, linking

Manhattan to the borough of Queens. It is 3,724 feet long and is open to cars, pedestrians, and bicycles.

St. Bartholomew's Episcopal Church (325 Park Ave.): During the recording of *Bridge Over Troubled Water*, the undeniably Jewish Art Garfunkel came here to pray during a break while recording the vocals for the now-classic title track at the nearby Columbia Studio on 52nd Street. He was having trouble getting the early verses right and sought support from above.

New York University (Washington Square): Beginning April 1970 Paul Simon taught a weekly course in how to write and record a popular song. It was not limited to NYU students and also open to working songwriters. Among his students were Melissa Manchester and Maggie and Terre Roche.

40 E. 68th St.: After living briefly in the Hampshire House (150 Central Park South), Garfunkel settled in a one-bedroom apartment here, with a terrace facing the street, during most of his tenure with Simon & Garfunkel (circa 1966 to 1970).

7 E. 94th St.: After Simon married Peggy Harper, the couple moved into this five-story brownstone in 1969. Paul moved to the West Side when they divorced in 1975. The album cover to *Simon and Garfunkel's Greatest Hits* was photographed here on the sidewalk in front.

Say Eng Look Restaurant (1 East Broadway): In a 1972 interview with *Rolling Stone*, Simon admitted that the title and lyrics of the song "Mother and Child Reunion" were inspired by a Chinese dish of that name, which contained both chicken and eggs.

16 Crosby St.: The photograph of Simon relaxing on a fire escape on the *Still Crazy After All These Years* album cover was taken outside the loft of photographer Edie Baskin.

NBC Studios (30 Rockefeller Plaza, Studio 8H): On October 18, 1975, Paul Simon hosted the second episode of what was then known as *NBC's Saturday Night*. In addition to playing basketball with NBA great Connie Hawkins, the show featured guests Phoebe Snow, Randy Newman, and the Jessy Dison Singers. Simon also performed "Scarborough Fair," "The Boxer," and "My Little Town" with Art Garfunkel. He would appear again the following year, singing "Still Crazy After All These Years" wearing a turkey suit. He would host twice more and appear as the musical guest another eight times, in addition to various cameos. Simon and SNL producer Lorne Michaels would also create *The Paul Simon Special* in 1977 at NBC, where Garfunkel would again make an appearance.

New York Hilton (1335 6th Ave.): At a ceremony on March 15, 1982, Paul Simon was inducted into the Songwriter's Hall of Fame.

Waldorf Astoria Hotel (301 Park Ave.): On January 17, 1990, Simon & Garfunkel were inducted into the Rock & Roll Hall of Fame by James Taylor. They performed "Bridge Over Troubled Water" and "The Boxer."

THE GAELIC PARK SPORTS CENTRE

W. 240th St., Bronx

Sometimes simply known as Gaelic Park, this expansive field has been largely devoted to hurling and football matches since its purchase in 1926 by the Gaelic Athletic Association of New York. In the late '60s and early '70s, Gaelic Park was also the site of numerous live concerts by the Beach Boys, the Four Tops, Jefferson Airplane, Yes, Deep Purple, Eagles, the Rascals, the Allman Brothers Band, and many others. Kiss guitarist Ace Frehley, who grew up in the Bronx, has spun a yarn about sneaking backstage at a Grateful Dead show at Gaelic Park to chat with Jerry Garcia, waking up the following day in the middle of the field.

Dion's childhood home

T-CONNECTION

3510 White Plains Rd., Bronx

T-Connection was a key late '70s/ early '80s hip-hop venue, with the Cold Crush Brothers, Grandmaster Flash, Jazzy Jay, Afrika Bambaataa, the Soulsonic Force MCs, the Funky 4 + 1, and DJ Red Alert all frequent performers.

DION'S HOME

749 E. 183rd St., Bronx

Rock & roll has always been a cacophony of sounds emanating from the streets. The fertile Italian-American enclave of Fordham in the Bronx was no exception. When young Dion Francis DiMucci first heard the likes of Hank Williams and Jimmy Reed on the radio in the early '50s, he was hooked. He was familiar with opera and the popular hits of the day, but what came over the airwaves spoke to him in a visceral way. Soon after, DiMucci and his friends

from the neighborhood began singing on street corners, improvising and refining their own vocal arrangements and harmonies. They heard other kids too, and were undoubtedly influenced by the vocal groups coming from the black neighborhoods just south of them in the Bronx and Harlem.

In 1956, Dion was invited to audition for a fledgling label that paired him with a lush arrangement and slick studio vocalists. The tune was a regional hit, but Dion knew he could do better. For his next outing, he assembled three of his neighborhood cohorts, Angelo D'Aleo, Fred Milano, and Carlo Mastrangelo, and they worked out the arrangements themselves in the house on 183rd Street. Since two of the guys lived on nearby Belmont Avenue, they named themselves Dion and the Belmonts. Their first outing, "I Wonder Why," hit big and the group appeared on *American Bandstand*. More hits followed, including "A Teenager in Love," and they toured the country with Buddy Holly, Bobby Darin, and the Coasters. In 1959, Dion narrowly missed being on the fateful flight that took the lives of Holly, Richie Valens, and the Big Bopper. Shortly after, he moved out of the house in the Bronx and moved to Manhattan. He also broke with the Belmonts and went solo, producing even bigger hits with "The Wanderer" and "Runaround Sue." His gritty, city-wise vocal style was to be hugely influential to later rockers like Lou Reed and Bruce Springsteen.

Dion worked his way through several styles, including folk and blues, and is still going strong today. The house on 183rd Street still stands, and the surrounding neighborhood retains much of the character it had in Dion's time. Nearby Arthur Avenue still boasts some of the best Italian dining in the city.

THE BIRTH OF HIP-HOP

1520 Sedgwick Ave., Bronx

One of the pivotal moments in the early history of hip-hop took place in the recreation center at 1520 Sedgwick Ave. On August 11, 1973, Clive Campbell, better known as DJ Kool Herc, spun records on a pair of turntables linked with a mixer at a "back to school jam" for his sister Cindy. Campbell's turntable technique, focused on the grooves in the beginning or middle of

records, along with Coke La Rock's rapping, was revolutionary, with everyone from Grandmaster Caz of the Cold Crush Brothers, Grandmaster Flash, KRS-One, Red Alert, Sheri Sher of the Mercedes Ladies, Afrika Bambaataa, Busy Bee, and Mean Gene reportedly in attendance.

In June 2017, the stretch of Sedgwick Avenue, which includes the high-rise at 1520, was renamed Hip Hop Boulevard by the city of New York.

ECSTASY GARAGE DISCO

1508 Macombs Rd., Bronx

Ecstasy Garage Disco was an early Bronx hip-hop club, with Starski, Afrika Bambaataa, Mean Gene, the Funky 4 + 1, and many others appearing during the genre's emergent era.

LAURA NYRO'S HOMES

1374 College Ave., Bronx/1504 Sheridan Ave., Bronx

Bronx native Laura Nyro (originally Nigro) produced a series of highly influential albums in the late '60s that merged pop, R&B, gospel, and soul. She grew up in a Jewish family and lived in an apartment on College Avenue until she was eight, moving nearby to Sheridan Avenue in 1956. Nyro was influenced by the multicultural nature of her neighborhood and often sang with school friends.

She developed a deep appreciation for music while a child at the **Ethical Culture School (33 Central Park West)**, and later attended the **High School of Music and Art**

York Giants football team and hosted many musical events. The stadium was the site of Sound-Blast '66, on June 10 of that year, a show featuring Stevie Wonder, Ray Charles, the Byrds, the Beach Boys, the Marvelettes, the Cowsills, and others. Pink Floyd, U2, James Brown, Madonna, Billy Joel, and Paul McCartney, among others, all played the original stadium. After years of civic debate, the original stadium was demolished and a new Yankee Stadium opened in 2009 next door, with a public park residing on the old grounds. In 2011 it was the NYC stop for the Big Four tour, with Metallica, Anthrax, Slayer, and Megadeth co-headlining.

(443-465 W. 135th St.). She sold her song "And When I Die" to Peter, Paul, and Mary and landed her own recording contract with Verve in 1966. Her first album, *More Than a New Discovery,* was critically acclaimed but not particularly successful. It did yield big hits for others, including "Stoney End" for Barbra Streisand, and "Wedding Bell Blues" for the Fifth Dimension. The album would be retitled and reissued after the success of her following releases. Her next album, *Eli and the Thirteenth Confession,* on Columbia, is often considered her finest work, and also produced hits for other artists: Both "Stoned Soul Picnic" and "Sweet Blindness" for the Fifth Dimension, and "Eli's Comin'" for Three Dog Night. Nyro would release three more albums and retire in 1971, having sold her song-publishing company, Tuna Fish Music, for millions. She made a comeback in the late '70s and recorded sporadically afterwards. In 1988 she released a live album from a gig at the **Bottom Line (15 W. 4th St.).** Nyro died of ovarian cancer at age 49 in 1997.

YANKEE STADIUM
1 E. 161st St., Bronx
Originally built in 1923 as the home of the New York Yankees, the "House that Ruth Built" also served for many years as the home of the New

BOBBY DARIN'S HOME ⊘
629 E.135th St., Bronx
Bobby Darin, born Walden Robert Cassotto, spent his earliest years in Harlem, but his formative years in the Bronx on 135th Street, and attended **PS 43 (165 Brown Pl.)** before entering the prestigious **Bronx High School of Science (120 E. 184th St.),** where he graduated in 1953. He would then enroll at **Hunter College (695 Park Ave.)** to study theater and moved in with a friend at 217 W. 71st St. in Manhattan. Darin performed in a few college productions but wanted to break into show business as soon as possible, so he quit after a year and joined a traveling children's theater group. Not long afterward, he formed a partnership with Don Kirshner, whom he met in a candy store, writing pop songs and commercial jingles. One of the artists they wrote for was a young Connie Francis, still looking for her first hit. She recorded their tune "My First Real Love," but it did nothing. Bobby scored a recording contract with Decca in 1956 and recorded a few singles, including "Rock Island Line," which he performed on the Dorsey Brothers Stage Show (1697 Broadway), but none were successful. He was reportedly inspired to invent his stage name from a neon sign for a Chinese restaurant.

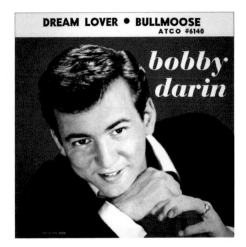

DREAM LOVER • BULLMOOSE
ATCO #6140

bobby darin

The first three letters in "Mandarin" were out, lighting only "darin." After failure at Decca, Darin landed a deal at **Atlantic Records (234 W. 56 St.)**, one of very few white artists to do so. He recorded for their Atco subsidiary and helped arrange material for other artists. In 1958 he finally had his breakthrough with "Splish Splash," a song he co-wrote with DJ Murray "the K" Kaufman. He followed that success in 1959 with his own tune, "Dream Lover," which sold even better. He then had a run of hits, including a jazzy version of Kurt Weill's "Mack the Knife," which sold two million copies and won him Grammy Awards for record of the year and best new artist in 1960. He followed that with "Beyond the Sea," a swing version of the French tune "La Mer." He would also headline at the **Copacabana (10 E. 60th St.)**, and he released a successful live album, *Darin at the Copa.* With success, he moved into a posh new penthouse apartment at **1175 York Ave**.

Darin had branched out, both creatively and career-wise. He formed his own publishing and production company and worked with younger artists, such as Wayne Newton. He also got back into acting. He made the film *Come September* in 1961 co-starring Rock Hudson and Gina Lollobrigida, where he met the 18-year-old actress Sandra Dee. The couple fell in love

and married almost immediately, producing a son. They would make a few more moderately successful films together but eventually divorce in 1967. His two most noteworthy film performances followed shortly thereafter; *Too Late Blues* for director John Cassavetes, and *Captain Newman MD,* for which he was nominated for an Academy Award in 1963. In later years his recordings encompassed country and folk, and he became politically active, campaigning for Robert Kennedy in 1968. He was with Kennedy when the candidate was assassinated in Los Angeles. Later Darin would establish his own record label Direction, with the express purpose of supporting politically active artists. He would later host seven episodes of a television variety show in 1972. Darin had health problems throughout his life, including a weak heart, and died in December 1973.

ST. ANTHONY OF PADUA SCHOOL
832 E.166th St., Bronx

After the Bobbettes, the Chantels were only the second girl group to have a hit on the pop charts. Teenagers Arlene Smith, Lois Harris, Sonia Goring, Rene Minus, and Jackie Landry had been singing together since they were kids in the St. Anthony choir. Arlene was classically

1027 Manor Ave.

trained and had performed in Carnegie Hall as a child. They were discovered by Richie Barrett of the Valentines, a Harlem vocal group, who brought them to the attention of George Goldner, the impresario behind several teen-oriented labels. He signed them to his End Records, where they would have a regional hit in 1957 with "He's Gone;" the Chantels would play the **Apollo (253 W. 125th St.)** shortly after its release. Their next single, "Maybe," was a huge national hit on both the pop and R&B charts in December 1957. It would prove to be a breakthrough, not only for the Chantels, but for female vocal harmony groups as a whole. Credited to Goldner and Barrett, it is generally believed that Arlene Smith was the actual songwriter. Smith would leave for a solo career in 1959, but the Chantels carried on for many years and recorded for several labels, with varying degrees of success.

PHIL SPECTOR CHILDHOOD HOMES
1029 Elder Ave. & 1027 Manor Ave., Bronx
Phil Spector had a humble and troubled early life in the Soundview neighborhood of the Bronx. His later years would be troubled as well, but in between, he had one of the most brilliant careers in rock & roll history. Harvey Philip Spector was born in 1939, the only son of Ben

and Bertha Spector, Russian Jewish immigrants. When he was born they were living at the Elder Avenue address, but moved to Manor Avenue soon thereafter. In 1949 Ben Spector drove his car to Brooklyn and committed suicide by asphyxiating himself with carbon monoxide poisoning. In 1953, Bertha took her son to Los Angeles, where he soon insisted upon being called Phil. At Fairfax High School he developed his musical prowess and formed a group, the Teddy Bears. He befriended Stan Ross, owner of Gold Star Recording Studios, who would tutor him in the art of record production. The Teddy Bears recorded a Spector-penned song, "Don't You Worry My Little Pet," which secured them a contract with Dore records. They then recorded "To Know Him Is to Love Him," another Spector composition, inspired by the inscription on his father's headstone. It would hit number 1 in December 1958. By the time Spector reached his early twenties he was the hottest producer in the country and had successfully formed his own label, with several big hits by artists ranging from The Crystals and Bob B Soxx & the Blue Jeans, featuring Darlene Love. He crafted a distinctive production style that came to be known as The Wall of Sound, which featured multitracked instrumentation, extensive background vocals, and a booming operatic quality. He did his recording at Gold Star in Los

Angeles but maintained an office and penthouse apartment in New York at 440 E. 62nd St. In New York he signed one of his most successful acts, the Ronettes, who would record "Be My Baby" and several other big hits. He would produce other legendary artists, including the Righteous Brothers, Ike and Tina Turner, and the Beatles. After the Beatles, Spector produced albums by former Fabs George Harrison and John Lennon. Spector's star began to fade as musical tastes changed, and by the late '70s, he was virtually a recluse in his California mansion. He produced Leonard Cohen's *Death of a Ladies Man* and the Ramones' *End of the Century* in 1977 and 1979, respectively. Both were critically slammed by fans of the artists. He worked only sporadically in the ensuing decades. In 2003, he shot actress Lana Clarkson in his home. After a protracted legal process, he was convicted of murder in 2009 and is currently doing time in a California prison.

James Monroe High School

JAMES MONROE HIGH SCHOOL
1300 Boynton Ave., Bronx

The Chiffons, one of the most successful and best loved girl groups of the '60s, got together here in 1960. Initially, Judy Craig, Barbara Lee, and Patricia Bennett formed a trio, but the addition of Sylvia Peterson, another Monroe student, in 1962 cemented their sound and they ultimately hit the top of the charts in March 1963 with "He's So Fine," written by Ronnie Mack. Several hits followed, including the Carole King–Gerry Goffin tune "One Fine Day," the Jeff Barry–Ellie Greenwich penned "I Have A Boyfriend," and Doug Morris's "Sweet Talkin' Guy." In 1964 they would open for both the Beatles and the Rolling Stones on their initial American tours. In 1970, George Harrison released "My Sweet Lord" and was quickly sued for plagiarizing "He's So Fine." A judge later found that Harrison had "subconsciously" copied the song, but a settlement wasn't ultimately reached until 1998.

KISS

Bob Gruen

Kiss, *Dressed to Kill*, at the corner of W. 23rd St. and 8th Ave. on Oct. 26, 1974

When they first entered a rehearsal loft at 10 E. 23rd St. in 1972, the ambitious rockers known today as Kiss were still calling themselves Wicked Lester. Guitarist and space cadet Ace Frehley auditioned for the rest of the band at their rehearsal loft sometime between December 1972 and January 1973, rounding out the classic lineup alongside starry-eyed guitarist Paul Stanley, demonic bass guitarist Gene Simmons, and feline drummer Peter Criss.

In the rehearsal loft, the group meticulously honed their sound and—perhaps more importantly—their showmanship. Kiss began dipping into tubs of greasepaint, taking the glam rock aesthetic to new extremes; fame was inevitable.

Days prior to entering **Bell Sound Studios (237 W. 54th St.)** ⊘ to cut rough demos for their first album in the summer of 1973, Kiss recorded an even rougher live tape in the 23rd Street rehearsal loft. Among the songs played that night were "Strutter," "Firehouse," and "Let Me Know," all of which eventually made it on to the eponymous debut. Also recorded at that rehearsal was "Watchin' You," which

10 E. 23rd St.

Peter Criss's childhood home, 365 Marcy Ave., Brooklyn

Ace Frehley's home, 2986 Marion Ave., the Bronx

Paul Stanley's childhood home, 531 W. 211th St.

appeared on the band's sophomore effort, *Hotter than Hell*. Both albums were released in 1974.

Kiss would return to Bell Sound Studios in late 1973 to properly record their debut album, one that set the stage for the group's catchy combination of destruction and drama.

MORE KISS

NOTEWORTHY LIVE PERFORMANCES

Henry LeTang School of Dance (236 W. 54th St.): Kiss successfully auditioned for Casablanca Records in a small rehearsal studio here in August 1973.

54 Bleecker St.: The first show in Manhattan for Kiss took place on May 4, 1973, in an eighth-floor loft here. It was a BYOB situation and tickets were inexpensive, in this case $1.

Hotel Diplomat (108 W. 43rd St.) ⊘: Kiss played showcase gigs in the Crystal Room at the Diplomat Hotel on July 13 and August 10, 1973.

Academy of Music (126 E. 14th St.) ⊘: Kiss didn't appear in any pre-show ads and they weren't even on the marquee when they played here on December 31, 1973. The headliner was Blue Öyster Cult, with support from Iggy Pop and Teenage Lust.

Fillmore East (105 2nd Ave.): The legendary Fillmore East had already shut down by the time Kiss formed, but the group would still manage to play there, both as a rehearsal space and, for one night only, a showcase gig on January 8, 1974.

Beacon Theatre (2124 Broadway): In an all-caps fan club letter, Kiss promised to "RAISE HELL WITH FIRE AND THUNDER" at a pair of shows at the Beacon Theatre on March 21, 1975.

Americana of New York (811 7th Ave.): Kiss played an impromptu and, remarkable for the time, unmasked show at guitarist Ace Frehley's wedding reception on May 1, 1976.

Madison Square Garden (4 Pennsylvania Plaza): Kiss first sold out Madison Square Garden on February 18, 1977, with support from Sammy Hagar.

Coventry (47-03 Queens Blvd., Queens) ⊘: Kiss made their live debut at Coventry on January 30, 1973, the first of three straight nights at a key Queens club that had just recently changed its name from the Popcorn Pub.

NOTEWORTHY RECORDING LOCATIONS

Electric Lady Studios (52 W. 8th St.): Kiss members were already familiar with Electric Lady Studios after recording demos there in 1973 when they set out to record their third album, *Dressed to Kill*, in February 1975.

Record Plant (321 W. 44th St.): Kiss completed work on *Destroyer* here in February 1976, returning the following May to record *Love Gun*.

OTHER NOTEWORTHY LOCATIONS

23rd St. and 8th Ave., southwest corner: A photo of the group shot by Bob Gruen before a lamppost was used for the cover of their third studio album, *Dressed to Kill*.

Sarge's Deli (548 3rd Ave.): In his autobiography, *Face the Music: A Life Exposed*, Paul Stanley recalled strolling in and wallowing in late-night loneliness over a bowl of Sarge's matzo ball soup following a 1977 gig at Madison Square Garden.

SIR Studios (240 W. 54th St.): Kiss rehearsed extensively for an upcoming tour at SIR Studios in November 1976.

Park Avenue United Methodist Church (106 E. 86th St.): The cover of Kiss' 1981 concept album, *Music From the Elder*, features a photograph of one of the doors of this church.

531 W. 211th St.: Paul Stanley, born Stanley Eisen, lived in this apartment building until his family moved to Queens when he was eight years old. While here he was in the shadow of PS 98, where he went to elementary school.

P.S. 75 (735 West End Ave.): In his pre-Kiss days, Gene Simmons taught Spanish to elementary school students at a public school at 735 West End Ave.

The Normandy (140 Riverside Dr.): Gene Simmons reportedly kept an apartment at the Normandy during the group's mid-'70s peak.

River Court (429 E. 52nd St.): Within spitting distance of the East River and views of his former borough of Queens, Paul Stanley had an apartment at River Court in the mid-'70s.

326 E. 30th St.: Peter Criss lived in a town house here during Kiss' heyday.

144-32 75th Rd., Queens: Paul Stanley's family decamped from Inwood to 144-32 75th Rd. in Queens when the future Starchild was just eight years old.

155-07 59th Ave., Queens: Born Chaim Witz in Israel, the future Gene Simmons of Kiss first reportedly lived in his uncle's modest brick home after his mother moved him to the US.

2986 Marion Ave., Bronx: Ace Frehley grew up in an apartment here.

Bronen's Music (2481 Webster Ave., Bronx): Ace Frehley worked at Bronen's Music in his pre-Kiss days. Founded in 1915, Bronen's has since moved to 2462 Webster Ave.

365 Marcy Ave., Brooklyn: Peter Criss lived in an apartment at 365 Marcy Ave. in Brooklyn as a child.

Kings Lounge (2081 Flatbush Ave., Brooklyn): Criss reportedly asked Simmons and Stanley to come see him play live here in 1972, leading to his joining the group, then known as Wicked Lester.

STATEN ISLAND

ST. GEORGE THEATRE
35 Hyatt St., Staten Island

Renowned for its ornate design and ideal acoustics, the St. George Theatre first opened in 1929 as a vaudeville circuit house and cinema. Though it was in constant operation since opening, it wasn't until the mid-'70s that artists such as Sly Stone and Chaka Khan began performing there.

On October 30, 1982, Scott Ian of Anthrax visited the St. George for the Headbangers Ball, featuring some of his favorite groups, Anvil, Riot, and Raven. While at the show, Ian met Jonny Z, a New Jersey record shop owner who also sold at flea markets. Z would become Anthrax's first manager, and he was also responsible for bringing Metallica to New York during their formative years.

Numerous attempts to revive the St. George Theatre over the years came up short, until it came back for good in 2004. Among the performers in the theater since its revival are Cyndi Lauper, the B-52s, Diana Ross, Tony Bennett, and Davy Jones of the Monkees. The

St. George was also the setting of the finale of *School of Rock,* a 2003 film starring Jack Black.

PARAMOUNT THEATRE
560 Bay St., Staten Island

Built as an art deco theater on the former site of Cornelius Vanderbilt's childhood farmhouse, the Paramount remained open as a theater until 1977, reopening two years later as a multipurpose hall and live music venue. Among the performers at the theater during the early '80s were Metallica, the Ramones, Flock of Seagulls, the Dead Kennedys, and Public Image, Ltd. The Paramount was shuttered for many years but has recently begun hosting occasional

A pair of griffons adorn the roof of the St. George

WU-TANG CLAN

Founded in Staten Island in 1992, Wu-Tang Clan is an influential hip-hop collective named after a martial arts film, a cinematic genre that helped inform their philosophies and has factored into their music, both lyrically and through creatively applied samples. Their 1993 debut album, *Enter the Wu-Tang (36 Chambers)*, was followed by several solo albums by the group's key members

67 Warren St., Staten Island

Robert Fitzgerald Diggs, better known as RZA, de facto leader of the Wu Tang Clan, lived in an apartment at 67 Warren during the group's formative years. He set up a home studio in the apartment, where members of the Wu-Tang cut demos, and where some of the songs would go on to be included on *Enter the Wu-Tang (36 Chambers)* gestated.

160 Park Hill Ave., Staten Island

Wu-Tang member Method Man, born Clifford Smith, grew up in an apartment here and, according to RZA, was nearly killed in front of the building in a drive-by shooting.

Stapleton Houses

Stapleton Houses (210 Broad St., Building 218, Staten Island)

Dennis Coles, a.k.a. Ghostface Killah of the Wu-Tang Clan, grew up here.

Wu-Wear Store (61 Victory Blvd., Staten Island)

Following the success of their debut album, *Enter the Wu-Tang (36 Chambers)*, the Wu-Tang Clan started Wu-Wear, with shops selling the clothes around the country. In Staten Island, a Wu-Wear shop operated for a few years at 61 Victory Blvd., with Wu-Nails, a salon run by RZA's sister, next door.

67 Warren St.

shows and serving as a location for television and film shoots.

MANDOLIN BROTHERS
629 Forest Ave., Staten Island

Mandolin Brothers, opened in 1971 by Stan Jay and Harold Kuffner, was long a destination for discerning musicians. Bob Dylan, Bruce Springsteen, and R.E.M.'s Peter Buck were all said to have ordered guitars from Mandolin Brothers. George Harrison visited the shop, which at one time also repaired a Höfner 500/1 violin bass for Paul McCartney. Mandolin Brothers, which closed in early 2017, was immortalized in song by Joni Mitchell, who sang "I went to Staten Island, Sharon, to buy myself a mandolin," in "Song for Sharon" from her 1976 album *Hejira*. Mitchell reportedly wrote that line while riding the Staten Island Ferry following her visit to the shop.

JOAN BAEZ'S HOME
20 Maine Ave., Staten Island

Joan Baez's father, Albert Baez, was a physics professor at nearby Wagner College when she was born in 1941 while the family lived on Maine Avenue in the neighborhood of Westerleigh. The family would move two years later. Due to Dr. Baez's work with UNESCO, the family would travel around the country and the world, eventually landing in Cambridge, Massachusetts. Baez would begin her music career as a teenager and go on to become one of the nation's preeminent folk singers and political activists.

UNGANO'S RITZ/THE RITZ THEATRE
255 Richmond Ave., Staten Island

For a few years in the early '70s, Manhattan's Ungano's had a relationship with the Ritz Theatre on Staten Island, sending many groups out there when they were in the area. Performers during this era included Captain Beefheart, the Allman Brothers, Yes, King Crimson, Fleetwood Mac, Procol Harum Grand Funk Railroad, Edgar Winter, the Byrds, T. Rex, and the post–Jim Morrison Doors.

Index

Acknowledgments

Rick Rinehart, Katie O'Dell, Kristen Mellitt, and everyone at Globe Pequot; Legs McNeil; Chris Stein; Chris Frantz; Jesse Malin; Lee Ranaldo; Bob Gruen; Sarah Field; Richelle DeLora; Cody Smyth; Oren Silverstein; James Marshall; Gillian McCain; Phillippe Marcade; Jim Waters; Mike Sinclair; Kevin McMahon; Spencer Gale; Elizabeth Howard; Helene Brenkman; James Fitzgerald; Jacob Hoye; Jason Kincade; the New York Public Library, especially the Cullman Center for the Performing Arts and the Schomburg Center for Research in Black Culture; Brooklyn Public Library; Nassau Library System; Scott Taylor, Georgetown University Library; The Wilson Library, University of North Carolina, Chapel Hill; Chris Carroll, Local 802, American Federation of Musicians.

My wife, Eve Levine, and my daughters, Madeline and Marguerite Kott; Claudia and Paul Andreassen; Gary and Karyn Kott; Suzanne McCombs; Andi Sumpter and Amy Chase; Chris Marron and Angela Challands; Nathaniel Kressen & the Greenpoint Writers Group; and my friend and writing partner, Mike Katz, for cooking up an idea that yielded years of agonizing, obsessive research. I've enjoyed practically every minute.

—Crispin Kott

My family, both immediate and extended, was a constant source of support, particularly my daughter Alison (the real scholar of the family), and my parents, Ron and Judith Katz. Marcy, Mark, and Stephanie Rothenberg, Marian Brown, Dan and Ellen Brown, Stuart Brown, Don and Roslyn Brown, Rebecca Pieken, and Adam Zaid were also invaluable in ways far too extensive to enumerate here. A great many friends, both personal and professional, provided support both moral and material, including Billy MacKay, Kate Krader, Wendy Marech and Chuck Loesner, Suzette Kaminski, Simon Astor, Will Murphy, Michael Longshore, Glenn Timony, Tom Nevins, Nicholas Sinisi, Richard Rosenberg, Steven Lee Beeber, J Greg Clark, Richard Ory, Tim Bartlett, Mary Beth Jarrad, Talya Salz and Claude Platton, and Ron Koury. Special thanks to my co-conspirator and fellow obsessive Crispin Kott. It's been a long, strange, winding trip, my friend.

—Mike Katz

Follow along with the Rock and Roll Explorers:

Facebook: www.facebook.com/RRExplorerNYC
Twitter: @RRExplorerNYC
Instagram: @rrexplorernyc